DATE D

D0730882

The Anti-Cancer Cookbook

How to Cut Your Risk With the Most Powerful, Cancer-Fighting Foods

JULIA B. GREER, MD, MPH

Library of Congress Cataloging-in-Publication Data

Greer, Julia B., 1970-
  The anti-cancer cookbook : how to cut your risk with the most powerful, cancer-fighting foods / Julia B. Greer.
      p. cm.
  ISBN 978-0-9624814-9-9
  1.   Cancer--Nutritional aspects. 2.   Cancer--Prevention. 3. Cancer--Diet therapy--Recipes. I. Title.
  RC268.45.G745 2008
  641.5'631--dc22

                              2008022457

ISBN-13 978-0-9624814-9-9
SRP149

39966 Grand Avenue
North Branch, MN 55056 USA
(651) 277-1400 or (800) 895-4585
www.sunriseriverpress.com

TABLE OF CONTENTS

Front Cover Photo:
Grilled Vegetable Pizza,
see recipe on page 128

Foreword

Only one third of adults in the United States maintain a "normal" weight. This is an amazing and distressing fact. Essentially, people in the normal range of weight are now a minority in this country. The remainder of the adult population is overweight or obese, leading to a wide range of health problems, including diabetes, heart disease, and cancer.

The relationship between our weight and the foods we eat is obvious but also complex. For Americans who do not smoke, weight control, food choices, and physical activity are the most important modifiable determinants of cancer risk. Food choices are important for two reasons. Many foods contribute directly to better health, such as fruits and vegetables and whole grains, while many others contribute directly to poorer health, such as trans-fatty acids and saturated fats. It is critical to know which foods to seek out and which to limit based on these direct effects. In addition, our food choices also determine our total caloric intake, which greatly influences body weight. Eating foods that are bulky, satisfying, and not high in calories and limiting foods that are high-calorie with little nutritive value is essential to maintaining healthy weight.

With *The Anti-Cancer Cookbook*, Dr. Julia Greer has given us an excellent cookbook to help us make better food choices and to explain how these choices can reduce our risk of cancer. She provides an informative and easy-to-read explanation of how cancer develops and how foods can play a role in the cancer process. The first section of the book gives an excellent foundation for healthier eating and guides the reader toward those foods that contribute to healthy eating and away from those foods that contribute empty or unhealthy calories. Dr. Greer also gives informed advice on healthy cooking methods and how to make the best choices when eating out.

Many poor food choices are made out of habit, perceived convenience, and a lack of understanding about the importance of different foods on our overall health and well-being. One need not be a scientist or understand all of the scientific studies (although many may find this information fascinating!) to appreciate the basic consensus that has been reached regarding healthy food choices: Choose foods and beverages in amounts that help achieve and maintain a healthy weight; eat a diet that is rich in fruits and vegetables and eat a variety of these plant foods; choose whole-grain rice, bread, pasta, and cereals and limit your intake of simple carbohydrates and sugar; when you eat meat, choose lean cuts and try to substitute fish, poultry, and beans for red and processed meats whenever possible

This book is not designed to be a diet book. The recipes included here taste great, are loaded with healthy ingredients, and tend to be low in saturated fat and sugar. The recipe portions are healthy, but not enormous, and are designed to suit an intelligently sized meal. Each recipe also includes comprehensive nutritional information (calories, grams of fat, protein, etc.) so that you can choose dishes that fit your energy needs and lifestyle. Enjoy!

— *Eugenia E. Calle, PhD, American Cancer Society*

Dedication

This book is dedicated to every individual whose life has been touched by cancer and the people working in the field to make a difference.

– Julia B. Greer, MD, MPH

About the Author

Julia B. Greer, MD, MPH, is an epidemiologist whose work focuses on pancreatic, ovarian, and breast cancers. She was born in Chicago, Illinois, and grew up in Pittsburgh, Pennsylvania, and was educated at Phillips Exeter Academy, Princeton University, Mount Sinai Medical School, Georgetown University Hospital, and the Graduate School of Public Health in Pittsburgh, Pennsylvania.

In addition to being a physician and an accomplished writer, some of her past jobs include aerobics instructor, short-order cook, research assistant, and translator of foreign documents. Her early cancer research concentrated on nutrition, body mass index, and hormonal exposures and ovarian cancer risk. Her more current work is focused in high-risk populations and the genetic predisposition to pancreatic cancer, particularly in relation to mutations in the breast and ovarian cancer genes, BRCA1 and BRCA2.

Greer has written numerous articles on pancreatic and ovarian cancer, speaks to local corporations about nutrition and disease, conducts peer review for a variety of medical journals, and is a member of the editorial board of the *World Journal of Gastroenterology*. She is presently a faculty member of the University of Pittsburgh Medical Center's Division of Gastroenterology, Hepatology, and Nutrition, and is also a member of the American Medical Writer's Association and Mensa International. And she is one darned good cook.

Acknowledgments

Thanks to the friends, colleagues, and professional chefs who provided input during this project, including donating their own recipes or testing mine. I would especially like to thank my parents (mother—purveyor of ingredients, and father—unbiased and adventurous recipe sampler), Dave Whitcomb and Jeanne Calle for supporting me in this rather unconventional endeavor, and my fabulous editor, Karin Hill, for guidance and comic relief. Finally, and most importantly, I would like to thank the friends who gave me those great kitchen gadgets as wedding presents. The marriage didn't last, but the bakeware is holding up beautifully.

Introduction

In the past century, the American diet has undergone a revolution, and it hasn't been a particularly healthy one.

Between the early and the late decades of the twentieth century, the fat content of the American diet increased by almost 40 percent. Rates of childhood obesity have grown from about 5 percent in 1980 to more than 15 percent in 2005, and current estimates are that about 60 percent of Americans are either overweight or obese. While our ancestors didn't have sugar-free muffins, fat-free dressings, calorie-free sodas, or today's constant stream of slimness-obsessed marketing messages, they somehow managed to be thinner than we are today.

Doctors and scientists have extensively researched the relationship between high caloric intake and fat consumption and the development of various cancers. They've reached a general consensus that diets that are rich in fruits and vegetables and lower in fats and meat (particularly fatty and processed meat) may protect against some forms of cancer in addition to heart disease, diabetes, and arthritis. Americans have been told to eat more fruits and vegetables and lean fish or poultry and to limit their intake of saturated fat; it really isn't enough to simply advise eating a 'balanced diet,' because many people have no idea what that is. Additionally, many say they don't have time to pay attention to what they eat because of their hectic family, career, and social lives. I recently came across the statistic that close to one in five (20 percent) of all meals in the United States is eaten in the car—and it's probably safe to say that the majority of these aren't salads!

I would like to believe that we all have a fairly good understanding of our bodies' nutritional needs, but unfortunately that belief is not always upheld. I recently discovered while chatting with a friend of mine, who is a successful businessman, that he had no idea what a carbohydrate was. This moment of enlightenment inspired me to want to share my own knowledge about diet—and specifically diet and cancer—with those who really want to improve their diets but honestly just don't know how. The fact that some forms of cancer are hereditary has led many people to seek preventative measures that may help them to avoid developing a certain type of cancer that runs in their family. Adding cancer-fighting foods to their diets is one of the most obvious and attainable of these measures.

In this book, I provide you with a thorough list of specific foods and their protective value for a number of cancers that occur in significant rates in the United States. The information included here is based on evidence from methodologically structured, scientific studies. This list is in no way comprehensive and undoubtedly can be debated by conflicting findings in the field of cancer research. Nonetheless, it may help you to establish a foundation for healthier eating and to target efforts against specific types of cancer.

In addition to explaining what we need to eat to live a longer life and help protect ourselves from cancer, I am including a myriad of recipes that include these specific cancer-fighting foods. While I do not claim to be a gourmet chef or a graduate of a prestigious culinary institute, I am a true food enthusiast and during my 25 years of cooking have developed or discovered an impressive collection of healthy and delicious recipes. Including these recipes as part of my healthy diet and sticking to a disciplined exercise routine has allowed me to maintain the same slim frame and body weight that I had during college. And, lastly, I am a cancer researcher with a fundamental knowledge of the physiology, genetics, and biochemistry that governs how the disease-fighting compounds found in some foods work on a molecular level to help prevent cancer or other types of disease.

Keep in mind that there is no one single nutrient that will make you healthy and no single food or beverage that will keep you from getting cancer. However, a diet that is rich in basic foods that are cooked by traditional methods may easily be tailored to suit one's health and nutrition needs. Our shelves are filled with "food stuffs" these days—cleverly packaged food-like substances such as cereal and yogurt bars, fruit roll-ups, and kids' colorful, pre-packaged lunch meals. Even items that are advertised as "nutrition bars" are often loaded with calories, fat, and oils such as palm kernel oil, the same partially saturated fat used to cook French fries, potato chips, and doughnuts. To me, the best food is *real* food that grows in the ground, comes off of a tree, or is raised on a farm. The fact that real food can also help ward off cancer is just a delightful bonus.

PART ONE

The Connection Between Nutrition and Cancer

What is Cancer?

Cancer, in basic terms, is uncontrolled cell growth. Most of the cells in your body divide and replenish themselves, with different types doing so at different rates. For instance, skin cells and those in your digestive tract divide often, while liver and brain cells divide rarely. Heart cells don't divide at all, which is why a heart attack has lasting effects and blocked arteries often need intervention in the form of bypass surgery. Every time your cells divide, they need to replicate their DNA—the genetic material in the center (nucleus) of the cell that controls how it will function. When a mistake is made in replicating this DNA—called a mutation—it is usually fixed by one of your body's many repair functions. But after dividing a certain number of times, cells start to lose their ability to prevent and repair the mistakes, so they are programmed to self-destruct. Once they have self-destructed, they are replaced with newborn cells. In cancer, cells have lost that ability to self-destruct, so they just keep on dividing and dividing, often making more mistakes along the way, which is what characterizes tumor growth.

Things that cause cancer are called **carcinogens**. Some carcinogens are substances such as asbestos or toxic chemicals found in things like cigarette smoke or pesticides. Sunlight contains ultraviolet rays that can cause DNA damage to skin cells, resulting in the occasional basal cell carcinoma or malignant melanoma. Other carcinogens are viruses, like hepatitis B that can cause liver cancer, or HPV, the human papillomavirus, which has been linked to some cases of cervical cancer. Cooking meat at very high temperatures can result in the formation of cancer-causing substances that develop from the proteins in meat. This is why a diet that contains a lot of fried or grilled meats has been associated with a number of cancer types, particularly colon and pancreatic cancer. Finally, some of the things that cause cancer are part of our own genetic make-up; in other words, some people are born with mutations that can cause cancer or other diseases. Some examples are the BRCA1 and BRCA2 genetic mutations, which have been linked to breast, ovarian, pancreatic, and a variety of other cancer types in some individuals who carry them.

In 2006, for the first time in the United States, deaths due to cancer in individuals age 85 and younger outnumbered deaths due to heart disease. About one out of every two American men and one out of every three American women can expect to develop cancer in his or her lifetime. Prostate and breast cancer lead the pack in new cases each year, but lung and colon cancers are the two that cause the greatest number of deaths in this country. Overall, in the year 2007, there were estimated to be more than 1,440,000 new cases of cancer and about 560,000 cancer-related deaths. Of those deaths, research has shown that at least one third may be attributed to diet or being overweight. **In other words, at least 186,600 deaths each year, in some way, may be related to our choices about what we eat or drink.**

How We Study Cancer

There are a number of different ways that scientists study cancer. There are so-called 'pre-clinical' studies, meaning that they take place before making it to the clinical setting and being tested on people. Also called **in vitro** studies, this type of research is typically done in the lab, on cells in a petri dish, or on animals. The studies that are performed on people (**in vivo** studies) can be broken down into three main types:

Present studies: these are often called **observational studies, cross-sectional studies,** or **empirical research**. These studies look at what people are doing at one point in time and relate it to cancer risks. For instance, researchers could observe that of 12 people buying grapefruit at the grocery store in one hour, 11 of them were thin, and thus conclude that grapefruit makes you thin. Observational studies are the weakest type of research for many reasons, the most important one being that chance can play a big role in these observations. Perhaps thin people just tend to eat more fruit than heavier people, and it is their overall diet and exercise habits that keep them trim, not just the grapefruit. Or, say that six patients who went to a doctor's office one day were wearing red shirts, and five of those six were there because they had a bad sore throat. If the doctor concluded that red shirts give people a sore throat, or that patients with sore throats tend to wear red, you might suspect that his conclusion was incorrect and that random choice was actually responsible for the apparent association.

Future studies: these are the best way to study food and cancer in terms of accuracy. One type of study that starts in the present and goes into the future is called a **prospective** or **prospective cohort study**. For food and cancer research, this study type surveys people on things such as their diet, medications they take, family history of cancer and illnesses, and exercise habits, and then follow them into the future, checking in at regular intervals and keeping track of who develops cancer. This way, researchers could relate what the people ate, drank, or did to why they might have developed cancer. Other types of future studies are **clinical trials**, like the Women's Health Initiative, in which people are given an "intervention," such as a certain diet to follow, and are again checked on regularly, noting who develops cancer and whether the diet seemed to influence the cancer development. This type of study tends to include a large number of people, and because of the long follow-up period, it can also be very expensive. The reasons are simple. If researchers were going to compare 300 people who were already diagnosed with cancer to 300 healthy people, they would only need to recruit 600 people into a study. But in order to *identify* 300 **new cases** of a certain cancer, especially a rare cancer, they might need to monitor 150,000 people over the course of about 10 years. Advertising the study, recruiting individuals, coordinating multiple study centers and health care professionals, paying interviewers to conduct interviews, and recording all of the data on participants all cost money. In the end, a prospective study such as a clinical trial can end up costing millions of dollars. And not only can it be difficult to acquire the funding dollars to support such a large prospective study, but it can also be tough to find people who are willing to invest so much of their time.

Past studies: these are probably the most feasible studies of diet and cancer. They are typically called **case-control studies** because what they do is compare people who have been diagnosed with cancer (cases) to people who do not have cancer (controls).

Researchers will usually give the cases and controls a similar questionnaire to complete, or they will interview them and record detailed information about their diet, lifestyle, past illnesses, and various behaviors. This information then helps them to make associations between dietary variables, behaviors, and lifestyle factors and their risk of developing cancer. One of the challenges in this study type is finding appropriate controls to participate. Often, healthy people who agree to participate in a study like this are more interested in their own health than the average person is and thus follow a diet or engage in certain activities (like exercising more) that aren't reflective of the population as a whole. What researchers do to remedy this issue is to match the controls with the cases based on things like race, age, socioeconomic status, education, and other factors, so that their study compares two people with very similar backgrounds, with one developing cancer and another not.

Challenges in Cancer Studies

Research on food and cancer has grown by monumental proportions in recent years. The results of cancer studies, however, are often contradictory. One study might show that a certain food is protective against a particular type of cancer, and then a subsequent study will show that there is no relationship, or, worse yet, that this food actually raises cancer risk. This contrast is often due to differences in study design, as described previously, and the way that data is collected and analyzed.

I work in pancreatic cancer research, for instance, and collecting accurate data on pancreatic cancer patients is fraught with complexities. The sickest pancreatic cancer patients often die within a few months of their diagnosis, so collecting survey information on their eating habits is difficult. If researchers are lucky, they can sometimes obtain information from what we call a 'proxy'—a spouse, partner or close relative—who knew the patient well enough to know approximately what they ate. Unfortunately, the information they receive from the proxy might not be entirely accurate. Because the dietary information on these sickest patients is often spotty or incomplete, researchers might end up analyzing food data only for the patients who are surviving and are healthy enough and willing to complete a lengthy questionnaire. As a result, the outcome might not accurately portray a relationship that could exist between foods and advanced-stage or more aggressive cancer. In other words, the results might just overlook the strongest dietary and cancer relationships.

What You Need to Know As You Design Your Diet

Although the field of investigation in the role of nutrition in the cancer process is very broad, a clear and recurring conclusion is that nutrition plays a major role in cancer. A daily diet that incorporates a good quantity of fruits, vegetables, and whole grains has been shown time and time again to be protective against a wide range of cancer types. Based on research evidence that these foods could decrease cancer risk, the National Cancer Institute implemented its 'Five A Day' program more than a decade ago, encouraging Americans to eat at least five servings per day of fruits and vegetables. Other organizations, such as the American Institute for Cancer Research, devote the majority of their energy to educating the public on nutrition and cancer risks. The strongest evidence of a relationship between diet and cancer has been shown in cancers of the breast, prostate, and lung, and in cancers of the gastrointestinal tract, such as esophageal, stomach, pancreas, and colon cancers.

Fruits and vegetables are the greatest sources of vitamins, minerals, and nutrients such as flavonoids and carotenoids, which are types of antioxidants. To understand what an antioxidant is, you need to understand that the cells in our bodies are constantly being damaged by oxidative stress, which is when oxygen molecules "steal" tiny, electrically charged particles, called electrons, from the molecules that make up our cells. Without these electrons, our cells lose the ability to function normally and become more likely to give rise to cancer. The damaging oxygen molecules carrying these extra electrons are called free radicals. Antioxidants work by binding to free radicals and transforming them into non-damaging compounds. If present in sufficient quantities, antioxidants can make a big difference in keeping our own cells healthy and functioning properly, lessening the likelihood that they'll become cancerous.

Why are plant-based foods so high in antioxidants? One main reason is that the antioxidants are necessary in order to protect the leaves, stems, shoots, and fruit of plants from cellular damage as a result of exposure to the sun's ionizing ultraviolet radiation. Antioxidants can also protect plants from insects and toxic metals found in the soil. Antioxidants called anthocyanins give plants their bright pink, purple, and bluish colors and, together with the orange and yellow carotenes, provide the varied colors characteristic of autumn foliage. The names of some antioxidants, such as beta carotene, folate, and selenium, might be familiar to you. Others, such as ellagic acid, myricetin, and resveratrol, sound rather foreign. The most important thing to remember is that a diet that is rich in fruits, vegetables, legumes, whole grains, and healthy sources of proteins and fats is the best way to eat—and the best way to teach your children to eat—to live a long and healthy life.

Saturated and Unsaturated Fat

When you think of a traditional American meal, you probably think of comfort foods like meatloaf and apple pie or ballpark fare such as hamburgers, French fries, and milkshakes. The "Western diet" that many Americans embrace typically contains a lot of refined sugar, white flour, and meats that are high in saturated fat. This type of diet has been linked to an increased risk of various cancers, as well as heart disease, obesity, diabetes, and arthritis. Refined sugar and white flour can be avoided by staying away from white bread and sugary baked goods and by paying greater attention to food labels. Fats are a little bit trickier. **Unsaturated fats** come in two main categories: **monounsaturated** and **polyunsaturated**—and both of these are much better for you than the saturated type. **Trans fats** are created when a fat that is in oil form at room temperature is pumped full of hydrogen atoms and made into a solid. Basically, trans fats are an unsaturated fat that has been turned into a saturated fat. Any food whose label includes the words **'hydrogenated oils'** or **'partially hydrogenated oils'** contains trans fats. They can contribute to cancer risk by promoting obesity, and they increase cholesterol levels and may lead to atherosclerosis—a main cause of heart disease. Here are some examples of foods high or low in saturated fats:

Foods high in saturated fat: **Bacon, pork chops, pork loin, regular cuts** of **beef, marbled meats, sausage, spare ribs, butter, cream, cream cheese** and **hard cheeses** like cheddar, **egg yolks** and **whole eggs, whipping cream, whole milk, buttermilk,** many brands of **chocolate milk, chicken wing meat/dark meat/giblets,** and oils such as **corn oil** and **cottonseed oil**

Foods low in saturated fat: **Chicken white meat,** most types of **fish and seafood (salmon, tuna, shrimp, tilapia, crab), very lean pork and beef, low-fat** and **nonfat dairy products** (such as nonfat or low-fat **cottage cheese, feta cheese, mozzarella cheese,** other **reduced-fat cheeses, skim** and **low-fat milk, nonfat** and **low-fat yogurt), egg whites, oils** (such as **safflower oil, olive oil, canola oil, peanut oil), nuts and seeds** (pecans, hazelnuts, almonds, cashews, Brazil nuts, pistachios, walnuts, sunflower kernels,** and **pine nuts. Macadamia nuts** are particularly high in polyunsaturated fat). **Avocados** carry the stigma of being a fatty food, but they contain mainly **monounsaturated fat**—a good fat.

Eat These Powerful "Anti-Cancer" Foods

Blueberries, blackberries, red and black raspberries, cranberries, strawberries, and lingonberries (popular in Europe and the Pacific Northwest) are chock full of cancer-fighting phenols. In the 1990s, Dr. Gary Stoner, a cancer scientist at Ohio State University, showed that concentrated black raspberry extract could fight colon and esophageal cancer. Now we know that the phenols in berries, such as the **anthocyanins** that give berries their blue or red color, can slow the growth and metabolism of cancerous and pre-cancerous cells. They can also inhibit the tumor's ability to form blood vessels, and, without a blood supply, tumors cannot survive. **Ellagic acid, coumaric acid, resveratrol, folate,** and **myricetin** are antioxidants found in berries that have demonstrated anti-cancer abilities in numerous lab-based studies. Ellagic acid extracts from raspberries have been shown to effectively inhibit cervical cancer growth; lab studies of ellagic acid show it may decrease pancreatic cancer risk and skin cancer cell division. Other studies have demonstrated that berries may inhibit or help to prevent oral and breast cancer, as well as leukemia and lymphoma. And one cup of raspberries has almost twice the **fiber** of a medium-sized baked potato—including the skin!

Berries are also loaded with the antioxidant **vitamin C,** and they are very low in calories. Frozen berries have an equivalent amount of cancer-fighting compounds and can be eaten when fresh berries are out of season.

Oranges, lemons, limes, tangerines, clementines, and grapefruit are the **citrus fruits** most commonly eaten in this nation, and for good reason. You can get them from Florida or California, ripe and juicy, year-round. Citrus fruits are rich in **vitamin C**, a powerful antioxidant long known for its ability to keep sailors from getting scurvy during extended periods of time at sea, and recent lab studies have shown it may fight breast cancer. It is better to peel an orange or grapefruit and eat it in sections rather than cutting it in half and spooning it out, because the white membrane that surrounds the fruit is packed with flavonoids—three times as much as is in the rest of the fruit. Citrus-fruit peel and pulp is also antioxidant-rich, and is particularly high in the flavanol **quercetin** as well as **limonoids,** phytochemicals with anti-cancer properties that give the citrus-fruit peel its fresh scent. In a recently published case-control study conducted in Northern Italy, individuals who ate the most citrus fruit had a 62 percent reduction in their esophageal cancer risk when compared to those who consumed the least citrus. Additionally, the **pectin** in citrus fruits has been shown to be a cancer-fighter and may delay the growth of cancerous cells in men diagnosed with recurrent prostate cancer. White grapefruit contains the flavonoid **naringenin.** In a large case-control study, people who ate the greatest average amounts of white grapefruit decreased their lung cancer risk by 50 percent compared to those who ate the least. Another citrus flavonoid, **luteolin** (also found in **basil**, **green peppers**, **celery**, **parsley**, **thyme**, **peppermint**, **pomegranates**, and **artichokes**) was studied in the Harvard-based Nurse's Health Study of more than 66,000 women. Results of this recent study showed that high luteolin intake was associated with a 34 percent reduction in ovarian cancer risk.

Red and pink grapefruit, pink guava, papaya, watermelon, and tomatoes all contain **lycopene.** Lycopene is one of the carotenoids whose intake has been correlated to a decreased risk of pancreatic and prostate cancers, among others. Botanically speaking, the tomato is actually a fruit, and it is the world's most popular fruit, with more than 60 million tons being produced each year. Each of these pink and reddish fruits also contains tons of **vitamin C** and **beta carotene**, which boost immunity and help fight infection by promoting free-radical scavenging. The white and greenish parts of watermelon also contain citrulline, which may assist in wound healing. Heating tomatoes does not destroy lycopene—in fact, it enhances it—so ounce for ounce, tomato paste, spaghetti sauce, and ketchup have even higher lycopene content than a raw tomato. Studies have also demonstrated that processed tomato products that contain a little bit of oil or fat (such as spaghetti sauce) are better foods for your body to absorb lycopene from, compared to raw tomato juice, from which the lycopene is poorly absorbed.

Apples have a high polyphenol quantity and contain the flavonoid **quercetin**, which is also found in onions, grapes, broccoli, and citrus fruit. Quercetin is a powerful antioxidant, and high quercetin intake has been associated with anti-inflammatory and anti-tumor activities, particularly in skin, prostate, esophageal, and lung cancers. Apples also contain antioxidants called **procyanidins,** and have been shown to have strong effects on the vascular system, improving blood flow to healthy cells and thereby lowering blood pressure and protecting the heart from damage.

Grapes have been receiving a lot of press lately because they contain high levels of the polyphenol **resveratrol**, which has been rumored to be the ingredient found in red wine as well as grape juice that just might help keep the French thin. Resveratrol can make muscle cells function at a higher rate and thus may accelerate the body's metabolism and ability to burn calories. While all grapes are good for you, **purple and red grapes** have about three times more antioxidants than green or white ones, including antioxidant **anthocyanins** (just like in berries), as well as **ellagic acid, myricetin, quercetin, and kaempferol**. In laboratory studies, resveratrol has been shown to be able to decrease or stop the growth of breast, prostate, pancreatic, stomach, liver, and colorectal cancers. A study of diet in Mediterranean countries showed that the more resveratrol-rich foods a woman consumes, the lower her breast cancer risk. Berries such as cranberries and raspberries are also high in resveratrol.

Tart cherries contain **anthocyanins**, the same cancer-fighting ingredient in berries, grapes, and plums, which also protect artery walls from the damage that leads to plaque buildup and heart disease. Studies have shown that cherries may help to decrease the risk of cardiovascular disease and 'metabolic syndrome' by improving cholesterol levels and the activity of insulin. Cherries have a high content of **perillyl alcohol**—a natural chemical that depletes the body of cancer-causing substances and helps to slow the growth of cancerous cells. The anthocyanin, **cyanidin**, contained in tart cherries has been shown to inhibit colon and breast cancer cell growth in lab studies. Cherries also contain a healthy dose of **melatonin,** the same hormone produced by your body's pineal gland that has been used to treat jet lag and insomnia and may play a role in cancer treatment. High levels of **fiber, vitamin C,** and **beta carotene** are also found in cherries.

Plums, peaches, pears, nectarines, apricots, kiwi fruit and melon are fruits known for their high antioxidant and fiber content and have been associated with a decreased risk of many types of cancers. As mentioned, plums contain **resveratrol**. Peaches and nectarines are high in **vitamin C**; apricots contain plenty of **beta carotene**; and ounce for ounce, kiwi fruit has more **vitamin C** than an orange and more **potassium** than a banana. Each of these fruits contains large amounts of polyphenols, which can scavenge free radicals and keep them from damaging healthy cells.

The botanical name for the **pomegranate** is *Punicum granatum*, though other names for it include Chinese apple, granada, and melo grano. Pomegranates are one of the oldest known fruits and are rich in folklore. Every pomegranate is composed of exactly 840 seeds, each surrounded by a sac of sweet-tart juice contained by a thin skin. Originally from India, they were introduced to the United States in the late 1700s and are now grown in California, Utah, Alabama, and Louisiana. Pomegranate juice has demonstrated potent antioxidant, anti-malarial, and anti-atherosclerotic properties. In laboratory studies, four important chemical components found in pomegranates, **ellagic acid**, **caffeic acid**, **punicic acid**, and **luteolin**, demonstrated the ability to inhibit prostate cancer cell growth and invasion. Pomegranates contain plenty of **folate** and **vitamin C**. There is also evidence that antioxidants found in pomegranate fruit and juice can help prevent breast and lung cancer cells from dividing and can even induce cancer cell death.

Vegetables known as **leafy greens** include kale, spinach, escarole, collard greens, Swiss chard, curly endive, watercress, mustard greens, and arugula. Just about any type of lettuce—such as bib, Boston, butter, leaf, and red or green romaine—also qualifies as a leafy green vegetable, even if the leaves have a lot of red or brownish color to them. Leafy greens are loaded with vitamins, such as **vitamin C**, and minerals, as well as two types of carotenoids called **lutein and zeaxanthin**. Studies have shown that consuming healthy quantities of leafy greens and other lutein-rich foods decreases the risk of breast, skin, lung, head and neck, and stomach cancer. Additionally, greens such as spinach, kale, and watercress contain the flavonoid **kaempferol**. The Iowa Women's Health Study, a large prospective study of more than 40,000 women, found that women with the highest intake of leafy greens decreased their risk of ovarian cancer by 56 percent. Watercress intake, in particular, was associated with decreased ovarian cancer risk. Leafy greens are also rich in **folate**, and large epidemiological studies have found that, compared to people who report low folate intake, individuals with the highest intake of folate-rich foods have, on average, a 40 percent decreased risk of colon cancer. And a Harvard-based study of more than 88,000 women found that folate decreased the risk of breast cancer in those women who drank at least one alcoholic beverage per day.

Broccoli, cauliflower, Brussels sprouts, cabbage, and bok choy are cruciferous vegetables, otherwise known as members of the Brassica family. The Brassica family of foods contains high levels of several chemical constituents called isothiocyanates, which stimulate detoxification enzymes in the liver. One example of a potent **isothiocyanate** is the antioxidant **sulforaphane**. Sulforaphane and other isothiocyanates are capable of revving up the cellular defense enzymes in your body and neutralizing free radicals. In basic terms, the broccoli and cabbage that you eat is digested and then goes on to protect your cells from DNA damage and inhibit carcinogenesis (the process by which normal cells transform into cancerous cells) and tumor formation. In laboratory studies, the compounds in cruciferous vegetables have been shown to keep cancers from forming, as well as to slow the growth of tumors that are already present. There is strong evidence that they can help ward off prostate, lung, breast, head and neck, and pancreatic cancer. A study of 300 Chinese women found that those with the highest isothiocyanate consumption had a 45 percent lower breast cancer risk compared to the women with the lowest. Certain isothiocyanates have also demonstrated the ability to induce tumor cell death in leukemia cells that are resistant to chemotherapy. Cruciferous vegetables are also rich in **vitamin C**, other polyphenol antioxidants and **quercetin**, as well as flavonoids. Cabbage, in particular, has very high levels of **kaempferol**—one of the most potent antioxidants known—and research has shown that eating cabbage just a few times a week may protect you from breast, lung, and colon cancer.

Orange and yellow vegetables such as carrots, yams, squash, and sweet potatoes are loaded with **beta carotene**, a well-known and studied antioxidant that is a precursor to vitamin A. They are also rich in **vitamin C**. High intake of carrots and yams has been associated with a lower risk of breast cancer as well as head and neck cancers (such as laryngeal). Cigarette smokers have been shown to have lower blood levels of beta-carotene as well as alpha-tocopherol (a form of vitamin E), but smokers with higher intake of beta-carotene rich foods have been shown to significantly decrease their risk of developing lung cancer compared to smokers who don't eat these types of foods.

Onions, **shallots**, **garlic**, **chives**, **scallions**, **and leeks** are all members of the onion, or *Allium*, family. Garlic has been known for centuries for its anti-inflammatory and immune-regulating properties, and some studies have shown that garlic may reduce cholesterol levels. The Iowa Women's Health study demonstrated that women who ate garlic regularly had a lower risk of colon cancer, and a Korean study showed that garlic consumption was linked to a lower risk of stomach cancer. Onions may be the greatest food source of the flavonol **quercetin**. A case-control study from the Journal of the National Cancer Institute of 582 patients with lung cancer and 582 age-, sex-, and ethnicity-matched healthy controls found that those with the highest onion intake had a 50 percent lower incidence of lung cancer. There is also evidence that onions may play a role in fighting colon, bladder, skin, prostate, stomach, and endometrial cancers as well as leukemia. Red and yellow onions have higher quercetin concentrations than white onion varieties. Other allium-based antioxidant compounds found in onions and garlic include **allicin**, **allyl sulfides**, **organosulfur compounds**, and **ajoene**. The potent antioxidant allicin in garlic, however, is destroyed by heating, while cooking garlic actually releases ajoene. To preserve some of the allicin, you can slice or mince garlic and let it sit at room temperature for about 10 minutes prior to cooking. Quercetin, on the other hand, is preserved when heated.

Lentils, **peas**, **and beans** of all varieties are known as **legumes**. Vegans, vegetarians, and people of various European, Mexican, and South American cultures consume legumes regularly. Legumes contain a great number of cancer-fighting compounds, including **lignans**, **saponins**, **phytic acid**, and **protease inhibitors**. A large study of Seventh Day Adventists whose diet included more fruits, vegetables, legumes, whole grains and fish than typical Americans consume, demonstrated that they had a 55 percent lower risk of pancreatic cancer compared to the general population, much of which was correlated to their high legume intake. Beans are one of the most nutritious foods known and are high in protein as well as minerals such as magnesium, copper, potassium, manganese and **calcium**. One serving of pistachios, for instance, has the same amount of dietary **fiber** as 1/2 cup of broccoli. They are also an excellent source of antioxidants such as **vitamin C, vitamin A** (from **beta-carotene**), and **folate**. Black beans, in particular, contain a quantity of **anthocyanins** equivalent to that of cranberries and grapes. A recent case-control study of over 3,000 ethnically diverse men found that men who ate the highest quantity of beans decreased their risk of prostate cancer by 38 percent. Other studies have shown that people who eat foods high in vitamin C, beta-carotene, and folate decrease their risk of lung, esophageal, and colon cancer.

The **soybean** is another type of legume that contains all of the same antioxidant compounds as described above, but also has some unique anti-cancer properties. Soy products contain **phytoestrogens**, which are plant-based weak estrogens similar to those that your body makes (men actually make a small amount of estrogen, too), but that can compete for the same estrogen receptor on tissues such as breast tissue. The most significant phytoestrogen is **isoflavone**, which contains two important compounds — **genistein and**

daidzein. Higher intake of soy-based foods has been shown to protect against pre-menopausal breast cancer as well as endometrial and prostate cancer, and it is likely to play a protective role for other cancer types. In a 20-year study of more than 12,000 American men, men who drank one or more servings of soymilk per day reduced their prostate cancer risk by 70 percent! Soybeans contain all the essential and non-essential amino acids, making them a complete protein equivalent to animal proteins. And soy products are low in saturated fat. **Examples of soy-based foods include soybeans, tofu, edamame, tempeh, miso, soy nut butter, soy-based veggie burgers, textured vegetable protein, and soymilk.** Tofu is an incredibly versatile food for cooking and baking, and provides protein and texture while taking on the flavor of other ingredients in the recipe.

Nuts are one of nature's most perfect foods. Nuts and seeds such as sunflower kernels and sesame seeds contain the healthy type of fat—**monounsaturated fat**—that has been shown to protect against breast cancer. Two of the **phytosterols** found in nuts, **beta-sitosterol** and **campesterol**—may suppress prostate and breast tumors. Nuts also have lots of **fiber**, are a good source of protein and B vitamins, and contain breast and colon cancer-fighting **lignans,** similar to flaxseeds and beans. Many types of nuts contain amino acids such as arginine that can give your immune system a boost. Pecans, pistachios, and Brazil nuts, among others, contain minerals such as zinc, magnesium, and **selenium**. Lab studies have found that selenium may inhibit the development or growth of prostate, lung, and bladder cancer cells, and both lab and human studies have shown that selenium may protect against colon cancer. Walnuts and walnut oil contain high levels of **ellagic acid**, the same potent antioxidant that is found in raspberries and pomegranates. Both nuts and seeds are also high in **vitamin E** content, an antioxidant that protects cell membranes, and nut oils contain **omega-6 fatty acids**.

Only one in 10 Americans eats the daily requirement of complex carbohydrates provided by **whole-grain foods.** Many of the carbohydrates that Americans consume are refined carbohydrates, such as bagels and pretzels. **Whole grains include wheat and rye, couscous, millet, bulgur, oats, popcorn, kasha, quinoa, tabouleh, barley, and buckwheat.** Whole-grain foods can be made into breads, cereals, muffins, pancakes, and other breakfast types of foods. Whole-grain **brown rice, couscous,** and **whole-grain pastas** should be a dinner staple on every American table. Whole grains are a great source of both soluble and insoluble **fiber** that helps you to feel full, improves regularity, and protects against pre-cancerous and cancerous disease of the small bowel and colon. Whole-grain foods contain the germ and bran parts of grain kernels, which have been removed from refined grains. Unlike simple sugars, such as glucose and fructose, the **complex carbohydrates** found in whole-grain foods are absorbed slowly and thus do not rapidly raise blood sugar levels and promote type II diabetes like simple sugars do. Type II diabetes increases the risk of developing some types of cancer, most notably the highly lethal pancreatic cancer. Whole grains are rich in **B vitamins** and **folate**, minerals such as iron and magnesium, and antioxidant phenols, **saponins, lignans,** and **phytoestrogens**. Many studies of whole grains have found high intake levels to correlate with reduced cancer risks. A recent case-control study of more than 2,000 individuals living in the San Francisco bay area, for instance, noted that adults who ate two or more servings per day of whole-grain foods decreased their risk of pancreatic cancer by 40 percent compared to individuals who ate less than one serving of whole grains per day. They also documented about a 35 percent reduction in pancreatic cancer risk among individuals who ate the highest amount of fiber (26.5 grams per day or more) compared with those who ate the least (15.6 grams per day or fewer). A separate study of more than 61,000 women showed that those with the highest whole-grain intake cut their colon-cancer risk by a third, while the prospective Iowa Women's Health Study found that increased whole-grain consumption decreased endometrial and ovarian cancer risk.

Flaxseeds themselves are not digestible. Thus, if they are eaten whole, you will get plenty of fiber but you will not attain the benefits of the **lignan** portion of them, which is the cancer-fighting **isoflavone phytoestrogen**. Flaxseed flour and flaxseed meal are the greatest lignan sources, and some flaxseed oils are supplemented with lignans. Flaxseeds are one of the greatest plant sources of **alpha-linolenic acid**, one of the heart-protective omega-3 fatty acids that demonstrate anti-inflammatory action. Consumption of flaxseed meal has been shown to protect against prostate cancer. A study of men diagnosed with prostate cancer who consumed 30 grams per day of ground flaxseed (about 3 tablespoons) had a 30 to 40 percent reduction in the rate of cancer-cell division—which was a greater reduction than in the sub-set of those who ate a reduced-fat diet but didn't eat the flaxseed meal. Lab-based studies have found that flaxseed consumption can decrease the growth rate of established breast-cancer tumors. Flaxseed meal and flour have a light, nutty flavor, and they can be used to make delicious baked goods.

Low-fat and nonfat dairy products, to a great degree, are synonymous with calcium. Although there are many other sources of **calcium**, dairy products provide one of the simplest and most readily available means of getting your calcium. For instance, spinach also contains calcium, but you would have to eat an awful lot of spinach to get the same amount of calcium as in a large glass of milk. Calcium intake was studied prospectively in 45,354 women by the National Cancer Institute and was shown to protect against colon cancer. Compared to those with a calcium intake of less than 400 milligrams a day, women who consumed more than 800 milligrams per day had a 25 percent reduction in colorectal cancer risk. Calcium and **vitamin D** have also been linked to lower rates of pre-menopausal breast cancer. On-going research will help to determine if vitamin D might decrease the risk of other types of cancer.

Fatty fish, such as **salmon**, **tuna**, **bluefish**, **mackerel**, **sardines**, and **raw herring** contain high levels of **omega-3 fatty acids**, **selenium**, **lignans**, **calcium**, and **vitamins A and D**. Omega-3 fatty acids are known for their ability to protect the heart from damage and maintain lower blood pressure. The nutrients in fatty fish may also help decrease cancer risk. The role of vitamin D and calcium has already been described as helping to lower colon and pre-menopausal breast cancer risk, and there is some evidence that it may be protective against lung cancer. Additionally, a study of more than 90,000 Swedish women conducted between 1987 and 2004 found that those women who ate at least one portion of fatty fish per week decreased their risk of kidney (renal) cancer by 74 percent, compared with those who did not regularly eat fatty fish. And a recent Swedish case-control study of more than 2,000 men demonstrated that men who ate fatty fish at least once a week had a 43 percent decreased risk of prostate cancer compared to those who never ate fatty fish.

Green tea has received a lot of press lately for its ability to lower the risk of many cancers, including breast, esophageal, and stomach cancer. People who live in Asian countries have been reaping the health benefits of green tea for more than 5,000 years. Green tea contains a multitude of cancer-fighting compounds, including **polyphenols** and **flavonoids**, **catechins** such as **tannins**, a variety of minerals and alkaloids, such as caffeine and theobromine. Tea is also the best source of anti-cancer compounds called catechins, and green tea contains about three times as much as black tea. Laboratory studies have demonstrated that green tea can slow or prevent colon-, prostate-, lung-, liver-, and breast-cancer development. One early study showed that drinking three or more cups of green tea per day reduced the recurrence rate of Stage I (early) breast cancer.

Red wine and red or purple grape juices contain polyphenol compounds such as **anthocyanosides**, **catechins**, **procyanidins**, **stilbenes**, and other phenolics. The stilbene called **resveratrol** was described in the section on grapes, but these other antioxidants have immune-modulating and anti-tumor effects and help to relax blood vessels—which is why drinking a little red wine may help to prevent heart disease and decrease the risk of stroke. Recent studies have shown that moderate red wine or grape juice intake may decrease the risk of kidney cancer as well as Hodgkin's and non-Hodgkin's lymphomas. **Note: drinking moderate to large amounts of alcohol has been shown to increase the risk of cancers of the upper airway and digestive tract (mouth, pharynx, larynx, and esophagus), as well as breast and colorectal cancer. Even one glass of alcohol a day may increase a woman's risk or developing breast cancer. Very heavy alcohol intake is associated with liver cancer. Current recommendations are that women drink no more than one alcoholic beverage per day and men no more than two beverages per day. A 12-ounce beer, 5-ounce glass of wine, or 1 ½-ounce shot of hard liquor qualifies as one alcoholic beverage.**

I was at the checkout counter of a store last week and saw a display of **dark chocolate** bars whose label read 'The Healthy Snack.' That was something that I would never have thought I would see, but it's true—dark chocolate has some proven health benefits. **Cocoa** products have been consumed since at least 460 A.D. and have been used to treat lung and liver diseases as well as indigestion, fever, and premenstrual syndrome. Cocoa and dark chocolate contain **procyanidins**, **catechins**, and **epicatechins**. Unsweetened cocoa powder appears to have the most, followed by dark chocolate. Milk chocolate contains fewer of these antioxidants because the milk binds to them and decreases the antioxidant activity (so don't wash down that piece of dark chocolate with a glass of milk!). Laboratory studies have shown that cocoa and extracts of dark chocolate can inhibit the formation of breast, colon, and prostate cancers and can decrease the division rate of liver cancer cells. Studies of dark chocolate consumption in humans have shown that it can lower your blood pressure. In 2003, scientists at Cornell University compared the chemical anti-cancer activity in certain beverages, and found that unprocessed cocoa has nearly twice the amount of antioxidants in red wine and up to three times of those found in green tea.

To decrease the risk of this cancer. . .	. . . definitely eat and drink these foods and beverages . . .	. . . and other foods and beverages that contain these nutrients
Lung	*White grapefruit, oranges, lemons, limes, and other citrus fruit *Onions, garlic, scallions, leeks, chives, apples, broccoli *Carrots, sweet potatoes, yams, squash, pumpkin, orange and red bell peppers, and other orange vegetables Pomegranates and pomegranate juice Broccoli, cauliflower, cabbage, Brussels sprouts, bok choy	Vitamin C, quercetin, limonoids, pectin, naringenin, luteolin Quercetin Beta carotene, vitamin C Ellagic acid, folate, vitamin C Isothiocyanates, quercetin, vitamin C, kaempferol
Breast	*Whole wheat, rye, barley, couscous, oats, bulgur, buckwheat, kasha, millet, popcorn, and other whole grains *Non-fat and low-fat dairy products, including cheese, milk, and yogurt *Cabbage, broccoli, bok choy, Brussels sprouts, cauliflower *Green tea *Carrots, sweet potatoes, yams, squash, pumpkin, orange and red bell peppers, and other orange vegetables Tart cherries Soybeans, tofu, edamame, tempeh, soy milk, soy-nut butter, and other soy-based foods Salmon, tuna, mackerel, trout, bluefish, sardines, and other fatty fish Pomegranates and pomegranate juice Red and purple grapes Unprocessed cocoa powder, dark chocolate Peas and beans of all types (legumes)	Fiber, lignans, selenium, B vitamins Calcium, vitamin D Isothiocyanates, quercetin EGCG, catechins (tannins) Beta carotene, vitamin C Anthocyanins, vitamin C, beta carotene Isoflavones Omega-3 fatty acids, lignans, vitamin D, calcium Ellagic acid, luteolin, caffeic acid, folate, vitamin C Resveratrol, anthocyanins, ellagic acid, myricetin, quercetin, kaempferol Catechins, epicatechins, procyanidins Fiber, saponins, lignans, protease inhibitors, vitamins A and C, folate, calcium
Prostate	*Soybeans, tofu, edamame, tempeh, soy milk, soy-nut butter, and other soy-based foods *Ground flaxseed meal *Watermelon, red grapefruit, pink guava, papaya, tomatoes, and tomato products—ketchup, spaghetti sauce *Oranges, lemons, limes, tangerines, grapefruit, and other citrus fruit *Salmon, tuna, mackerel, trout, bluefish, sardines, and other fatty fish Broccoli, cauliflower, cabbage, Brussels sprouts, bok choy Pomegranates and pomegranate juice Green tea Unprocessed cocoa powder, dark chocolate Peas and beans of all types (legumes)	Isoflavones Lignans, alpha-linolenic acid Lycopene, polyphenols Vitamin C, quercetin, limonoids, pectin, naringenin, luteolin Omega-3 fatty acids, selenium, lignans, vitamins A and D, calcium Isothiocyanates, quercetin, vitamin C, kaempferol Ellagic acid, folate, vitamin C EGCG, catechins (tannins) Catechins, epicatechins, procyanidins Fiber, saponins, lignans, protease inhibitors, vitamins A and C, folate, calcium
Colon	*Non-fat and low-fat dairy products, including cheese, milk, and yogurt *Whole wheat, rye, barley, couscous, oats, bulgur, buckwheat, kasha, millet, popcorn, and other whole grains *Peas and beans of all types (legumes) *Raspberries, black raspberries, blackberries, cranberries, strawberries, blueberries *Garlic, onions, chives, scallions, leeks *Lettuce, spinach, kale, Swiss chard, arugula, watercress, mustard greens, escarole, endive, collards, and other leafy greens Unprocessed cocoa powder, dark chocolate Tart cherries Almonds, pecans, walnuts, hazelnuts, pistachios, filberts, macademia nuts, peanuts, sesame seeds, sunflower kernels Oranges, lemons, limes, tangerines, grapefruit, and other citrus fruit	Calcium, Vitamin D Fiber, lignans, selenium, B vitamins Fiber, saponins, lignans, protease inhibitors, vitamins A and C, folate, calcium Anthocyanins, quercetin, ellagic acid, coumaric acid, vitamins C, folate, resveratrol, myricetin Quercetin, allicin and other allium compounds Kaempferol, lutein, folate, vitamin C, beta carotene Catechins, epicatechins, procyanidins Anthocyanins, vitamin C, beta carotene Vitamin E, phytosterols, lignans, fiber, selenium, ellagic acid, omega-6 fatty acids (in nut oils) Vitamin C, quercetin, limonoids, pectin, naringenin, luteolin

The Anti-Cancer Cookbook

Pancreas	Whole wheat, rye, barley, couscous, oats, bulgur, buckwheat, kasha, millet, popcorn, and other whole grains	Fiber, lignans, selenium, B vitamins
	*Watermelon, red grapefruit, pink guava, papaya, tomatoes, and tomato products—ketchup, spaghetti sauce	Lycopene, beta-carotene
	*Peas and beans of all types (legumes)	Fiber, saponins, lignans, protease inhibitors, vitamins A and C, folate, calcium
	*Lettuce, spinach, kale, Swiss chard, arugula, watercress, mustard greens, escarole, endive, collards, and other leafy greens	Folate
	Red and purple grapes	Resveratrol, anthocyanins, ellagic acid, myricetin, quercetin, kaempferol
	Berries and pomegranates	Ellagic acid, folate, vitamin C
	Broccoli, cauliflower, cabbage, Brussels sprouts, bok choy	Isothiocyanates, quercetin, vitamin C, kaempferol
Ovarian	*Black and green tea (non-herbal), broccoli, watercress, spinach	Kaempferol, lutein
	*Cabbage, carrots, celery, artichokes, citrus fruit, green peppers	Luteolin
	Whole wheat, rye, barley, couscous, oats, bulgur, buckwheat, kasha, millet, popcorn, and other whole grains	Fiber, lignans, selenium, B vitamins
Liver	*Carrots, sweet potatoes, yams, squash, pumpkin, orange and red bell peppers and other orange vegetables	Beta carotene, vitamin C
	Non-fat and low-fat dairy products, including cheese, milk, and yogurt	Calcium, vitamin D
	*Fatty fish such as salmon, mackerel, trout, bluefish and sardines	Omega-3 fatty acids, selenium, lignans, vitamins A and D, calcium
	Unprocessed cocoa powder, dark chocolate	Catechins, epicatechins, procyanidins
Endometrial	*Soybeans, tofu, edamame, tempeh, soy milk, soy nut butter, and other soy-based foods	Isoflavones
	Whole wheat, rye, barley, couscous, oats, bulgur, buckwheat, kasha, millet, popcorn and other whole grains	Fiber, lignans, selenium, B vitamins
	Garlic, onions, chives, scallions, leeks	Quercetin, allicin, and other allium compounds
Esophageal	*Oranges, lemons, limes, tangerines, grapefruit, and other citrus	Vitamin C, quercetin, limonoids, pectin, naringenin, luteolin
	*Green tea	EGCG, catechins, polyphenols
	*Raspberries, black raspberries, blackberries, cranberries, strawberries, blueberries, lingonberries	Anthocyanins, quercetin, ellagic acid, coumaric acid, vitamins C, folate, resveratrol, myricetin
Stomach	*Lettuce, spinach, kale, Swiss chard, arugula, watercress, mustard greens, escarole, endive, collards, and other leafy greens	Kaempferol, lutein, folate, vitamin C, beta carotene
	*Garlic, onions, chives, scallions, leeks	Quercetin, allicin, and other allium compounds
	*Green tea	EGCG, catechins (tannins)
	Almonds, pecans, walnuts, hazelnuts, pistachios, filberts, macadamia nuts, peanuts, sesame seeds, sunflower kernels	Vitamin E, lignans, fiber, selenium, ellagic acid, B vitamins, omega-6 fatty acids (in nut oils)
Skin	*Lettuce, spinach, kale, Swiss chard, arugula, watercress, mustard greens, escarole, endive, collard greens, frisee, and other leafy greens	Kaempferol, lutein, folate, vitamin C, beta carotene
	Berries and pomegranates	Ellagic acid, folate, vitamin C
	*Carrots, sweet potatoes, yams, squash, pumpkin, orange and red bell peppers, and other orange vegetables	Beta carotene, vitamin C
	Garlic, onions, chives, scallions, leeks	Quercetin, allicin and other allium compounds
Bladder	*Broccoli sprouts and cruciferous vegetables such as cauliflower and Brussels sprouts	Isothiocyanates, quercetin, vitamin C, kaempferol
	*Raspberries, black raspberries, blackberries, cranberries, strawberries, foblueberries, lingonberries	Anthocyanins, quercetin, ellagic acid, coumaric acid, vitamins C, late, resveratrol, myricetin
Kidney	*Salmon, tuna, mackerel, trout, bluefish, sardines, and other fatty fish	Omega-3 fatty acids, selenium, lignans, vitamins A and D, calcium
	Red wine	Resveratrol, catechins

* These foods are particularly high in nutrients that may help prevent this type of cancer.

Limit Your Red-Meat Intake

There has also been a lot of debate about **meat**, particularly **red meat**, and whether regular consumption increases cancer risk. **Red meat means beef, lamb, veal, and pork**. Although pork looks more white than red, its chemical properties place it in the category of a red meat. Some studies have found a link between high intake of red meat and gastrointestinal cancers—particularly stomach, colon, and pancreatic cancer. A 2006 study from the United Kingdom found that people who consumed red meat on a daily basis had a significantly higher risk of colon cancer than those who ate it only once a week. Another recent study from the United States demonstrated that survivors of colon cancer who continued to eat lots of red meat each week greatly increased their risk of having a recurrence of colon cancer. Legumes, soy protein, low- or non-fat dairy products, and lean chicken and poultry should be your main protein sources, with an occasional three-ounce (cooked) serving of red meat being an acceptable part of a healthy diet.

Grill Meats Wisely to Avoid Carcinogens

If you have been reading the newspaper lately, you may have learned that grilling meat, fish, and poultry can create carcinogens in your food. The results of a case-control study published in the journal *Epidemiology* in May 2007 demonstrated that postmenopausal women who consumed large amounts of grilled, barbecued, or smoked meats each week had a 47 percent increased risk of breast cancer compared with women who ate small quantities of these types of meats. Additionally, their breast-cancer risk was increased by 74 percent if they also reported low fruit and vegetable intake. The carcinogenic substances created by cooking at high temperatures are produced when the amino acids in the protein are heated, and they have names like polycyclic aromatic hydrocarbons (PAHs) and heterocyclic amines (HCAs). However, if you want to grill food more safely, here are a few things that you can do:

- **Trim any excess fat** from meat prior to grilling and **remove the skin** from chicken or other poultry.
- **Grilling fruits and vegetables** doesn't create these same cancer-associated compounds, so combine a small amount of grilled meat, poultry, or fish with a larger portion of grilled fruits and veggies to get the same flavor.
- **Marinate** meat, poultry, or fish **for 30 minutes** prior to cooking. This will help form a barrier between the meat and the heat. (**Never** reuse marinade as a sauce because the raw meat contaminates it!)
- **Pre-cook meat**, either in an oven or microwave, and then grill just briefly to get the flavor.
- **Turn food often** to avoid charring it. Any charred or black bits should be removed prior to eating.
- Cook meats only to a **rare or medium-rare** degree.

Be Cautions About What Supplements You Take

Based on the fact that foods containing antioxidants may decrease the risk of some cancers and the discovery that people diagnosed with cancer often have low levels of antioxidants in their bloodstream, the idea was born that, perhaps, taking a nutrient-containing supplement might decrease cancer risk. To date, there has not been enough conclusive evidence that supplements can decrease cancer risk. Research has shown that vitamin D may lower pancreatic and invasive breast-cancer risk and calcium may decrease colon and breast cancer risk, but these findings need to be confirmed in large-scale prospective studies.

A few studies have even found that supplements may **INCREASE** cancer risk. The Alpha-Tocopherol, Beta-Carotene Cancer Prevention Trial was a cancer-prevention trial conducted from 1985 to 1993 to determine whether certain vitamin supplements would prevent lung cancer in a group of almost 30,000 male smokers. What the researchers found, in fact, was that men who took a beta-carotene supplement for five to eight years had an 18 percent increased incidence of lung cancers and an 8 percent increased overall mortality (death rate)! Furthermore, a study in 2007 by researchers at the National Cancer Institute followed 295,344 men over five years and found that men who exceeded the recommended dose of multivitamins—taking more than seven a week—increased their risk of advanced prostate cancer by about 30 percent.

It is almost impossible to get too much of any given vitamin through food alone, but loading up on some vitamins in pill form can cause significant problems. The fat-soluble vitamins—A, D, E, and K—are called fat-soluble because they are absorbed best in the digestive tract when fat is present. They also tend to accumulate in the fat in your body, particularly in your liver, where they can build up to dangerous levels. If a certain amount of a nutrient is good for you, two or three times as much is not necessarily better.

Buying Organic: More Important For Some Foods Than Others

People wonder whether buying organic foods makes sense in a disease-fighting context. Unfortunately, there isn't an easy answer to this question because there have been few, if any, scientific studies that compared health outcomes of people who eat **only organic foods** and those who eat **nothing that is organic**. The term 'organic' means that food is grown or animals are raised without the use of synthetic pesticides or herbicides (weed-killers), fertilizers, antibiotics, growth hormones, genetically modified organisms, or the use of irradiation. Organic farmers use manure or compost as fertilizer, and they kill weeds with plant-based weed killers. Some past studies have demonstrated that organically grown foods have higher levels of vitamins, minerals, and other antioxidants than conventionally grown or raised foods. A recent study showed that eating organic foods could help patients with Crohn's disease suffer fewer intestinal problems. Here is a breakdown of the foods that the Environmental Working Group and other experts recommend to purchase organically and those that are acceptable in non-organic versions:

Organic is best: **apples**, **peaches**, **bell peppers**, **celery**, **nectarines**, **cherries**, **strawberries**, **imported grapes**, **pears**, **spinach**, **lettuce**, **potatoes**, **carrots**, and **baby food** because conventional versions have higher pesticide levels; **milk, dairy products, meat,** and **poultry** because of growth hormones and antibiotics.

Non-organic is okay: **onions, broccoli, bananas, frozen sweet peas, frozen sweet corn, asparagus, avocados, pineapples, cabbage, papaya, mangoes, and kiwifruit** because conventional versions have low pesticide-residue levels; **seafood** because no USDA organic certification yet exists and any seafood contains mercury, PCBs and other contaminants; **processed foods** such as **bread, chips, pasta,** and **oils** because, while they do often contain whole grains or other healthy ingredients, processed foods sometimes still include non-organic ingredients, and the processing itself can remove some of the vital nutrients.

Organic food manufacturing is now on an industrial scale. In fact, General Mills owns one of the largest organic food companies in the nation, Cascadian Farms. I opt for many organic foods in the grocery store, but I am even more likely to visit the local farmers market in the summer seasons and support the small, regional organic farmer.

Tips for Making Healthy Choices When Eating Out

Eating out can be a touchy issue for Americans. While most of us strive to be health-conscious, we often view an evening of dining at a nice restaurant as a treat or reward and thus tend to over-indulge. The National Restaurant Association estimates that on a typical day, more than four out of 10 adults patronize restaurants. When people eat out at restaurants, they consume a greater quantity of saturated fat and calories, fewer nutrients, and less fiber than when they eat at home. Children eat almost twice as many calories in the average restaurant meal compared to a home-cooked meal (770 versus 420 calories). There are some easy ways to stay on track when dining out:

- Try to **avoid large chain restaurants** that typically have many higher-fat entrees and avoid **buffet-style dining.** Enormous salad bars often have unhealthy choices—like mayonnaise-loaded macaroni or potato salad—that can easily corrupt a healthy plate of greens, vegetables, and fruits.
- **Limit portion sizes,** share a large main course, or get an appetizer size of a desired dish and a big salad.
- Choose **whole-grain bread** in the bread basket, order sandwiches with **whole-grain or -wheat bread**, and choose a **wheat or whole-grain tortilla or wrap** over one made of white flour.
- **Try to incorporate leafy greens and vegetables into your meal as much as possible.** If you can have a main course of salmon, or salmon served on a bed of greens, go for the greens. Instead of fries or chips on the side, opt for **steamed vegetables** or a **mixed green salad.**
- If ordering a **dinner salad**, go for a **harvest-type salad** that contains **berries, fruit and nuts**, rather than a Caesar or other lettuce and dressing-only salad.
- Anything can be **served on the side** and, for the sake of flavor, should be: dressings, sauces, even cheese on a salad can be put on the side—that way, you control how much you get.

- Use **balsamic vinegar** on salads and add a little bit of dressing. Balsamic doesn't have that acidic taste of other vinegars and will enhance the flavor.
- Ask for the **skin to be removed** from chicken or other poultry before serving. Ask for **minimal oil or butter** to be used. **Opt for lemon juice** if you are having broiled, baked, or steamed fish.
- Anything in a Chinese restaurant can be **steamed.** Beware especially of sweet-and-sour sauces, as they are often loaded with sugar, fat, and calories.
- Try to have **berries or other fruit** if you choose to have dessert. Instead of cake or pie or other caloric desserts, have a scoop of **sorbet** or **frozen yogurt** with berries, if it is available.
- If having an alcoholic beverage, choose **red wine** if available. Many restaurants now have **iced green tea** or **citrus-based cold beverages**. Hot **green tea** is a great way to end a meal.
- **Healthy condiments:** mustard, lemon juice, chutney, salsa, soy sauce (though it is high in sodium), cocktail sauce, ketchup (in moderation), vinegar, horseradish
- **Less healthy condiments:** butter or clarified butter, cheese, margarine, bacon or bacon bits, regular or creamy salad dressings, cream, sour cream, whipped cream, hollandaise sauce, cream cheese (unless it is low-fat)

Foods cooked by healthy cooking methods include those described as:
Baked
Broiled
Steamed
Lightly sautéed (make sure it is a healthy oil)
Garden fresh
Au jus
Roasted
Poached
Pan-seared
Aglio-Olio (if light on the oil)

Less healthy cooking methods will appear on the menu as:
In cheese sauce or au gratin
Buttered, in butter, au beurre
Alfredo
In cream sauce, in vodka cream sauce, in tomato cream sauce
Fried, chicken-fried (as in 'chicken-fried steak')
Candied, glazed, maple-glazed
Béarnaise sauce
Stuffed
Pesto

PART TWO: RECIPES

Introduction to the Recipes

This book is not designed to be a diet book. However, if you are a typical American, you are probably eating a somewhat unbalanced diet, and if you incorporate some of these recipes into your daily routine, you may just lose a few pounds. The book is not a guarantee that you will not get cancer. Cancer develops due to many factors—how much you weigh, whether you smoke cigarettes or exercise regularly, and your genetic make-up. Even what you ate or how much you weighed as a child may influence your risk of some types of cancer and other diseases. However, making changes in your eating habits at any age can only be a positive step toward maintaining good health.

The recipes in this book come from a variety of sources, including cookbooks, magazines, websites, friends and family members, and my own creative mind. I have included a few dishes from famous chefs, and have obtained permission to include them. I will frankly admit that I have been cooking and accumulating recipes for close to 30 years, and I honestly do not know where each and every recipe came from, although I have done my best to list the sources. All of the recipes have a few things in common:

· They are loaded with nutrients and antioxidants that have been shown to be health protective.
· They contain ingredients that should be relatively easy to find in local supermarkets.
· They are not incredibly difficult to prepare (though a few of them take a good investment of time).
· They taste fantastic.

The recipe portions are healthy, but not enormous, and are designed to suit an intelligently sized meal. The comprehensive nutrition information lists calories, grams of fat, saturated fat, protein, carbohydrate, total sugars and dietary fiber, and milligrams of sodium and cholesterol so that you can choose dishes that fit your energy needs and lifestyle. It is recommended that the average person should consume no more than 30 percent of calories of fat per day and no more than 10 percent of calories of saturated fat per day. If you are eating about a 2,000-calorie daily diet, this comes to 60 grams of fat, including 20 grams of saturated fat at maximum. Fiber recommendations are about 25 grams per day for women and about 30 for men; children need to get plenty of fiber in their diets as well.

Almost all of these dishes are low in saturated fat and total sugar, although a few of the main dishes and casual dining recipes (sandwiches, pizza, burgers, burritos, etc.) contain upwards of 300 to 400 calories. This may seem like a lot of calories, until you consider that a large double burger with cheese at a well-known U.S. fast food restaurant has 1,070 calories and 70 grams of fat, which is more than most people's daily recommended fat intake. The recipes are designed so that you can mix and match various beverages, soups, salads, side dishes, main courses, and dessert items to get a totally nutritious and fulfilling daily diet.

Substitutions: I have chosen to use sugar and natural sweeteners, such as maple syrup, rather than low-calorie sweeteners in most of these recipes. When I do use a low-calorie sweetener, I tend to choose Splenda® rather than another sweetener, because the sugar-to-Splenda® conversion is one-to-one, so you would use the same quantity of Splenda® as the recipe lists for sugar. If you are diabetic or on a low-sugar diet, feel free to use your sugar substitute of choice. And, if you prefer to use sugar instead of Splenda® or another sweetener, feel free to do so. I use mainly monounsaturated and polyunsaturated oils in the dishes, although a few do contain butter or trans-fat–free butter alternatives. There are many butter alternatives on the grocery shelves these days, each with its own particular health claim, and you are free to use the one that you prefer. Bear in mind, however, that changing an ingredient may alter the nutritional information for the recipe.

If you are vegetarian or vegan, feel free to substitute a plant-based protein such as tofu or tempeh for animal protein in appropriate dishes. Soy yogurt, soy milk, and soy margarine can all be substituted for dairy products quite easily. If you require a gluten-free diet, choose wheat-free soy sauce or tamari (or use Bragg's amino acids), rice, potato, tapioca or corn breads, cereals, and flours where appropriate, and use gluten-free flour mixes for baked goods. I have a touch of gluten sensitivity, and I can tell you that almost all of these recipes can be made quite successfully with a gluten-free alternative.

One other point to make: This book is not the best recipe book for individuals who are actively getting cancer treatment, such as chemotherapy and radiation. Your protein needs increase during treatment, and because of side effects such as mouth and esophageal sores, eating acidic foods such as tomatoes and citrus fruit is a very bad idea. However, toward the back of the book, I have made a list of recipes that would be appropriate for people in active cancer treatment. PLEASE check with your own doctor before cooking any of these dishes, however, to ensure that they will not aggravate any of your symptoms from treatment.

Finally, try to have fun with the recipes. Cooking with antioxidant-rich ingredients will soon become natural to you. Like me, over time you will probably find that you can look at just about any recipe and figure out how to make it a bit healthier and better suited to your own tastes and to achieving longevity.

BREADS AND BREAKFAST FOODS

Many of my recipes call for whole-wheat pastry flour, which is typically found in the organic section of the grocery store if it is not in the regular baking section. It is also widely available in any health-food store.

Apple Bran Mini Muffins

These bite-size bran muffins are ideal for children or adults of any age and are the perfect portion for wholesome snacking. You can also bake this batter as full-size muffins in regular muffin tins by increasing the baking temperature to 375°F and the time to 20 minutes. You'll only get 6 to 8 muffins, though.

Ingredients:
Nonstick cooking spray
1-1/4 cups natural bran (not bran cereal)
2/3 cup all-purpose white flour
1/3 cup whole-wheat pastry flour
1/3 cup brown sugar
2-1/2 teaspoons baking powder
1/2 teaspoon cinnamon
1/2 cup reduced-fat (2%) milk
1/3 cup canola oil
2 eggs
1 medium Gala or Jonagold apple, peeled and finely chopped

Preparation: Preheat oven to 350°F. Spray cups in two miniature muffin pans with nonstick cooking spray or line with mini muffin papers. In a large bowl, stir together bran, flour, brown sugar, baking powder, and cinnamon. In a smaller bowl, whisk together milk, oil, and eggs. Add milk mixture to bran mixture, stirring until just combined. Fold in chopped apple. Spoon batter into prepared muffin pans, filling each cup to the top. Bake 12 to 14 minutes or until a toothpick inserted in the middle of a muffin comes out clean. Makes 20 miniature muffins.

Nutritional information per muffin:
Calories: 101.5
Fat: 4.7 g
Saturated fat: 0.6 g
Carbohydrate: 12.4 g
Total sugars: 3.4 g
Protein: 2.4 g
Sodium: 11 mg
Cholesterol: 19 mg
Dietary fiber: 1.4 g

Apple Pecan Baked Pancakes

This recipe is credited to Beverly and Doug Breitling, innkeepers of the Arsenic and Old Lace Bed and Breakfast in Eureka Springs, Arkansas, and reprinted with their permission.

Ingredients:
1-1/2 cups prepared buckwheat pancake batter
2 tablespoons unsalted butter, melted
1 cup Granny Smith apples, peeled and sliced
1/3 cup pecans, chopped
2 tablespoons maple syrup
1/2 teaspoon ground cinnamon

Preparation: Heat oven to 350°F. Prepare buckwheat pancake mix according to package directions and set aside. Pour melted butter into a 9-inch pie plate. Place apple slices in bottom of pie plate. Sprinkle cinnamon and pecans and drizzle syrup over apples; carefully pour batter on top of apple-nut mixture. Bake 30 to 35 minutes or until top springs back when touched. Loosen edges and invert onto serving plate. Cut in wedges and serve with warm maple syrup or fresh apple butter. Makes 4 servings, 1/4 pancake each.

Nutritional information per serving:
Calories: 262.8
Fat: 14.8 g
Saturated fat: 5.2 g
Carbohydrate: 28.7 g
Total sugars: 12.6 g
Protein: 3.7 g
Sodium: 55 mg
Cholesterol: 107.6 mg
Dietary fiber: 1.5 g

Carrot Raisin Flax Muffins

In addition to their anti-cancer effects, ground flaxseeds and flaxseed oil may be able to lower blood pressure.

Ingredients:
1 cup all-purpose flour
1/2 cup whole-wheat flour
3/4 cup ground flaxseed meal
3/4 cup oat bran (can substitute rolled oats)
1/2 cup brown sugar, packed
2 teaspoons baking soda
1 teaspoon baking powder
1/4 teaspoon salt
2 teaspoons cinnamon
1-1/2 cups grated carrots (about 3 medium carrots)
1 cup pineapple tidbits, drained (save the juice)
1/2 cup raisins
2 eggs
1 cup reduced-fat (2%) milk
1 tablespoon juice from the drained pineapple
2 tablespoons unsweetened applesauce
1 teaspoon vanilla

Preparation: Preheat oven to 350°F. Spray two regular 12-muffin tins with nonstick cooking spray or line with paper liners. In a large bowl, combine white flour, wheat flour, flaxseed, oat bran or oats, brown sugar, baking soda, baking powder, salt, and cinnamon. Stir in carrots, pineapple, and raisins. In a separate bowl, combine eggs, milk, drained pineapple juice, applesauce, and vanilla. Add liquid ingredients to dry ingredients and stir until moist (the batter should be lumpy). Pour into 18 prepared muffin-tin cups (fill any empty ones with water). Bake 16 to 20 minutes, or until lightly browned and a toothpick comes out clean. Makes 18 muffins.

> The lignans (flaxseeds) and fiber (oat bran) in this recipe may help prevent the following cancers: **prostate and pancreas.**

Nutritional information per muffin:
Calories: 145.4
Fat: 3.0 g
Saturated fat: 0.4 g
Carbohydrate: 25.4 g
Total sugars: 10.7 g
Protein: 4.2 g
Sodium: 197 mg
Cholesterol: < 1 mg
Dietary fiber: 4.0 g

Cherry Bran Muffins

This recipe's fiber (bran flakes) and anthocyanins (cherries) may help prevent the following cancers: **colon and breast.**

There are two types of fiber—soluble and insoluble. Insoluble fiber, which is found in foods like wheat bran and bran flakes, is thought to help reduce the risk of colorectal cancer. Soluble fiber, such as the fiber in oat bran, helps reduce blood cholesterol, lowering the risk of heart disease. You should eat fiber from a variety of sources every day to obtain the greatest health benefits.

Ingredients:
Nonstick cooking spray
3 cups bran flakes cereal
2 cups oat bran
2 cups whole-wheat pastry flour
1/2 cup brown sugar
2 teaspoons baking powder
2 teaspoons baking soda
1 cup cholesterol-free egg substitute (such as Egg Beaters)
2 cups low-fat (1%) milk
1/4 cup honey
1/4 cup molasses
1-1/2 cups dried cherries

Preparation: Preheat oven to 400°F and spray 18 cups of 2 regular 12-muffin tins with nonstick cooking spray or line with paper liners (or use nonstick muffin tins). In a large mixing bowl, combine bran flakes, oat bran, flour, brown sugar, baking powder and baking soda. Stir until evenly distributed. Add egg substitute, milk, honey, and molasses and stir until blended. Fold in dried cherries. Fill 18 muffin cups about 2/3 full with batter (put some water in any remaining unfilled cups) and bake 18 to 20 minutes or until a toothpick inserted in muffin center comes out clean. Makes 18 large muffins.

Nutritional information per muffin:
Calories: 215.6
Fat: 1.6 g
Saturated fat: 0.3 g
Carbohydrate: 44.0 g
Total sugars: 21.7 g
Protein: 6.3 g
Sodium: 237 mg
Cholesterol: < 1 mg
Dietary fiber: 5.1 g

Cherry Granola Bread

Ingredients:
1-1/4 cups water
2-1/2 teaspoons active dry yeast
2 tablespoons canola oil
2 tablespoons honey
1-1/2 teaspoons salt
2 cups bread flour, divided
1-1/4 cups whole-wheat flour, divided
3 tablespoons nonfat dry milk powder
2/3 cup granola (natural or berry flavor, preferably)
1/2 cup dried tart cherries

Preparation: Preheat oven to 350°F. Heat water until warm (105° to 115°F). In a large mixing bowl, dissolve yeast in warm water. Add oil, honey, and salt; mix well. Add 1 cup bread flour, 3/4 cup whole-wheat flour and dry milk powder to warm liquid mixture. Beat on low speed with an electric mixer until moistened; beat an additional 3 minutes at medium speed. Stir in granola, cherries, remaining 1 cup bread flour, and remaining 1/2 cup whole-wheat flour. Mix until dough pulls cleanly away from sides of bowl. On lightly floured surface, knead dough until smooth and elastic, adding more bread flour if needed. Place dough in a lightly oiled mixing bowl; cover loosely with plastic wrap and a cloth towel. Let rise in a warm place (80° to 85°F) about 1 hour, or until about double in size. Punch down dough several times to remove all air bubbles. Let rest 15 minutes. Shape into a loaf. Place in nonstick or lightly oiled 8-1/2 x 4-1/2-inch loaf pan. Cover and let rise in a warm place 45 to 60 minutes or until double in size. Bake 35 to 45 minutes, or until golden and loaf sounds hollow when lightly tapped. Remove from pan immediately and cool on a wire rack. Serve warm or at room temperature. Makes 1 loaf, about 16 slices.

This recipe's fiber (wheat flour) and resveratrol (cherries) may help prevent the following cancers: **colon and breast.**

Nutritional information per slice:
Calories: 171.5
Fat: 3.5 g
Saturated fat: 0.4 g
Carbohydrate: 29.6 g
Total sugars: 6.1 g
Protein: 5.4 g
Sodium: 229 mg
Cholesterol: < 1 mg
Dietary fiber: 3.6 g

Chilled Apple Oatmeal

Top this oatmeal with some fresh raspberries or dried cherries to add sweetness and get an extra antioxidant boost.

Ingredients:
1/2 cup rolled oats (quick or old-fashioned)
1/2 cup reduced-fat (2%) milk
1/2 cup plain non-fat yogurt
1/4 cup natural (unsweetened) applesauce
1 teaspoon almonds, coarsely chopped
1 teaspoon pumpkin seeds
1/4 teaspoon low-calorie sugar substitute
1/8 teaspoon ground cinnamon

Preparation: Combine all ingredients in a medium bowl. Stir well, cover with plastic wrap, and refrigerate overnight. Serve chilled. Makes 2 servings, about 3/4 cup each.

This recipe's lignans (oats) and calcium (milk) may help prevent the following cancers: **pancreas and liver.**

Nutritional information per serving:
Calories: 179.9
Fat: 4.3 g
Saturated fat: 0.8 g
Carbohydrate: 25.6 g
Total sugars: 11.1 g
Protein: 9.7 g
Sodium: 72 mg
Cholesterol: 4.2 mg
Dietary fiber: 2.8 g

Cranberry Breakfast Bars

These delightful bars keep for several days if stored in an air-tight container. Additionally, you can freeze them and thaw overnight in the refrigerator for the next day's breakfast treat.

Ingredients:
Nonstick cooking spray
1 cup whole-wheat pastry flour
2 cups rolled oats
2 tablespoons sunflower kernels
1 teaspoon baking powder
1 teaspoon ground cinnamon
1/8 teaspoon salt
2/3 cup brown-rice syrup
3 tablespoons canola oil
1 egg
1/3 cup dried cranberries
3 tablespoons dark raisins
1/4 cup walnuts, coarsely chopped
1/4 cup pecans, coarsely chopped

Preparation: Preheat oven to 325°F. Use a nonstick 9-inch square baking pan or line a 9-inch square baking pan with aluminum foil and lightly spray with nonstick cooking spray. Set aside. In a large mixing bowl, combine flour, oats, sunflower kernels, baking powder, cinnamon, and salt. In a separate bowl, combine brown-rice syrup, oil and egg; stir. Mix in dried cranberries, raisins, walnuts, and pecans. Spread batter into prepared baking pan using a rubber spatula to create an even thickness. Bake 30 to 35 minutes, until firm to touch in center and lightly brown. Cool 10 minutes on a wire rack, then invert onto a cutting board. Use a large serrated knife to cut into quarters; cut each quarter into three separate bars. Makes 12 breakfast bars.

Nutritional information per bar:
Calories: 234.8
Fat: 8.0 g
Saturated fat: 0.7 g
Carbohydrate: 35.8 g
Total sugars: 15.0 g
Protein: 4.9 g
Sodium: 44 mg
Cholesterol: 0 mg
Dietary fiber: 3.0 g

Cranberry Orange Oat-Nut Muffins

Just about everything in these delicious muffins, from the oats to the pecans to the cranberries, is good for you. Enjoy one with a glass of soy milk or some low-fat yogurt for an energy-rich breakfast.

Ingredients:
2 cups quick oats
1-1/4 cups plain low-fat yogurt
1-1/4 cups warm water
1 cup pecans, chopped
1 cup fresh cranberries, coarsely chopped
1 tablespoon orange zest, grated
1/2 cup canola oil
1/2 cup whole-wheat pastry flour
1 cup unbleached white flour
1 tablespoon baking powder
1/2 teaspoon baking soda
1/4 teaspoon salt
1/4 cup brown sugar

Preparation: Preheat oven to 375° F. Use either two large nonstick muffin pans, 18 cups total, or lightly coat two large muffin pans with nonstick cooking spray. In a large bowl, combine oats, yogurt, and water. Add pecans, cranberries, orange zest, and oil to oat mixture and stir. In a separate bowl, combine whole-wheat and white flours, baking powder, baking soda, salt, and brown sugar, and stir until evenly distributed. Pour dry ingredients into wet ingredients and mix gently (only a few stokes). Spoon mixture evenly into muffin cups. Bake 20 to 25 minutes in the center rack of oven, until lightly browned and firm to the touch. Cool in pans on rack 5 minutes; run a knife around edges of muffins and turn out onto rack. May be eaten immediately, at room temperature, or refrigerate and reheat in microwave or toaster oven. Makes 18 muffins.

This recipe's vitamin E (pecans) and pectin (orange zest) may help prevent the following cancers: **breast and esophageal.**

Nutritional information per muffin:
Calories: 193.2
Fat: 11.4 g
Saturated fat: 1.1 g
Carbohydrate: 18.8 g
Total sugars: 3.8 g
Protein: 4.0 g
Sodium: 81 mg
Cholesterol: 1 mg
Dietary fiber: 2.3 g

Crunchy Peanut Butter Muffins

These healthy, whole-grain and nut muffins are sweetened with apple juice and bananas rather than sugar. Eating less refined sugar may help you maintain a healthy weight and protect you from developing insulin resistance and diabetes.

This recipe's vitamin D (milk) and selenium (peanut butter) may help prevent the following cancers: **breast and stomach.**

Ingredients:
2 eggs
1 cup reduced-fat (2%) milk
1 ripe banana, mashed with a fork
1/4 cup natural peanut butter
1/3 cup canola oil
1/4 cup frozen apple juice concentrate, thawed until soft
1/4 cup nonfat dry milk
1-1/2 cups all-purpose (white) flour
3/4 cup whole-wheat pastry flour
1-1/2 teaspoons baking powder
1 teaspoon baking soda
Nonstick cooking spray

Preparation: Preheat oven to 350° F. In a small bowl, beat eggs gently with a fork. In a large bowl, combine milk, mashed banana, peanut butter, canola oil, apple juice, and dry milk. Add beaten eggs and mix with a large spoon until creamy. Add flour, baking powder, and baking soda and mix. Line a muffin tin with paper liners or lightly spray with nonstick spray. Fill each muffin cup about 2/3 full with muffin mix. Bake 15 to 17 minutes, until browned on top and a toothpick comes out clean. Cool on wire rack. Makes 12 muffins.

Nutritional information per muffin:
Calories: 192.2
Fat: 9.3 g
Saturated fat: 1.1 g
Carbohydrate: 22.4 g
Total sugars: 6.9 g
Protein: 4.9 g
Sodium: 133 mg
Cholesterol: 1.2 mg
Dietary fiber: 2.5 g

Easy Cranberry Nut Granola

You can eat this granola alone as a snack, as a breakfast cereal, or use it to top some bran flakes or vanilla yogurt.

Ingredients:
1/2 cup sunflower kernels
1/3 cup cashew pieces
1-1/2 cups rolled oats
1/4 cup ground flaxseed
1/3 cup almonds, sliced or slivered
1/2 cup unsweetened coconut, shredded
3 tablespoons natural peanut butter
1/2 cup dried cranberries
1/4 teaspoon salt
1/3 cup honey
1/2 teaspoon vanilla extract

Preparation: Preheat oven to 300°F. In a large bowl, combine all ingredients. Mix thoroughly until ingredients are evenly distributed. Press mixture into a deep baking pan or dish and bake 40 to 45 minutes. Let cool and store in a resealable container. Makes 12 servings, about 1/3 cup each.

The vitamin E (almonds) and lignans (flaxseed) in this recipe may help prevent the following cancers: **colon and prostate**

Nutritional information per serving:
Calories: 180.1
Fat: 8.1 g
Saturated fat: 2.0 g
Carbohydrate: 22.3 g
Total sugars: 11.4 g
Protein: 4.6 g
Sodium: 70 mg
Cholesterol: 0 mg
Dietary fiber: 3.5 g

Homemade Banana Bread

This is my own recipe for banana bread that my mother and I have been making together since I was a teenager.

Ingredients:
Nonstick cooking spray, canola-oil flavor
1 cup all-purpose white flour
1/2 cup whole-wheat pastry flour
1/4 cup sugar
2 teaspoons baking powder
1 teaspoon baking soda
1/8 teaspoon salt
1/2 cup wheat germ
4 medium-large, very ripe bananas (about 1-1/2 cups)
1/4 cup low-fat buttermilk
1/4 cup canola oil
4 egg whites
3 tablespoons honey
2 tablespoons walnuts, chopped or pieces

Preparation: Preheat oven to 350°F. Spray an 8x4-inch loaf pan with nonstick cooking spray (or use a nonstick loaf pan). In a large mixing bowl, sift together white and wheat flour, sugar, baking powder, baking soda, and salt. One by one, add remaining ingredients except walnuts; beat with a hand or stand mixer or stir with a large wooden spoon until well blended. Pour into prepared loaf pan and sprinkle walnuts on top. Bake 1 hour or until golden brown on top and an inserted toothpick comes out clean. If you use very large bananas, it may take an extra 5 to 10 minutes to cook through. Makes 12 slices.

This recipe's ellagic acid (walnuts) and calcium (buttermilk) may help prevent the following cancers: **colon and breast.**

Nutritional information per slice:
Calories: 191.7
Fat: 6.1 g
Saturated fat: 0.9 g
Carbohydrate: 29.4 g
Total sugars: 12.4 g
Protein: 4.8 g
Sodium: 153 mg
Cholesterol: 0.2 mg
Dietary fiber: 2.3 g

Low-fat Blueberry Muffins

There is just about nothing better to wake you up than moist, warm blueberry muffins. By using a limited amount of heart-healthy canola oil and low-fat buttermilk, I've created a lower-fat version of traditional muffins that is still packed with flavor. For variation, try making them with 1/2 heaping cup of blueberries and 1/2 heaping cup of fresh, chopped strawberries.

Ingredients:
1-1/3 cups all-purpose white flour
2/3 cup whole-wheat pastry flour
1/3 cup sugar
1 teaspoon baking powder
1/2 teaspoon baking soda
1/4 teaspoon salt
1 cup low-fat buttermilk
2 tablespoons canola oil
1 large egg, lightly beaten
1 heaping cup fresh blueberries

Preparation: Preheat oven to 400° F. Lightly spray a regular 12-cup muffin tin with cooking spray or line with paper liners. In a large bowl, combine white and wheat flour, sugar, baking powder, baking soda, and salt. In a small bowl, combine milk, canola oil, and egg. Make a well in the center of dry ingredients and add wet ingredients. Stir until just moist. Fold in blueberries. Fill muffin cups about 2/3 full. Bake for 18 to 22 minutes or until golden brown. Cool on wire rack. Makes 12 muffins.

This recipe's calcium (buttermilk) and anthocyanins (blueberries) may help prevent the following cancers: **breast and colon.**

Nutritional information per muffin:
Calories: 140.8
Fat: 3.2 g
Saturated fat: 0.4 g
Carbohydrate: 24.5 g
Total sugars: 7.8 g
Protein: 3.4 g
Sodium: 77 mg
Cholesterol: 18.4 mg
Dietary fiber: 0.9 g

Morning Glory Muffins

One of the best ways to achieve a diverse and healthy diet is to get your fiber from a variety of different foods, including whole grains, nuts, fruits, and vegetables—and these muffins contain all of those ingredients!

This recipe's fiber (wheat flour) and quercetin (apples) may help prevent the following cancers: **colon and lung.**

Ingredients:
1/2 cup raisins
1-1/3 cups all-purpose white flour
2/3 cup whole-wheat pastry flour
1 cup sugar
2 teaspoons baking soda
2 teaspoons ground cinnamon
1/2 teaspoon salt
2 medium carrots, grated
1 medium Granny Smith apple, cored and finely diced
1/2 cup sliced almonds
1/2 cup shredded unsweetened coconut
3 eggs
2/3 cup natural applesauce
2 teaspoons vanilla extract
Nonstick cooking spray

Preparation: Place raisins in a bowl and soak in warm water to 2 inches covered for 30 minutes; drain thoroughly. Preheat oven to 350°F. In a large bowl, combine white and whole-wheat flour, sugar, soda, cinnamon, and salt. Stir in raisins, carrots, apple, almonds, and coconut. In a separate small bowl, beat eggs with applesauce and vanilla to blend. Stir egg mixture into flour mixture until just combined. Line 12 muffin cups with paper liners or spray with nonstick cooking spray. Fill cups 2/3 full with muffin batter. Bake until golden brown, about 20 to 22 minutes. Let cool 5 minutes before removing from pan. These muffins are delicious hot or at room temperature, and they also freeze well. Makes 12 muffins.

Nutritional information per muffin:
Calories: 219.4
Fat: 3.4 g
Saturated fat: 1.2 g
Carbohydrate: 42.7 g
Total sugars: 23.9 g
Protein: 4.5 g
Sodium: 121 mg
Cholesterol: 0 mg
Dietary fiber: 3 g

Multigrain Banana-Berry Pancakes

This is a recipe that I found on a health website and adapted a bit to fit my own tastes. These pancakes are the perfect meal to eat before a day of physical activity, like hitting the slopes or riding your bike. They are also one of my favorite "breakfast-for-dinner" meals.

Ingredients:
Nonstick cooking spray
1-1/4 cups unbleached flour
1/4 cup cornmeal
1/4 cup rolled oats
1/3 cup packed brown sugar
1 teaspoon baking soda
1/4 teaspoon salt
2 egg whites from extra-large eggs, slightly beaten
1 cup nonfat buttermilk
1 cup low-fat sour cream
2 ripe bananas, sliced
1/2 cup strawberries, hulled and sliced
1/2 cup fresh blueberries

Preparation: In a mixing bowl, combine flour, cornmeal, oats, brown sugar, baking soda, and salt. In another mixing bowl, combine egg whites, buttermilk, and sour cream. Mix dry ingredients with wet ingredients until just moistened. Spray a skillet with nonstick cooking spray and place over medium heat until hot. Ladle batter onto skillet, using about 3 tablespoons per cake. Cook about 2 minutes, flip carefully, and cook about 2 minutes more, until lightly browned. Repeat with remaining batter. Place 3 pancakes on plate and top with sliced banana and berries. Makes 4 servings, 3 medium-size pancakes each.

Nutritional information per 3-pancake serving:
Calories: 454.5
Fat: 8.9 g
Saturated fat: 5.4 g
Carbohydrate: 81.1 g
Total sugars: 31.3 g
Protein: 12.5 g
Sodium: 88 mg
Cholesterol: 9.5 mg
Dietary fiber: 1.5 g

The Anti-Cancer Cookbook

Oatmeal Maple Pecan Muffins

These are some of the most delectable muffins you will ever bake. Try them once and I am sure that you will be hooked. Feel free to substitute walnuts, hazelnuts, or other nuts for the pecans.

Ingredients:
1-1/4 cups rolled oats
1 cup whole-wheat pastry flour
1/2 cup all-purpose white flour
1 teaspoon baking powder
1 teaspoon baking soda
1/4 teaspoon salt
1 large egg plus 2 egg whites
1 cup low-fat buttermilk
1/2 cup canola oil
1/2 cup pure maple syrup
1/2 cup pecans, finely chopped

Preparation: Preheat oven to 400°F. Lightly spray a regular 12-muffin tin with nonstick cooking spray or line with paper liners (or use a nonstick muffin pan). Place oats in a blender or food processor and process until they become a coarse powder (some larger flakes may remain). Measure 1 cup (precisely) of this oat flour and place in a large bowl; add whole-wheat flour, white flour, baking powder, baking soda, and salt, and stir until evenly distributed. (Discard remaining oat flour or save for another use.) In a separate small bowl, lightly beat the egg and egg whites. Stir in buttermilk, maple syrup, and canola oil. Make a well in middle of dry ingredients and pour in wet ingredients; stir until just blended and fold in pecans. Divide batter evenly among 12 muffin cups. Bake 20 to 24 minutes, until golden brown. These are delicious served either hot or at room temperature. Makes 12 muffins.

This recipe's fiber (oats) and calcium (milk) may help prevent the following cancers: **colon and breast.**

Nutritional information per muffin:
Calories: 244.3
Fat: 13.1 g
Saturated fat: 1.3 g
Carbohydrate: 26.7 g
Total sugars: 10.1 g
Protein: 4.9 g
Sodium: 192 mg
Cholesterol: 18.4 mg
Dietary fiber: 2.5 g

Orange-Banana Whole-Wheat Pancakes

I sometimes toss some blueberries into the pancake batter to get an extra burst of flavor.

This recipe's calcium (yogurt) and pectin (orange) may help prevent the following cancers: **colon and lung.**

Ingredients:
2 eggs
1/4 cup canola oil
1-1/4 teaspoons vanilla extract
2 cups whole-wheat pastry flour
1/2 tablespoon baking soda
1 tablespoon brown sugar
About 1-3/4 cups orange juice (more if needed)
2 bananas, sliced into about 1/4-inch slices
6 ounces low-fat vanilla yogurt
1 orange, peeled and sectioned

Preparation: In a large bowl, beat eggs, oil, and vanilla. Combine whole-wheat flour, baking soda, and brown sugar in a separate bowl and stir; add to egg mixture. Gradually add orange juice to desired consistency. Drop about 1/4 cup batter onto a hot griddle and place banana slices on top. Cook bottom side to a golden brown and flip to brown top. Bananas will brown first and melt slightly. Serve with a dollop of low-fat vanilla yogurt and a few orange sections on the side. Makes 6 servings, 2 large pancakes per serving.

Nutritional information per 2-pancake serving:
Calories: 354.5
Fat: 12.1 g
Saturated fat: 1.4 g
Carbohydrate: 53.1 g
Total sugars: 17.5 g
Protein: 8.3 g
Sodium: 41 mg
Cholesterol: 63.6 mg
Dietary fiber: 5.7 g

The Anti-Cancer Cookbook

Pumpkin-Cranberry Bread

Ingredients:
Nonstick cooking spray
1 cup all-purpose white flour
1/2 cup whole-wheat pastry flour
1/4 cup cornmeal
3/4 cup sugar
3/8 teaspoon salt
1 teaspoon baking soda
1/4 teaspoon baking powder
1/4 teaspoon ground cloves
1/2 teaspoon ground cinnamon
1/2 teaspoon ground ginger
1 cup canned 100% pumpkin purée
5 tablespoons canola oil
2 teaspoons grated orange zest
3 tablespoons water
1-1/2 cups fresh cranberries, chopped

Preparation: Preheat oven to 350°F. Lightly spray a 9x9-inch baking pan with nonstick cooking spray. In a medium bowl, combine white flour, whole-wheat flour, cornmeal, sugar, salt, baking soda, baking powder, cloves, cinnamon, and ginger and set aside. In a large mixing bowl, combine pumpkin, canola oil, orange zest, and water. Add dry ingredients to wet ingredients; gently stir in chopped cranberries until thoroughly combined. Pour mixture into baking pan and bake 40 to 50 minutes or until an inserted toothpick comes out clean. Allow bread to cool about 5 minutes before removing from pan; place bread on a rack to cool completely before serving. Makes 16 small squares.

This recipe's beta carotene (pumpkin) and ellagic acid (cranberries) may help prevent the following cancers: **skin and colon.**

Nutritional information per square:
Calories: 138.2
Fat: 4.6 g
Saturated fat: 0.4 g
Carbohydrate: 22.6 g
Total sugars: 10.3 g
Protein: 1.6 g
Sodium: 57 mg
Cholesterol: 0 mg
Dietary fiber: 1.5 g

Pumpkin Scones

Most scones that you find in the bakery are made with loads of butter and are fairly high in fat. These healthy and hearty scones are delicious and practically fat-free.

This recipe's fiber (whole-wheat flour) and beta carotene (pumpkin) may help prevent the following cancers: **colon and lung.**

Ingredients:
1-1/2 cups white flour
1 cup whole-wheat pastry flour
2 teaspoons baking powder
2 teaspoons baking soda
3/4 cup sugar
1/2 teaspoon salt
1/2 teaspoon ground cinnamon
1/4 teaspoon ground nutmeg
1/4 teaspoon ground ginger
2 eggs
1 cup plain low-fat yogurt
1/2 cup canned 100% pumpkin

Glaze:
2 tablespoons trans-fat–free margarine
1 tablespoon confectioners' sugar
1 tablespoon maple syrup

Preparation: Preheat oven to 425°F. Combine white and whole-wheat flour, baking powder, baking soda, sugar, salt, and spices in a large bowl. Stir dry ingredients with a fork until well blended. Add eggs, yogurt, and pumpkin and continue to stir. Dough will become a sticky mass. To make scones, scoop batter using an ice cream scoop, and place each scoop onto a nonstick baking sheet, about 2 inches apart. Make 12 scoops. Bake 15 to 20 minutes, until golden brown. Meanwhile, for glaze, melt margarine (I use the microwave) and combine with sugar and maple syrup. After removing scones from the oven and cooling for 1 to 2 minutes, spread glaze over top and sides of scones. Makes 12 scones.

Nutritional information per scone:
Calories: 172.3
Fat: 0.7 g
Saturated fat: 0.3 g
Carbohydrate: 36.7 g
Total sugars: 16.0 g
Protein: 4.8 g
Sodium: 138 mg
Cholesterol: 1.2 mg
Dietary fiber: 2.0 g

Strawberry French Toast

Ingredients:
2 cups low-fat (1%) milk
1 large egg plus 4 egg whites
1 cup bran flakes cereal
1-1/2 teaspoons ground cinnamon
12 slices Challah bread (or thickly sliced whole-wheat or peasant bread)
Nonstick cooking spray
1 cup fresh strawberries, thinly sliced

Preparation: In a medium bowl, combine milk, egg, and egg whites; mix well. Place bran flakes and cinnamon in a zip-lock bag, crunch up flakes, and shake to distribute cinnamon. Pour cereal mixture into a large baking dish or rimmed plate. Dip bread in egg mixture and dredge both sides of bread with cereal mixture. Spray a skillet with nonstick cooking spray and place over medium heat. Heat each slice of bread on both sides until golden brown. Serve topped with sliced strawberries. Makes 6 servings, 2 slices of French toast each.

This recipe's calcium (milk) and vitamin C (strawberries) may help prevent the following cancers: **breast and pancreas.**

Nutritional information per 2-slice serving:
Calories: 241.6
Fat: 4.4 g
Saturated fat: 1.4 g
Carbohydrate: 38.1 g
Total sugars: 18.2 g
Protein: 12.4 g
Sodium: 430 mg
Cholesterol: 39.2 mg
Dietary fiber: 6.0 g

Super Strawberry Bread

I've had this bread for breakfast, as a snack, and with a little scoop of low-fat frozen yogurt for dessert. It has been a hit with everyone who has tried it.

Ingredients:
1-1/3 cups all-purpose white flour
2/3 cup whole-wheat flour
1/3 cup sugar
1-1/2 teaspoons baking powder
1/2 teaspoon salt
1/4 teaspoon baking soda
1 egg, slightly beaten
1/4 cup trans-fat free margarine
3/4 cup nonfat (skim) milk
2 tablespoons strawberry all-fruit preserves or jam
1 cup fresh strawberries, hulled and coarsely chopped

This recipe's fiber (whole-wheat flour) and vitamin C (strawberries) may help prevent the following cancers: **breast and esophageal.**

Nutritional Information per slice:
Calories: 121.1
Fat: 0.7 g
Saturated fat: trace
Carbohydrate: 25.3 g
Total sugars: 7.9 g
Protein: 3.4 g
Sodium: 142 mg
Cholesterol: 15.8 mg
Dietary fiber: 1.5 g

Preparation: Preheat oven to 350°F. Spray a 9x5x3-inch loaf pan with nonstick cooking spray or use a nonstick loaf pan. In a medium bowl, combine white and whole-wheat flour, sugar, baking powder, salt, and baking soda. Mix well. Add egg and margarine and beat with hand or stand mixer at low speed until well blended. Gradually blend in milk and strawberry preserves or jam. Fold in strawberries. Pour batter into prepared loaf pan and bake 60 to 70 minutes until top is lightly brown and toothpick inserted in middle comes out clean. Remove from oven and let cool at least 5 minutes before removing from pan to cooling rack. Serve warm or at room temperature. Makes 12 slices.

Tex-Mex Cornbread Muffins

These cornbread muffins are made with regular and soy flour as well as soy milk, which provide some valuable phytoestrogens.

Ingredients:
Nonstick cooking spray
3/4 cup all-purpose white flour
1/4 cup soy flour
1 cup yellow cornmeal
1/4 cup sugar
4 teaspoons baking powder
1 teaspoon salt
1 teaspoon chili powder
1 cup plain soy milk
1/4 cup vegetable oil
1 egg plus 3 egg whites, slightly beaten
3/4 cup shredded reduced-fat cheddar cheese
3 tablespoons jalapeño pepper, chopped
1/4 cup green chiles, chopped

Preparation: Preheat oven to 425°F. Coat muffin tin with non-stick cooking spray or line with paper liners. In medium bowl, combine white flour, soy flour, cornmeal, sugar, baking powder, salt, and chili powder. In a separate bowl, stir together soy milk, oil and egg/egg-white mixture. Add wet ingredients to dry ingredients and blend gently. Stir in cheese, pepper, and green chiles. Pour into muffin cups. Bake 20 to 24 minutes or until a toothpick inserted in center comes out clean. Remove muffins from tin and cool on wire rack. Makes 12 muffins.

This recipe's isoflavones (soy milk) and vitamin D (cheddar) may help prevent the following cancers: **prostate and colon.**

Nutritional information per muffin:
Calories: 166.4
Fat: 6.8 g
Saturated fat: 1.1 g
Carbohydrate: 21.0 g
Total sugars: 5.0 g
Protein: 5.3 g
Sodium: 237 mg
Cholesterol: 18 mg
Dietary fiber: 1.6 g

The Anti-Cancer Cookbook

Whole-grain Mixed Berry Muffins

These muffins contain the whole-grain goodness of wheat, wheat germ, and flaxseed, as well as powerful berry antioxidant polyphenols. They are also low in calories and fat and contain virtually no saturated fat. These muffins store and travel nicely for the lunchbox or snacks.

Ingredients:
Nonstick cooking spray
1-3/4 cups whole-wheat pastry flour
3/4 cup rolled oats (not quick oats)
1/4 cup wheat germ
1/4 cup ground flaxseed
1/4 cup sugar
1 teaspoon baking powder
1 teaspoon salt
2 eggs
2 tablespoons canola oil
2 tablespoons orange juice
1/4 cup nonfat (skim) milk
1/2 cup plain low-fat yogurt
1/2 cup fresh strawberries, hulled and chopped
1/2 cup fresh raspberries
1/2 cup fresh blueberries

Preparation: Preheat oven to 350°F. Spray two regular muffin tins with nonstick spray or line with paper liners. In a large bowl, combine whole-wheat flour, oats, wheat germ, ground flaxseed, sugar, baking powder, and salt. In a separate bowl, combine oil, orange juice, milk, and yogurt. Pour wet ingredients into dry ingredients and stir until moistened. Gently fold in berries. You may add more milk or yogurt if batter does not appear to be moist. Divide batter among muffin cups, filling each cup about 2/3 full. If batter doesn't fill every muffin cup, put a few tablespoons of water in empty cups. Bake 18 to 22 minutes or until a toothpick inserted in muffins comes out clean. Makes about 18 muffins.

This recipe's lignans (flaxseed) and anthocyanins (berries) may help prevent the following cancers: **breast and esophageal.**

Nutritional information per muffin:
Calories: 110.6
Fat: 3.0 g
Saturated fat: 0.3 g
Carbohydrate: 17.4 g
Total sugars: 4.2 g
Protein: 3.5 g
Sodium: 143 mg
Cholesterol: < 1 mg
Dietary fiber: 2.7 g

Whole-grain Waffles

This recipe comes courtesy of Lorna Sass and can be found in her cookbook The New Vegan Cookbook (Chronicle Books 2001). It has been reprinted with the author's permission.

Ingredients:
1-1/3 cups soy milk (not the light variety), plus more if needed
1-1/2 tablespoons freshly squeezed lemon juice
1-1/4 cups whole-wheat pastry flour, plus more if needed
1/2 cup cornmeal
3/4 teaspoon salt
1/2 teaspoon baking soda
1/2 teaspoon baking powder
1/2 teaspoon ground cinnamon
3 tablespoons neutral oil, such as corn or canola, plus additional oil or cooking spray to oil the waffle iron
2 tablespoons maple syrup

Preparation: In a 2-cup liquid measure, combine soy milk and lemon juice. Set aside. (Mixture will curdle.) Set a sifter over a bowl. Measure in flour, cornmeal, salt, baking soda, baking powder, and cinnamon; sift dry ingredients into bowl. Stir oil and maple syrup into soy milk. Make a well in center of dry ingredients and add wet ingredients. Stir with a fork just until blended. Batter should be medium-thick but still pourable. If too runny, stir in an additional 1 or 2 tablespoons of wheat pastry flour. Alternatively, if batter becomes very thick as it stands, add 1 or 2 tablespoons of soy milk. Preheat waffle iron. When iron is ready, brush top and bottom with oil or mist with nonstick spray. Pour a generous 1/2 cup of batter over surface. Bake according to iron manufacturer's directions until crisp, usually 5 to 6 minutes. Serve immediately. Makes 4 servings, one 7-inch waffle each.

This recipe's isoflavones (soy milk) and fiber (whole-wheat flour) may help prevent the following cancers: **prostate and ovarian.**

Nutritional information per serving:
Calories: 344.2
Fat: 12.3 g
Saturated fat: 1.7 g
Carbohydrate: 50.5 g
Total sugars: 6.9 g
Protein: 8.0 g
Sodium: 610 mg
Cholesterol: 0 mg
Dietary fiber: 6.1 g

SAUCES, DIPS, AND DRESSINGS

Apple-Pecan Dip with Horseradish

This dip is great with crusty, whole-grain bread or raw vegetables. This recipe combines three main disease-fighting ingredients: nuts, apples, and dairy products. The amount of horseradish that you add can be guided by your personal taste. If you are vegan or you want the added benefit of soy, simply replace the regular dairy yogurt with soy yogurt.

Ingredients:
1/3 cup pecans
4 apples, peeled and cored
2 tablespoons lemon juice
6 ounces plain low-fat yogurt
2 tablespoons prepared horseradish
2 tablespoons red onion, minced
2 tablespoons celery, minced
Salt and pepper

Preparation: In a small nonstick skillet, dry-sauté pecans over medium heat 3 to 4 minutes, until lightly toasted. Remove from pan and set aside. While pecans cool, grate apples into a bowl and drizzle with lemon juice; toss well (this will prevent apples from turning brown). When pecans have cooled, place in a blender or food processor, and finely grind. Add pecans, yogurt, horseradish, red onion, and celery to grated apple and stir well to combine. Season with salt and pepper as desired and serve. Makes 3 cups or 16 servings, 3 tablespoons each.

This recipe's quercetin (apples) and calcium (yogurt) may help prevent the following cancers: **lung and colon.**

Nutritional information per serving:
Calories: 49
Fat: 2.0 g
Saturated fat: 0.13 g
Carbohydrate: 7.1 g
Total sugars: 0.7 g
Protein: 0 .7 g
Sodium: 2 mg
Cholesterol: 0.2 mg
Dietary fiber: < 1 g

Avocado-Onion Vegetable Dip

Low-fat dairy products are a great source of calcium and vitamin D and keep this dip's calorie count low.

Ingredients:
1/2 medium avocado, peeled and pitted
1 tablespoon fresh lemon juice
1 cup low-fat cottage cheese
3/4 cup plain nonfat yogurt
1/4 cup reduced-fat mayonnaise
1/2 cup green onions, white and green parts, sliced
1/3 cup carrots, shredded

Preparation: Dice avocado into small pieces, toss with lemon juice and set aside. In a food processor or blender, blend cottage cheese, yogurt, and mayonnaise until smooth. Add cottage-cheese mixture to avocado; gently stir in onions and carrots. Cover and chill. Serve with vegetable crudités such as carrot or celery sticks or slices of cucumbers or bell peppers. Makes about 25 servings, 2 tablespoons each.

This recipe's quercetin (onions) and beta carotene (carrots) may help prevent the following cancers: **lung and skin.**

Nutritional information per serving:
Calories: 24
Fat: 1.7 g
Saturated fat: 0.2 g
Carbohydrate: 1.7 g
Total sugars: 0.9 g
Protein: 1.4 g
Sodium: 84 mg
Cholesterol: 0.9 mg
Dietary fiber: 1.9 g

Balsamic Blueberry Vinaigrette

Blueberries are antioxidant-rich fruits that contain anthocyanins—disease-fighting ingredients that give them their bright blue color. Walnut oil is a healthier type of oil that contains mainly monounsaturated fat. This dressing is especially good with salmon, shrimp, or crab salads.

Ingredients:
1 cup fresh blueberries (about 6 ounces), coarsely chopped
1/3 cup balsamic vinegar
1/4 cup honey
2 tablespoons walnut oil
1 Serrano pepper, minced (about 1 teaspoon)
1/2 teaspoon freshly grated orange peel

Preparation: Whisk together all ingredients in a bowl and pour into a resealable container. Vinaigrette can be stored for up to 1 week. Makes about 14 servings, 2 tablespoons each.

This recipe's ellagic acid (blueberries) and pectin (orange peel) may help prevent the following cancers: **colon and lung.**

Nutritional information per serving:
Calories: 52
Fat: 2.0 g
Saturated fat: 0.2 g
Carbohydrate: 7.4 g
Total sugars: 5.7 g
Protein: 0.8 g
Sodium: < 1 mg
Cholesterol: 0
Dietary fiber: < 1 g

Blackberry-Sage Sauce

This is a fantastic marinade for tofu, poultry, or salmon and an excellent addition to a summer barbecue.

Ingredients:
1/2 tablespoon olive oil
2 garlic cloves, peeled and minced
1/2 cup chopped shallots (about 2)
1 cup red wine
1-1/2 cups low-sodium vegetable broth
1-1/2 cups fresh or frozen and thawed blackberries
1/4 cup fresh sage, chopped
1 tablespoon honey
1/4 teaspoon salt
1/4 teaspoon freshly ground black pepper

Preparation: Heat olive oil in a large saucepan over medium heat. Add garlic and shallots and sauté until lightly browned. Add red wine. Increase heat to medium-high and boil until reduced by half. Add broth, blackberries, sage, honey, salt, and pepper and continue to boil. Cook for about 10 minutes, until mixture reaches a thick and sauce-like consistency. Serve warm. Makes 6 servings, 1/4 cup each.

This recipe's lutein (blackberries) and resveratrol (wine) may help prevent the following cancers: **stomach and kidney.**

Nutritional information per serving:
Calories: 113.8
Fat: 1.2 g
Saturated fat: 0.2 g
Carbohydrate: 12.6 g
Total sugars: 2.5 g
Protein: 0.5 g
Sodium: 138 mg
Cholesterol: 0 mg
Dietary fiber: 1.5 g

Nutritional information per serving:
Calories: 79.9
Fat: 1.9 g
Saturated fat: trace
Carbohydrate: 14.9 g
Total sugars: 11.1 g
Protein: 0.8 g
Sodium: 170 mg
Cholesterol: 0 mg
Dietary Fiber: 1.2 g

Blueberry-Bourbon Sauce

This is a delicious, antioxidant-rich sauce that I adapted from a recipe that a friend gave me. It pairs nicely with poultry, pork, and red meat. Try it with the spice-rubbed filet mignon (page 174).

Ingredients:
1 tablespoon canola oil
1/2 cup red onion, diced
5 small garlic cloves, chopped
1/2 small jalapeño pepper, seeded and chopped
1/2 cup bourbon
2-1/4 cups fresh or frozen (not thawed) blueberries
1/2 cup ketchup
1/3 cup cider vinegar
1-1/2 tablespoons brown sugar
1 tablespoon molasses
1/8 teaspoon ground cumin
1/8 teaspoon freshly ground black pepper

Preparation: Place a large saucepan over medium heat; add canola oil and heat until hot. Add onion and cook, stirring occasionally, until tender and just starting to brown, 3 to 4 minutes. Add garlic and jalapeño; cook, stirring, until fragrant, about 30 seconds. Add bourbon, increase heat to high and bring to a boil; cook until most liquid has evaporated, about 5 minutes. Stir in blueberries, ketchup, vinegar, brown sugar, molasses, cumin, and black pepper; return to a boil. Reduce heat and simmer, stirring occasionally, until thickened, about 20 minutes. Remove from heat and let cool 5 minutes. Serve immediately or store in an air-tight container up to 1 week. Makes about 8 servings, 1/4 cup each.

Brandied Raspberry-Cherry Sauce

This tart and sweet sauce is a fantastic way to top frozen yogurt, whole-grain waffles, or pound cake. It contains antioxidants such as melatonin, ellagic acid, and anthocyanins. For a non-alcoholic sauce, simply omit the brandy and add 1 teaspoon of almond extract.

This recipe's anthocyanins (cherries) and vitamin C (raspberries) may help prevent the following cancers: **breast and colon.**

Ingredients:
2 cups Bing cherries, pitted and coarsely chopped
2 cups fresh raspberries or thawed frozen unsweetened raspberries, divided
1/4 cup sugar
2 cinnamon sticks, broken in half
1 tablespoon brandy

Preparation: Combine cherries, 1 cup raspberries, sugar, and cinnamon in saucepan over medium-high heat. Bring to a boil, stirring until sugar dissolves. Reduce heat; simmer until cherries soften, about 15 minutes. Remove from heat. Stir brandy and 1 cup raspberries into sauce. Discard cinnamon sticks. Serve warm or at room temperature. Makes about 4 cups or 8 servings, 1/2 cup each.

Nutritional information per 1/2 cup serving:
Calories: 67.3
Fat: 0.4 g
Saturated fat: 0 g
Carbohydrate: 11.5 g
Total sugars: 10.8 g
Protein: 4.0 g
Sodium: 0 mg
Cholesterol: 0.3 mg
Dietary fiber: 7.5 g

Caponata

Caponata is a traditional Sicilian appetizer or side dish whose main ingredient is eggplant. Many of the store-bought brands in the United States contain so much oil that they mask the flavor of the eggplant and spices. Caponata can be served warm or cool over toasted Italian or crusty whole-grain bread, or as a sauce for fish, meat, poultry, or tofu.

Ingredients:

1 medium eggplant, cut into approximately 1/2-inch slices
1 tablespoon regular or garlic-infused olive oil
1/4 cup pine nuts
1/4 cup balsamic or red wine vinegar
1 small yellow onion, chopped
1/3 cup celery, finely diced
1 can (14 or 14-1/2 ounces) diced tomatoes, drained
1/4 cup black olives, sliced
1 tablespoon capers (drained)
1 tablespoon dried oregano leaves
1/4 teaspoon freshly ground black pepper

Preparation: Preheat broiler. Evenly brush both sides of sliced eggplant with olive oil. Arrange eggplant on baking sheet and broil at least 4 to 5 inches from heat until browned and tender, turning once, about 15 minutes. Toast pine nuts in a small, dry nonstick skillet over medium-low heat until lightly browned, about 5 minutes. In a medium nonstick skillet, heat vinegar over medium heat. Add onion and celery and sauté 5 minutes. Stir in remaining ingredients and simmer 2 minutes, stirring occasionally. Mix in eggplant and pine nuts. Remove from heat and let cool while stirring occasionally. Makes about 4 cups or 16 servings, 1/4 cup each.

Nutritional information per serving:

Calories: 46.1
Fat: 2.5 g
Saturated fat: 0.4 g
Carbohydrate: 4.8 g
Total sugars: 2.0 g
Protein: 1.1 g
Sodium: 100 mg
Cholesterol: 0 mg
Dietary fiber: < 1 g

Cherry-Peach Salsa

This salsa is delightful with Mexican dishes or as a topping for fish, chicken, or pork. It has the cancer-fighting ingredients of garlic and onions, as well as the antioxidant anthocyanins and vitamin C found in peaches and Bing cherries.

Ingredients:
8 fresh peaches, peeled and diced
1 cup fresh Bing cherries, pitted and cut in half
1/3 cup fresh cilantro, finely chopped
2 shallots, finely chopped
1 small jalapeño pepper, seeded and finely chopped
1 garlic clove, minced
1 tablespoon rice wine vinegar
1 teaspoon fresh lime juice
Salt and pepper to taste

Preparation: Place peaches in a large bowl. Add cherries, cilantro, shallots, jalapeño pepper, garlic, vinegar, and lime juice and mix well. Season with salt and pepper as desired. Refrigerate tightly covered and serve chilled. Makes about 4 cups or 16 servings, 1/4 cup each.

This recipe's anthocyanins (cherries) and quercetin (shallots) may help prevent the following cancers: **colon and lung.**

Nutritional information per serving:
Calories: 26
Fat: 0.6 g
Saturated fat: 0 g
Carbohydrate: 6.1 g
Total sugars: 4.2 g
Protein: 0.6 g
Sodium: < 1 mg
Cholesterol: 0 mg
Dietary fiber: 0.5 g

Chipotle Tomato Ketchup

The chipotle chile is a smoked, dried form of the ripened jalapeño pepper. It is full-bodied and rich in flavor and can be found in canned form in the international section of most grocery or specialty stores. This ketchup is perfect with any type of burger. Try it with a thick slice of red onion and some melted mozzarella cheese.

Ingredients:
1 teaspoon olive oil
1 small onion, thinly sliced
1 tablespoon plus 2 teaspoons brown sugar
1 can (12 ounces) tomato purée
2 teaspoons tomato paste
2 chipotle chiles (canned), seeded and minced
2 tablespoons cider vinegar
2 teaspoons ground coriander

Preparation: In a small skillet or fry pan, heat oil over medium heat. Add onion and sauté until translucent, about 3 to 4 minutes. Add brown sugar and cook 2 minutes. Stir in tomato purée, tomato paste, chipotle chiles, cider vinegar, and coriander; simmer about 25 minutes, until thickened. Taste and adjust seasonings if necessary. Let cool and serve or store. Makes about 20 servings, 2 tablespoons each.

This recipe's lycopene (tomato purée) and quercetin (onion) may help prevent the following cancers: **pancreas and lung.**

Nutritional information per serving:
Calories: 16.2
Fat: 0.2 g
Saturated fat: trace
Carbohydrate: 3.3 g
Total sugars: 2.2 g
Protein: 0.3 g
Sodium: 73 mg
Cholesterol: 0 mg
Dietary fiber: 0.4 g

Nutritional information per serving:
Calories: 14
Fat: 0 g
Saturated fat: 0 g
Carbohydrate: 2.2 g
Total sugars: 1.3 g
Protein: 1.3 g
Sodium: 38 mg
Cholesterol: 1.3 mg
Dietary fiber: < 1 g

Nutritional information per serving:
Calories: 102
Fat: 10.5 g
Saturated fat: 1.5 g
Carbohydrate: 2.9 g
Total sugars: 0.5 g
Protein: 0.1 g
Sodium: 0.3 mg
Cholesterol: 0 mg
Dietary fiber: < 1 g

Cilantro-Yogurt Dressing

The antioxidant compounds in garlic, such as allicin and ajoene, and the vitamin D in dairy products have been shown to be disease-fighting. This appealing dressing is great with any salad that could use a spicy boost.

Ingredients:
3/4 cup (6 ounces) plain nonfat yogurt
1/3 cup cilantro, stems removed
2 small garlic cloves, sliced or minced
1 medium Serrano chile, seeded and diced
1/2 teaspoon salt

Preparation: Add all ingredients to a blender or food processor. Blend until smooth. Refrigerate 3 to 4 hours to allow flavors to blend before serving. Makes 6 servings, 2 tablespoons each.

Citrus Vinaigrette

This vinaigrette is loaded with healthy vitamin C, and the monounsaturated fats in olive oil will help you to better absorb the vitamins and minerals in the salad's vegetables.

Ingredients:
1 orange (preferably a seedless juice orange), peeled
1 lemon, peeled
1 lime, peeled
1/4 cup champagne vinegar or other white wine vinegar
1 shallot, peeled and coarsely chopped
1 tablespoon sugar
3/4 cup extra virgin olive oil
Salt and freshly ground pepper to taste

Preparation: Place orange, lemon, and lime in blender or juicer. Juice the fruit; remove pulp or seeds and add juice back to blender. Add vinegar, shallot, sugar, and a pinch of salt and pepper. Set blender to medium speed, and blend while slowly pouring in olive oil. Season to taste with additional salt and pepper, if desired. Refrigerate several hours, preferably overnight, to allow flavors to meld. Makes about 16 servings, 2 tablespoons each.

Creamy Low-Calorie Herb Dressing

Calcium and vitamin D in dairy products have recently been associated with a lower risk for breast cancer, especially invasive breast cancer. I frequently add this dressing to albacore tuna, hard-boiled egg whites, celery, and red onion to make a nutritious and calorie-saving tuna salad.

Ingredients:
2 green onions, finely chopped
1/2 cup parsley leaves, finely chopped
2 tablespoons fresh dill, finely chopped (or 1 teaspoon dried dill)
1 cup low-fat buttermilk
1/2 cup low-fat cottage cheese, preferably small-curd
1/3 cup plain low-fat yogurt
1 teaspoon dried oregano
1/4 teaspoon salt
1/4 teaspoon freshly ground black pepper

Preparation: In a large bowl, combine onions, parsley, and fresh dill; set aside. In a food processor or blender container, process buttermilk, cottage cheese, yogurt, oregano, and salt and pepper until smooth. Transfer to bowl containing onion-and-herb mixture and stir until thoroughly combined. Pour into a covered container and keep refrigerated for up to 1 week. Makes 2 cups or 16 servings, 2 tablespoons each.

This recipe's vitamin D (milk) and allicin (onion) may help prevent the following cancers: **colon and lung.**

Nutritional information per serving:
Calories: 15.1
Fat: 0.3 g
Saturated fat: 0.2 g
Carbohydrate: 1.3 g
Total sugars: 0.9 g
Protein: 1.6 g
Sodium: 84 mg
Cholesterol: 1.3 mg
Dietary fiber: 0 g

Creamy Tahini Sauce

Tahini is a smooth paste of ground, toasted sesame seeds popular in Middle Eastern and East Asian cultures. You can find it in the organic or International sections of most groceries stores or in specialty food stores. Occasionally it is on the shelves right next to the peanut butter. This sauce can be made with more water to achieve a thin consistency perfect for a spinach, arugula, or romaine lettuce salad, or it can be made thicker with less water and serve as a dip for vegetables. It is great over vegetables (try it on baby green peas) or with some brown rice and sunflower kernels.

Ingredients:
3/4 cup sesame tahini
5 tablespoons fresh lemon juice
1/2 teaspoon garlic, minced
1 cup spring or filtered water (more as necessary)
1/4 teaspoon salt
2 tablespoons fresh parsley, minced
1/8 teaspoon paprika
Pinch of cayenne pepper (optional)

Preparation: Place tahini, lemon juice, and garlic in a blender or food processor fitted with a metal blade. Begin to process. With the motor running, slowly add water, checking the consistency of the sauce occasionally; when tahini mixture is at desired consistency, stop processing and transfer to a medium bowl or resealable container. Add the salt, parsley, paprika, and cayenne pepper (if using). Cover tightly and refrigerate until ready to use. The sauce keeps for 3 or more weeks if stored in an airtight container. Makes about 2 cups, or 16 servings, 2 tablespoons each.

Nutritional information per serving:
Calories: 69.3
Fat: 5.7 g
Saturated fat: 0.8 g
Carbohydrate: 2.7 g
Total sugars: trace
Protein: 1.8 g
Sodium: 49 mg
Cholesterol: 0 mg
Dietary fiber: 1.0 g

Garlicky Basil-Ricotta Sauce

This sauce is a great alternative to heavy cream sauces, which may have twice the fat and calories. The sauce can be served over pasta at room temperature or warmed before serving.

Ingredients:
15 ounces part-skim ricotta cheese
1/2 cup fresh basil, chopped
1/2 cup green onions, sliced
1/2 cup roasted red peppers (jarred, packed in water), drained and diced
1/4 cup Parmesan cheese
1/4 cup low-sodium chicken broth
2 tablespoons extra-virgin olive oil
2 tablespoons white wine
2 garlic cloves, minced
Salt and pepper as desired

Preparation: Combine all ingredients in a large bowl and season to taste with salt and pepper. Makes 4 servings, about 3/4 cup of sauce each (enough for about 1 pound of dry pasta total).

> This recipe's calcium (ricotta) and luteolin (basil) may help prevent the following cancers: **breast and ovarian.**

Nutritional information per serving:
Calories: 253.3
Fat: 17.0 g
Saturated fat: 7.5 g
Carbohydrate: 7.3 g
Total sugars: 0 g
Protein: 14.8 g
Sodium: 479 mg
Cholesterol: 14.4 mg
Dietary fiber: 0.4 g

Garlicky White Bean Dip

This is a perfectly seasoned appetizer or dip for fresh veggies. I love it with raw vegetables, such as broccoli, cauliflower, celery, and carrot sticks. It contains no saturated fat, unlike many store-bought bean dips.

Ingredients:
1 can (15 ounces) Great Northern Beans, drained and rinsed
2 teaspoons freshly squeezed lemon juice
3 small garlic cloves, sliced or minced
3 tablespoons fresh basil
1 teaspoon balsamic or red wine vinegar
2 teaspoons Dijon mustard
1/4 teaspoon dried oregano
1/2 teaspoon salt
Pinch of white pepper

Preparation: Place all ingredients in a blender or food processor and blend until smooth. Makes about 10 servings, 2 tablespoons each.

> This recipe's folate (beans) and vitamin C (lemon juice) may help prevent the following cancers: **pancreas and prostate.**

Nutritional information per serving:
Calories: 18.5
Fat: 0 g
Saturated fat: 0 g
Carbohydrate: 4.0 g
Total sugars: 0.1 g
Protein: 1.3 g
Sodium: 182 mg
Cholesterol: 0 mg
Dietary fiber: 1.3 g

Guilt-free Guacamole

A friend sent this recipe my way. It is adapted from a Good Housekeep-ing *recipe and has fewer calories than traditional guacamole, mainly be-cause it uses a can of white beans and only one avocado. Its rich, oniony flavor and smooth texture go great with any chicken, fish, or Mexican dish, or serve it with baked blue-corn tortilla chips.*

Ingredients:
1 can (15 ounces) cannellini beans, drained and rinsed
Juice of 2 limes
1/2 cup cilantro leaves, loosely packed
1/4 cup Vidalia or other sweet onion, coarsely chopped
1 jalapeño pepper, seeded and chopped
1/4 teaspoon salt
1 ripe avocado, cut in half and pitted
3 small plum tomatoes

Preparation: In a blender or food processor, using a knife-blade at-tachment, puree beans and lime juice until smooth. Transfer to a medium-size bowl. In the same blender or processor, add cilantro, onion, jalapeño, and salt. Pulse or blend until thick and juicy. Use a spoon to scoop avocado from its peel and place in bowl with bean mixture. Use a fork to mash mixture until it is blended, with some small chunks remaining. Cut tomatoes crosswise and squeeze halves to remove seeds and juice. Coarsely chop tomatoes. Stir tomato-and-onion mixture into avocado mixture until well blended. You can add extra lime juice for more tang. Guacamole is best to serve when just made, but it can also be covered and refrig-erated until serving. Makes 16 servings, about 1/4 cup each.

Nutritional information per serving:
Calories: 48
Fat: 1.8 g
Saturated fat: 0.3 g
Carbohydrate: 6 g
Total sugars: 0 g
Protein: 2.2 g
Sodium: 67 mg
Cholesterol: 0 mg
Dietary fiber: 2.3 g

Lime-Cilantro Salad Dressing

This is a great recipe for Southwestern or Mexican salads. You can play around with the recipe ingredients to achieve the flavor that you like. More olive oil can be used to make it richer. As outlined below, it is fairly low-fat and very healthy. I use Splenda® to keep the sugar and calorie content low.

Ingredients:
10 ounces (1-1/4 cups) lime juice
4 teaspoons celery seeds
2 tablespoons olive oil
1 tablespoon plus 1 teaspoon honey
4 tablespoons Splenda®
1-1/4 cups red onion, finely chopped
1 cup cilantro, chopped

Preparation: Whisk all ingredients together in a medium bowl and chill. The dressing keeps for up to a week in the refrigerator and the longer the flavors meld together, the better the taste. Makes about 3-1/2 cups or 28 servings, 2 tablespoons each.

> This recipe's vitamin C (lime juice) and quercetin (onion) may help prevent the following cancers: **prostate and skin.**

Nutritional information per serving:
Calories: 16.4
Fat: 1.0 g
Saturated Fat: 0.2 g
Carbohydrate: 1.8 g
Total sugars: trace
Protein: trace
Cholesterol: 0 mg
Sodium: 1 mg
Dietary fiber: < 1 g

Pecan-Cranberry-Orange Relish

This relish is wonderful to have as a side dish at the holidays. I love it with turkey or chicken or as a sweet and zesty bread spread. Sometimes I top a cup of plain or vanilla yogurt with it to have a protein-rich snack.

Ingredients:
12 ounces fresh cranberries
1/2 cup reduced-sugar orange marmalade
1/3 cup honey
1/2 cup pecans, chopped
Pinch of ground cloves
Pinch of ground ginger
Zest of 1 whole orange

Preparation: Place cranberries and orange marmalade in a microwaveable bowl and heat 1 minute on high. Stir and heat 1 additional minute on high. Add chopped nuts and heat additional 2 minutes. Stir in honey, nuts, orange zest, and spices. Let cool. Chill until ready to serve. Relish will congeal to a semi-solid state. Makes 3 cups or 24 servings, 2 tablespoons each.

> This recipe's resveratrol (cranberries) and vitamin E (pecans) may help prevent the following cancers: **breast and stomach.**

Nutritional information per serving:
Calories: 37.6
Fat: 1.7 g
Saturated Fat: 0.3 g
Carbohydrate: 11.8 g
Total sugars: 8.3 g
Protein: 0.5 g
Sodium: < 1 mg
Cholesterol: 0 mg
Dietary fiber: 0.8 g

Red Pepper Hummus

Hummus is a fantastic Middle Eastern dish that can be used as a dip or bread spread. I love it on whole-grain or pita bread and often use it as a topping for my falafel pita sandwiches.

This recipe's fiber (beans) and vitamin E (peanut butter) may help prevent the following cancers: **pancreas and colon.**

Ingredients:
1 can (15 ounce) garbanzo beans (chickpeas), drained and rinsed
1 tablespoon natural peanut butter
1/3 cup lemon juice
1/2 cup warm water
2 teaspoons garlic, minced
1/4 teaspoon salt
1/2 teaspoon ground cumin
3 tablespoons parsley, finely minced
3 tablespoons basil leaves, finely minced
1 teaspoon sesame-seed oil
3 ounces chopped red peppers (from a jar, packed in water and drained)
Sprinkle of paprika

Preparation: In a food processor or blender, place garbanzo beans, peanut butter, water, lemon juice, garlic, cumin, and salt. Blend until puréed. Remove to bowl and mix in parsley, basil, sesame seed oil, and roasted peppers. Sprinkle paprika on top. Refrigerate in bowl or resealable container for several hours before serving. Makes approximately 1-1/2 cups or 12 servings, 2 tablespoons each.

Nutritional information per serving:
Calories: 50
Fat: 1.4 g
Saturated fat: trace
Carbohydrate: 7.1 g
Total sugars: 0.2 g
Protein: 2.1 g
Sodium: 88.4 mg
Cholesterol: 0 mg
Dietary fiber: 1.8 g

Savory Lentil Tomato Sauce

This flavorful sauce can be served as a filling for lasagna or crepes, over angel hair or whole-wheat penne, or even as a unique pizza sauce. I've often served it over a dish of steamed broccoli, cauliflower, carrots, snow pea pods, and Brussels sprouts.

Ingredients:
3 tablespoons extra-virgin olive oil
1 large yellow onion, chopped
2 garlic cloves, crushed
2 carrots, coarsely grated
2 celery stalks, chopped
2/3 cup lentils
1 can (14 or 14-1/2 ounces) tomatoes, chopped
2 tablespoons tomato paste
2 cups reduced-sodium vegetable stock
1 tablespoon fresh marjoram, chopped (or 1 teaspoon dried marjoram)
Salt and freshly ground black pepper to taste

Preparation: Place a large saucepan over medium heat and add olive oil. Add onion, garlic, carrots, and celery and heat until soft—about 5 to 6 minutes. Add lentils, tomatoes, tomato paste, vegetable stock, marjoram, and season with salt and pepper as desired. Bring to a boil, partially cover, and simmer 20 minutes until thickened. Note: If you don't wait for it to thicken, it will be more of a soup than a sauce. Makes 8 servings, about 1/2 cup each.

This recipe's beta carotene (mango) and luteolin (celery) may help prevent the following cancers: **liver and prostate.**

Nutritional information per serving:
Calories: 118.8
Fat: 5.2 g
Saturated Fat: < 1 g
Carbohydrate: 14.2 g
Total sugars: 2.3 g
Protein: 3.8 g
Sodium: 132 mg
Cholesterol: 0 mg
Dietary fiber: 4.7

Strawberry-Herb Marinade

This light sauce is perfect as a marinade for tofu, fish, or chicken and can be ladled on top of roasted or grilled vegetables. The ingredient quantities can be doubled to make enough marinade to serve a larger group.

Ingredients:
1/2 cup all-fruit strawberry preserves
1 tablespoon red wine vinegar
2 tablespoons capers, drained and chopped
1/2 teaspoon dried Italian herbs
1/2 teaspoon cracked black pepper
1/4 teaspoon salt

Preparation: Combine all ingredients in a small bowl and mix well. Serve at room temperature or refrigerate for up to 1 week. Makes 6 servings, 2 tablespoons each.

This recipe's anthocyanins (strawberries) may help prevent the following cancers: **esophageal and skin.**

Nutritional information per serving:
Calories: 56.0
Fat: 0 g
Saturated fat: 0 g
Carbohydrate: 14.0 g
Total sugars: 11.0 g
Protein: 0 g
Sodium: 96 mg
Cholesterol: 0 mg
Dietary fiber: 0 g

Nutritional information per serving:
Calories: 104.8
Fat: 6.9 g
Saturated fat: 1.3 g
Carbohydrate: 7.1 g
Total sugars: 3.0 g
Protein: 3.6 g
Sodium: 171 mg
Cholesterol: 0 mg
Dietary fiber: 2.5 g

Nutritional information per serving:
Calories: 20
Fat: 0.2 g
Saturated fat: 0 g
Carbohydrate: 4.0 g
Total sugars: 3.0 g
Protein: 0.2 g
Sodium: 5 mg
Cholesterol: 0 mg
Dietary fiber: < 1 g

Spicy Spinach and Peanut Sauce

This sauce is great over fish, poultry, whole-grain pasta, brown rice, or couscous. You can add more jalapeños or hotter peppers if you want a really spicy sauce.

Ingredients:
2 tablespoons canola oil
1 medium yellow onion, chopped
3 small garlic cloves, minced
1/2 small jalapeño pepper, seeded and minced
1 can (14-1/2 ounces) diced tomatoes, drained and finely chopped
1 pound fresh spinach, coarsely chopped
1/4 cup natural peanut butter
Salt and freshly ground pepper

Preparation: Place a large skillet or fry pan over medium heat and add oil. Add onion, garlic, and jalapeño; cover and cook about 7 to 8 minutes. Stir in tomatoes and spinach and heat just until spinach wilts, stirring occasionally. When wilted, stir in peanut butter and season with salt and pepper as desired. Makes about 9 servings, 1/3 cup each.

Strawberry-Tarragon Dressing

This dressing has all the berry benefits of strawberries and some citrus juice to boot! It is great with grilled chicken or steak salads.

Ingredients:
1-1/2 cups strawberries, hulled
1/4 cup lemon juice
1 tablespoon sugar
1 tablespoon shallots, finely chopped
1 teaspoon fresh tarragon, chopped (or 1/2 teaspoon dried)
1/2 teaspoon cornstarch
2 tablespoons orange juice

Preparation: Purée strawberries in a blender or food processor. Press through a fine wire strainer into a 2-cup glass measure. Add lemon juice and enough water to make about 1 cup. Transfer mixture to a small pan and add sugar, shallots, and tarragon. In a separate container, mix cornstarch and orange juice until smooth. Add orange-juice mixture to pan with strawberry mixture while stirring. Bring to a boil over high heat while stirring constantly. Remove from heat and let cool or chill quickly by placing pan into bowl or large baking dish of ice water (up to 2/3 side of pan) about 5 minutes. Transfer to a jar or other re-sealable container and refrigerate before using. Makes 1 cup or 8 servings, 2 tablespoons each.

Tomato-Ginger Dressing

Aside from the antioxidants lycopene and vitamin C, tomatoes also contain vitamin K, which helps wounds to heal, as well as coumaric acid, which can counteract carcinogens such as nitrosamines, which are found naturally in the body as well as in cigarette smoke.

Ingredients:
2 large plum tomatoes, seeded and roughly chopped
1/2 cup oil-packed sun-dried tomatoes, drained and chopped
2 tablespoons fresh ginger, minced
4 garlic cloves, chopped or sliced
3 tablespoons balsamic vinegar
1 cup water
1/2 teaspoon salt
1/2 teaspoon freshly ground black pepper

Preparation: In a blender, combine tomato, sun-dried tomatoes, ginger, garlic, and vinegar. Process until finely chopped. Add water, salt, and pepper and purée until smooth. Makes about 2 cups or 16 servings, 2 tablespoons each.

This recipe's lycopene (tomatoes) and allicin (garlic) may help prevent the following cancers: **pancreas and stomach.**

Nutritional information per serving:
Calories: 14
Fat: 0.5 g
Saturated fat: 0 g
Carbohydrate: 2.3 g
Total sugars: 0.5 g
Protein: 0.3 g
Sodium: 83 mg
Cholesterol: 0 mg
Dietary fiber: < 1 g

Tropical Kiwi Salsa

This salsa is absolutely perfect with any steamed, baked, broiled, or grilled fish. The mango and pineapple are packed with vitamin C, onion and scallions contain quercetin, and red pepper is full of the antioxidant lycopene.

Ingredients:
5 kiwi fruit, peeled and diced into 1/2- to 3/4-inch pieces
1 mango, peeled and diced
1/2 cup pineapple (fresh preferably), diced
1/4 cup sweet red pepper, diced
1 small stalk celery, finely diced
3 tablespoons red onion, finely diced
3 tablespoons fresh chives, minced
2 tablespoons scallions, chopped
1 cup reduced-sodium vegetable stock or broth
Dash of salt and freshly ground pepper

Preparation: Combine all ingredients in a medium mixing bowl and toss until thoroughly mixed. Cover and chill before serving. Makes 3 cups or 12 servings, 1/4 cup each.

This recipe's beta carotene (mango) and luteolin (celery) may help prevent the following cancers: **lung and ovarian.**

Nutritional information per serving:
Calories: 38.2
Fat: trace
Saturated fat: 0 g
Carbohydrate: 9.0 g
Total sugars: 2.1 g
Protein: 0.5 g
Sodium: 17 mg
Cholesterol: 0 mg
Dietary fiber: 1.5 g

SIDES AND VEGGIES

Almond-Vegetable Couscous

This healthy dish can be served hot, cold, or at room temperature. It makes a great side dish for fish or a light lunch entrée with a cup of soup or a small salad.

Ingredients:
1 tablespoon olive oil
1 cup yellow or red onion, diced
4 cups broccoli, half small florets and half chopped stems, divided
1-1/2 cups red bell pepper, diced
3 garlic cloves, minced
2 cups water
3 tablespoons lemon juice
1/2 teaspoon each: salt and freshly ground black pepper
1-1/2 cups couscous
3/4 cup almonds, coarsely chopped
1/4 cup fresh dill, chopped
1/4 cup fresh parsley, chopped

Preparation: Place a large saucepan over medium heat. Add olive oil and sauté onion 3 to 4 minutes until softened and translucent. Add broccoli stems and sauté mixture 3 minutes. Add broccoli florets, red pepper, and garlic; sauté about 4 minutes, stirring frequently. Add water, lemon juice, salt, and pepper; bring to a boil. Once boiling, add couscous and stir. Cover, remove saucepan from heat, and set aside. After 5 minutes, use a fork to fluff couscous while stirring in almonds, dill, and parsley. Serve immediately. Makes 6 servings, 1 cup each.

This recipe's allicin (onions) and sulforaphane (broccoli) may help prevent the following cancers: **lung and pancreas.**

Nutritional information per serving:
Calories: 244.3
Fat: 8.3 g
Saturated fat: 0.8 g
Carbohydrate: 34.5 g
Total sugars: 9.6 g
Protein: 7.8 g
Sodium: 404 mg
Cholesterol: 0 mg
Dietary fiber: 1.2 g

Amazing Stuffed Peppers

These peppers can be served as a main dish, side dish, or appetizer. For a vegan option, substitute your choice of grated soy cheese for the provolone cheese.

Ingredients:
Nonstick cooking spray, preferably olive-oil flavor
2 large onions, finely chopped
2 cups white button mushrooms, sliced
1/2 tablespoon each: dried basil and dried oregano
1 teaspoon each: dried thyme and dried marjoram
2 cups cooked brown rice
2 tablespoons sunflower kernels, coarsely ground
2 cups tomato sauce of choice, divided
6 large red bell peppers, sliced in half length-wise, cored and seeded
1/4 teaspoon salt
1/4 teaspoon freshly ground black pepper
1/4 cup grated part-skim provolone cheese

Preparation: Preheat oven to 350°F. Spray a large skillet with non-stick cooking spray and place over medium heat. Add onions, mushrooms, and herbs, and sauté until vegetables are tender. Add brown rice, ground sunflower kernels, and 2 tablespoons tomato sauce and stir until well-blended. Remove from heat. Arrange pepper halves in a shallow baking dish and fill with rice mixture. Pour water into baking dish until it is about 2 inches deep. Bake for 25 minutes, until tops are browned. Meanwhile, heat remaining tomato sauce until almost boiling. When peppers finish cooking, remove from oven and top with hot tomato sauce and grated cheese. If desired, return peppers to the oven for 3 to 4 minutes until cheese has melted. Makes 6 stuffed peppers.

This recipe's fiber (brown rice) and lycopene (tomato sauce) may help prevent the following cancers: **colon and pancreas.**

Nutritional information per 1 pepper (two halves) serving:
Calories: 204.1
Fat: 3.4 g
Saturated fat: 1.2 g
Carbohydrate: 37.2 g
Total sugars: 13.2 g
Protein: 6.4 g
Sodium: 243 mg
Cholesterol: 3.8 mg
Dietary fiber: 8.3 g

Apple-Carrot Stir-Fry

Canola oil contains healthy monounsaturated fats which, aside from being heart-healthy, have been shown to decrease the frequency and severity of migraine headaches. Carrots, onions, and apples contain antioxidants such as quercetin, which have been associated with a decreased risk of many types of cancer.

This recipe's beta carotene (carrots) and procyanidins (apples) may help prevent the following cancers: **lung and liver.**

Ingredients:
1 tablespoon canola oil
2 medium carrots, thinly sliced (about 1 cup)
1 medium onion, cut into wedges
3 medium apples, peeled, cored, and sliced (about 3 cups)
2 teaspoons sugar
1/4 teaspoon salt
2 tablespoons water
1/8 teaspoon ground nutmeg

Preparation: Pour canola oil into a wok or large skillet. Heat oil over medium-high heat. Add carrots and stir-fry 2 minutes. Add onion and stir-fry 2 to 3 minutes or until crisp-tender. Remove vegetables from wok. Add apples to hot wok and stir-fry 2 minutes. Sprinkle with sugar and salt. Carefully add water. Cover and cook over medium heat 3 minutes or until apples are just tender. Return cooked vegetables to wok. Cook and stir until heated thoroughly. Sprinkle with nutmeg and serve immediately while warm. Makes 4 servings.

Nutritional information per serving:
Calories: 126.5
Fat: 3.7 g
Saturated fat: 0.3 g
Carbohydrate: 20.0 g
Total sugars: 14.4 g
Protein: 0.8 g
Sodium: 167 mg
Cholesterol: 0 mg
Dietary fiber: 2.6 g

Baked Sweet Potato Wedges

This dish goes great with any of the burgers listed in the Casual Dining section, as well as with just about any main courses. You can probably get 6 servings out of it as a family side dish, but the nutrition info is listed for 4 larger servings.

Ingredients:
Nonstick cooking spray, olive-oil flavor
2 pounds organic, unpeeled sweet potatoes, cut into wedges
1 tablespoon extra-virgin olive oil
2 small garlic cloves, minced
1/2 teaspoon chili powder
1/4 teaspoon paprika
1/4 teaspoon salt
1/4 teaspoon ground black pepper

Preparation: Preheat oven to 425°F. Line a baking sheet with aluminum foil and lightly spray with nonstick olive-oil cooking spray. Place potato pieces in a single layer on baking sheet. Lightly baste with olive oil and sprinkle with minced garlic, chili powder, paprika, salt and pepper to taste. Bake 30 minutes or until browned and crispy. Let cool a few minutes and serve. Makes 4 generous servings.

Nutritional information per serving:
Calories: 234.5
Fat: 3.7 g
Saturated fat: 0.6 g
Carbohydrate: 46.5 g
Total sugars: 9.5 g
Protein: 3.7 g
Sodium: 275 mg
Cholesterol: 0 mg
Dietary fiber: 7.1 g

Barley and Spring Greens

Barley is often thought of as an ingredient in bread and cereals, although it is a whole grain that is high in fiber and antioxidants that can be used in numerous healthy dishes.

Ingredients:
Nonstick cooking spray, canola-oil flavor
3/4 cup yellow onion, chopped
1 fennel bulb, chopped
2 teaspoons olive oil
3 garlic cloves, finely chopped
3/4 cup red or orange bell pepper, thinly sliced
1-1/4 cups pearl barley
1 teaspoon dried thyme
1 teaspoon dried marjoram
4-1/2 cups low-sodium chicken broth
Salt and freshly ground black pepper
1 cup fresh spinach leaves, torn into pieces (or use baby spinach)
3 tablespoons grated Parmesan cheese
2 tablespoons fresh basil, finely chopped

Preparation: Generously coat a large, heavy stock pot with non-stick cooking spray and place over medium-high heat. Add onions and fennel and sauté until tender, 5 to 10 minutes. Add olive oil and heat until hot. Add garlic and bell peppers; sauté lightly 1 to 2 minutes. Stir in barley, thyme, marjoram, and chicken broth. Bring to a boil, immediately reduce heat to low and simmer until liquid is almost absorbed and barley is tender, stirring occasionally, 40 to 50 minutes. Midway through cooking, sprinkle with salt and pepper as desired. When barley is finished cooking, add spinach, Parmesan cheese, and basil. Stir to blend and season with salt and pepper as desired. Serve warm. Makes 6 servings.

This recipe's fiber (barley) and lutein (spinach) may help prevent the following cancers: **colon and ovarian.**

Nutritional information per serving:
Calories: 203.1
Fat: 3.9 g
Saturated fat: 1.0 g
Carbohydrate: 34.6 g
Total sugars: 22.5 g
Protein: 9.7 g
Sodium: 121.5 mg
Cholesterol: 2.2 mg
Dietary fiber: 8.4 g

Basted Grilled Vegetables

This is a wonderful dish to accompany any meat, fish, poultry, or vegetarian main dish. These vegetables are loaded with vitamins and minerals, and each serving is high in fiber.

This recipe's quercetin (onion) and lycopene (red pepper) may help prevent the following cancers: **stomach and prostate.**

Ingredients:
12 small red potatoes, halved
3 tablespoons honey
3 tablespoons dry white wine
1 garlic clove, minced
1/2 teaspoon crushed dried thyme leaves
1/4 teaspoon salt
1/4 teaspoon freshly ground pepper
2 medium zucchini (unpeeled), halved lengthwise
1 medium eggplant (unpeeled), cut into 1/2-inch-thick slices
1 yellow or orange bell pepper, halved, stemmed, and seeded
1 red bell pepper, halved, stemmed, and seeded
1 large yellow onion, cut into wedges

Preparation: Preheat oven to 400°F. Place potatoes in a large saucepan and cover with water. Bring water to a boil over medium-high heat and cook 5 minutes; drain. Combine honey, wine, garlic, thyme, salt, and pepper in a small bowl; stir to mix thoroughly. Place potatoes and other vegetables in a Dutch oven or other deep baking dish. Coat with honey/wine mixture and stir. Bake, uncovered, about 25 minutes or until tender, stirring every 8 to 10 minutes to prevent burning. Makes 8 servings.

Nutritional information per serving:
Calories: 254.1
Fat: 0.6 g
Saturated fat: trace
Carbohydrate: 56.9 g
Total sugars: 27.0 g
Protein: 6.7 g
Sodium: 95.8 mg
Cholesterol: 0 mg
Dietary fiber: 8.0 g

Bean Sprouts and Bok Choy

This tasty side dish is full of antioxidants and is quick and easy to prepare.

Ingredients:
2-1/2 tablespoons peanut oil
3 tablespoons reduced-sodium soy sauce or tamari
1 tablespoon sesame oil
2/3 cup cold water
3/4 teaspoon honey
1 teaspoon cornstarch
1/8 teaspoon freshly ground black pepper
1-inch cube of fresh ginger, cut into slivers
3 scallions, sliced
3 small garlic cloves, thinly sliced
1 carrot, peeled and cut into thin sticks
2/3 cup fresh bean sprouts
8 ounces bok choy, shredded
1/3 cup cashews, chopped

Preparation: Place a large wok over medium heat. Add peanut oil and heat about 3 minutes until warm. Add ginger, garlic, scallions and carrots and heat 2 to 2-1/2 minutes. Add the bean sprouts and heat 2 more minutes, stirring and tossing continuously. Add bok choy and cashews and heat until bok choy leaves are just beginning to wilt. Mix all of the sauce ingredients quickly in a bowl and pour into the wok while stirring. Once the vegetables are lightly covered in sauce, serve immediately. Makes 6 servings.

This recipe's quercetin (scallions) and isothiocyanates (bok choy) may help prevent the following cancers: **endometrial and pancreas.**

Nutritional information per serving:
Calories: 143.4
Fat: 11.0 g
Saturated fat: 1.9 g
Carbohydrate: 8.2 g
Total sugars: 2.8 g
Protein: 2.9 g
Sodium: 335 mg
Cholesterol: 0 mg
Dietary fiber: 1.4 g

Braised Brussels Sprouts

This is a recipe from Beverly Lynn Bennett, accomplished vegan chef (website for other great recipes: www.veganchef.com). It will make you see Brussels sprouts in an entirely new light.

Ingredients:
1 cup almonds, sliced
2 pounds (32 ounces) Brussels sprouts
2 tablespoons peanut or sunflower oil
2 slices ginger
3 tablespoons unbleached cane sugar
1 teaspoon salt
1/4–1/2 cup water

Preparation: Place almonds in a dry wok or large nonstick skillet and cook over medium heat 3 to 4 minutes or until lightly toasted and fragrant. Remove almonds from wok or skillet; set aside. Remove any tough outer leaves from Brussels sprouts, trim ends, cut each into quarters lengthwise, and set aside. In same wok or skillet used to toast almonds, heat oil. When hot, add slices of ginger and cook for 1 to 2 minutes to flavor oil. Remove ginger and discard. Add Brussels sprouts, toss well to thoroughly coat with flavored oil; stir-fry 2 minutes. Add sugar and salt, stir well, and stir-fry an additional 2 minutes. Add a little water to pan and stir-fry 1 to 2 minutes until the liquid cooks off. Repeat procedure, adding water 1 or 2 more times, until Brussels sprouts are tender and lightly browned. Add toasted almonds and stir well to combine. Transfer to a large bowl or platter and serve. Makes 8 servings.

Nutritional information per serving:
Calories: 154.3
Fat: 8.3 g
Saturated fat: 1.0 g
Carbohydrate: 13.7 g
Total sugars: 4.5 g
Protein: 6.2 g
Sodium: 318 mg
Cholesterol: 0 mg
Dietary fiber: 5.5 g

Broccoli and Cauliflower with Cheddar

This recipe comes courtesy of Elaine Devlin, fiscal manager of the department where I work. It is a great way to get kids to eat their broccoli. I've modified it slightly to reduce the fat content.

Ingredients:
4 cups fresh broccoli florets
4 cups fresh cauliflower florets
Nonstick cooking spray
1/4 cup olive oil, divided
2 large garlic cloves, minced
1/8 teaspoon ground red pepper
2 tablespoon black olives, coarsely chopped
8 ounces (about 2 cups) reduced-fat, shredded sharp cheddar cheese, divided
3/4 cup coarse whole-wheat dry breadcrumbs
Salt and pepper to taste

Preparation: Preheat oven to 400°F. Bring a large saucepan of salted water to a boil; add broccoli and cauliflower. Cook until crisp-tender, about 3 minutes. Drain. Spray a 2-inch-deep 2-quart baking dish with nonstick cooking spray. In a large skillet, heat 2 tablespoons olive oil over medium heat. Add garlic and ground red pepper; cook until fragrant. Remove from heat and toss broccoli and cauliflower with oil mixture. Toss olives and 1 cup cheese with vegetable mixture. Transfer to baking dish and sprinkle with remaining cheese. In a small bowl, toss bread crumbs with remaining olive oil and season with salt and pepper. Sprinkle breadcrumb mixture over cheese in baking dish. Bake in upper section of oven approximately 12 to 15 minutes or until cheese bubbles and crumbs are golden brown. Serve hot. Makes 6 servings.

This recipe's isothiocyanates (broccoli) and calcium (cheese) may help prevent the following cancers: **pancreas and breast.**

Nutritional information per serving:
Calories: 196.2
Fat: 12.1 g
Saturated fat: 3.0 g
Carbohydrate: 9.3 g
Total sugars: 4.3 g
Protein: 12.5 g
Sodium: 313.4 mg
Cholesterol: 8 mg
Dietary fiber: 2.2 g

Cauliflower and Spinach Au Gratin

Healthy fat, plenty of protein, and complex carbohydrates . . .
what more can I say?

This recipe's isothiocyanates (cauliflower) and lutein (spinach) may help prevent the following cancers: **lung and ovarian.**

Ingredients:
Nonstick cooking spray
1 tablespoon olive oil
3/4 cup sweet onion, finely chopped
1 teaspoon garlic, minced
1/2 teaspoon salt
1 cup baby spinach leaves
1 head cauliflower, divided into florets
1 cup plain low-fat yogurt
2 tablespoons flour
1/4 cup shredded reduced-fat cheddar cheese
Pinch of kosher salt and freshly cracked black pepper
1/2 cup whole-wheat bread crumbs
2 tablespoons grated Parmesan cheese
1 tablespoon chopped parsley

Preparation: Preheat oven to 375°F. Spray a baking dish with non-stick cooking spray. Place a small sauté pan over medium heat and add olive oil. Add onions and garlic and slowly caramelize 15 to 20 minutes, lowering heat as necessary and stirring occasionally. Season with 1/2 teaspoon salt. Toward end of cooking, add spinach and cook until it begins to wilt. Remove from heat. Place cauliflower in boiling water and blanch 3 to 4 minutes. Drain and cool. Whisk together yogurt and flour; stir in cheddar cheese, salt, and pepper. Toss yogurt mixture with cauliflower, caramelized onions, and spinach. Place in baking dish. Sprinkle breadcrumbs, Parmesan cheese, and parsley over cauliflower mixture. Bake 20 minutes. Makes 6 servings.

Nutritional information per serving:
Calories: 120.9
Fat: 4.1 g
Saturated fat: 1.3 g
Carbohydrate: 14.1 g
Total sugars: 6.8 g
Protein: 6.1 g
Sodium: 335 mg
Cholesterol: 4.9 mg
Dietary fiber: 3.1 g

Chinese Lettuce Wraps

This is a light and easy appetizer or side dish that is high in protein and low in calories. For a vegan option, substitute about 1-1/2 cups of tofu lightly sautéed in canola oil for the chicken.

Ingredients:
12 large butter-lettuce leaves, washed and dried
2 tablespoons fresh ginger, grated
2 tablespoons rice wine vinegar
2 tablespoons reduced-sodium soy sauce or tamari
1 tablespoon plus 1 teaspoon honey
1/2 teaspoon cornstarch
Nonstick cooking spray
1/3 cup yellow onion, chopped
2 cups carrots, grated
1 cup fresh snow-pea pods, sliced lengthwise
2 skinless, boneless chicken breasts, cooked and cut into thin strips

Preparation: Lay out 4 plates with 3 butter-lettuce leaves on each plate. In a medium bowl, combine ginger, vinegar, soy sauce or tamari, honey, and cornstarch. Spray a skillet with nonstick cooking spray and place over medium heat. Add onions, carrots, and pea pods to skillet and heat 3 to 4 minutes, stirring continuously. Add ginger mixture and heat about 1 minute, stirring, to thicken the sauce. Add chicken and heat thoroughly. Spoon about 1/4 cup of chicken mixture onto the center of each lettuce leaf and serve warm. Makes 4 servings.

This recipe's zeaxanthin (lettuce) and beta carotene (carrots) may help prevent the following cancers: **ovarian and lung.**

Nutritional information per serving:
Calories: 135.2
Fat: 1.2 g
Saturated fat: 0 g
Carbohydrate: 16.4 g
Total sugars: 10.4 g
Protein: 14.7 g
Sodium: 135 mg
Cholesterol: 35 mg
Dietary fiber: 3.1 g

Cowboy Potatoes

This recipe, courtesy of amateur vegan chef Rob Felty, is very similar to rice and beans, except it uses potatoes instead of rice. The beans, onions, and peppers are a great combination, and the potatoes make it a satisfying side dish.

Ingredients:
1-1/2 tablespoons olive oil
8 medium red potatoes, diced (unpeeled)
1 teaspoon each: ground cumin, ground coriander, and chili powder
1/4 teaspoon cayenne pepper
1 large onion, minced
1/2 medium green bell pepper, diced
1/2 medium red bell pepper, diced
1 can (15 ounces) black beans, drained and rinsed
1/3 cup mild or medium-heat tomato salsa
1/4 cup chopped fresh cilantro

Preparation: Heat olive oil in a large nonstick skillet over medium-high heat. Add potatoes and sauté about 10 minutes. Add cumin, coriander, chili powder and cayenne powder and stir. Add onion and peppers and continue cooking until potatoes are fully cooked and lightly crispy and browned, and onions and peppers have softened a bit. Add beans and salsa and stir, heating another 3 to 4 minutes, until heated through. Add cilantro and serve. Makes 6 servings.

Nutritional information per serving:
Calories: 333.8
Fat: 4.6 g
Saturated fat: 0.7 g
Carbohydrate: 62.8 g
Total sugars: 6.0 g
Protein: 10.3 g
Sodium: 336 mg
Cholesterol: 0 mg
Dietary fiber: 11.1 g

Cranberry-Almond Quinoa

Quinoa is a South American grain, once a staple of the Incas, rich in protein and minerals. The Incas referred to it as the "mother grain." Quinoa is a small and light grain that has a very pleasant texture. You can find it in most health-food stores. Quinoa is light, easily digested, and has the most complete nutrition and highest protein content of any grain. This dish is perfect with fish or poultry.

This recipe's lignans (quinoa) and vitamin E (almonds) may help prevent the following cancers: **prostate and colon.**

Ingredients:
1 cup quinoa
1/2 cup almonds, sliced
1/2 cup dried cranberries
1-1/2 cups reduced-sodium vegetable stock
1/4 teaspoon salt
1 bay leaf
1 cinnamon stick

Preparation: Soak quinoa about 1 hour in cold water. Rinse thoroughly in water several times and drain through a large fine-mesh strainer. Shake dry in strainer. Place a medium nonstick skillet or fry pan over medium heat. Add almonds; stir and toast until golden. Remove from pan. Add quinoa and stir and toast until dry and turning color. Transfer toasted quinoa, toasted almonds, and cranberries to a 2-quart saucepan. In a separate pot, heat vegetable stock over medium heat until boiling. To the 2-quart saucepan, add boiling stock, salt, bay leaf, and cinnamon stick and return to a boil. Cover, reduce heat to simmer, and cook 20 minutes. Remove from heat and let stand 5 minutes with lid on. Remove cinnamon stick. Fluff gently with a fork and serve. Makes 6 servings.

Nutritional information per serving:
Calories: 157.9
Fat: 1.5 g
Saturated fat: 0.5 g
Carbohydrate: 30.7 g
Total sugars: 7.1 g
Protein: 5.4 g
Sodium: 212 mg
Cholesterol: 0 mg
Dietary fiber: 3.3 g

Curried Lentils, Sweet Potatoes, and Spinach

Ingredients:
1 tablespoon olive oil
1 medium yellow onion, diced
1 tablespoon curry powder
3 garlic cloves, minced
1 teaspoon ground cumin
1 cup green lentils, rinsed in water a few times
2-1/2 cups reduced-sodium vegetable broth
1 medium sweet potato (about 8 to 9 ounces), peeled and cubed into 1/4-inch pieces
4-1/2 cups baby spinach
Pinch of salt and pepper
6 ounces plain low-fat yogurt
1/3 cup cashews, chopped

Preparation: In a medium soup pot, heat olive oil over low-medium heat. Add onion and garlic and sauté about 5 minutes, until soft. Stir in curry powder, garlic, and cumin and cook about 1 minute. Add lentils and broth and stir; bring to a boil, reduce heat, and simmer, covered, 10 minutes. Add sweet potato, cover, and cook an additional 10 minutes, until sweet potatoes are tender and water is absorbed. Stir in baby spinach and cook about 1 minute until just wilted. Season with salt and pepper. Serve in 6 large soup bowls or soup plates; top with low-fat yogurt and chopped cashews. Makes 6 servings.

Nutritional information per serving:
Calories: 282.3
Fat: 9.1 g
Saturated fat: 1.6 g
Carbohydrate: 35.8 g
Total sugars: 7.5 g
Protein: 14.3 g
Sodium: 105 mg
Cholesterol: 1.7 mg
Dietary fiber: 12.3 g

Edamame and Braised Greens

I found this recipe in a magazine called Delicious Living, *which I picked up from my local health food store, and then made a number of changes to suit my tastes. This delicious dish is very high in protein and antioxidants.*

Ingredients:
1/4 teaspoon salt
2 cups frozen shelled edamame
2 tablespoons extra-virgin olive oil
3 small to medium shallots, thinly sliced
1 small head escarole (about 8 ounces), trimmed and cut crosswise into thin strips
4 small garlic cloves, minced
1/8 teaspoon salt
1/8 teaspoon freshly ground pepper
3 cups baby arugula
3 cups baby spinach
1/8 teaspoon crushed red pepper flakes
3 tablespoons reduced-fat feta cheese, crumbled

Preparation: Place a large stockpot of water over medium heat and add 1/4 teaspoon salt. Bring to a boil; add edamame and cook 5 minutes. Drain and rinse under cold water to stop cooking. Drain again and pat dry. Place a large, heavy skillet or fry pan over medium heat and add olive oil. Add shallots and sauté over medium heat 2 minutes. Add escarole and garlic, toss and stir until coated with oil and sprinkle with 1/8 teaspoon each of salt and pepper; cook 2 minutes. Add edamame, spinach, red pepper flakes; cook about 1 minute until spinach is just wilted. Season with additional salt and pepper if desired. Top with feta cheese and serve. Makes 6 servings.

This recipe's isoflavones (edamame) and folate (spinach) may help prevent the following cancers: **breast and colon.**

Nutritional information per serving:
Calories: 160.3
Fat: 7.5 g
Saturated fat: 1.5 g
Carbohydrate: 8.1 g
Total sugars: 1.3 g
Protein: 15.1 g
Sodium: 230 mg
Cholesterol: 1.3 mg
Dietary fiber: 2.9 g

Garbanzo, Tomato, and Red Onion Mélange

Ingredients:
1 can (19 ounces) garbanzo beans, drained and rinsed
2 garlic cloves, minced
3 tablespoons red onion, finely chopped
1 ripe medium tomato, seeded and diced
1/3 cup fresh parsley, chopped
3 tablespoons olive oil
1 tablespoon bottled lemon juice or juice of one fresh lemon
Salt and freshly ground pepper

Preparation: Combine all ingredients except salt and pepper in a large salad bowl and toss to distribute evenly. Season with salt and pepper as desired and toss again. Chill for 1 hour or more before serving to allow flavors to meld. Makes 4 generous servings.

Nutritional information per serving:
Calories: 326.2
Fat: 12.6 g
Saturated fat: 1.8 g
Carbohydrate: 43.7 g
Total sugars: 9.3 g
Protein: 9.5 g
Sodium: 544 mg
Cholesterol: 0 mg
Dietary fiber: 8.6 g

Hazelnut-Cranberry Sweet Potatoes

Ingredients:
2 tablespoons trans-fat-free butter
2 pounds sweet potatoes, peeled and sliced into 1/2 inch slices
1/4 teaspoon ground cloves
1 cup fresh cranberries
1/2 cup apricot nectar
1 teaspoon grated orange peel
1/3 cup maple syrup
1/4 cup hazelnuts, toasted

Preparation: In a large skillet over medium heat, melt butter. Add potatoes and cloves; cover and cook about 8 or 9 minutes or until nearly tender. Stir occasionally. Add cranberries, apricot nectar, and orange peel. Bring potatoes to a boil; reduce heat. Simmer, covered, about 5 minutes. Remove from heat. Gently stir in maple syrup and hazelnuts and serve immediately. Makes 6 servings.

Nutritional information per serving:
Calories: 183.8
Fat: 4.2 g
Saturated fat: 2.5 g
Carbohydrate: 33.4 g
Total sugars: 23.9 g
Protein: 3.1 g
Sodium: 43 mg
Cholesterol: 10 mg
Dietary fiber: 6.9 g

Healthy Home Fries

Ingredients:
4 medium baking potatoes, thinly sliced
1 tablespoon each: garlic powder, onion powder, paprika, salt, and dried oregano
1 teaspoon black pepper
1 small yellow onion, chopped
1 small green bell pepper, chopped
1 small red bell pepper, chopped
1 cup mushrooms, thinly sliced
2 tablespoons olive oil

Preparation: Place potatoes and spices in a container with a tight-fitting lid or a large, heavy-duty zip-lock plastic bag. Shake 30 seconds, until potatoes are well coated. Set aside. In a large frying pan, sauté chopped onion, bell peppers, and mushrooms in olive oil until onion is translucent and slightly browned, about 7 to 10 minutes. Add spiced potato slices to sautéed vegetables. Toss well. Let sit about 8 to 10 minutes, browning over low heat, without stirring. Flip potatoes and allow to cook another 8 to 10 minutes, or until both sides are crispy brown. Serve immediately. Makes 6 side-dish servings

This recipe's quercetin (onion) and luteolin (green pepper) may help prevent the following cancers: **lung and ovarian.**

Nutritional information per serving:
Calories: 272
Fat: 7.1 g
Saturated fat: 1.0 g
Carbohydrate: 45.5 g
Total sugars: 4.8 g
Protein: 6.3 g
Sodium: 15 mg
Cholesterol: 0 mg
Dietary fiber: 5.0 g

Heirloom-Tomato and Olive Salad

This flavorful salad is low in calories and rich in monounsaturated fat.

Ingredients:
7 medium heirloom tomatoes (combination of red and orange, preferably)
3/4 cup pitted Kalamata olives, quartered
1 medium shallot, peeled and finely diced
Salt and freshly ground pepper
1 tablespoon sherry vinegar
1 tablespoon fresh basil, coarsely chopped
1-1/2 teaspoons fresh oregano, chopped
1 teaspoon fresh chives, chopped
3 tablespoons extra virgin olive oil

Preparation: Core tomatoes and slice into large cubes or bite-size wedges. In a large ceramic bowl, combine tomatoes, olives, and diced shallot and season with salt and pepper. Add sherry vinegar, basil, oregano, and chives. Add olive oil and toss. For best flavor, prepare 1 to 2 hours ahead of time and let stand at room temperature. Toss again just prior to serving. Makes 6 servings.

This recipe's lycopene (tomatoes) and luteolin (basil) may help prevent the following cancers: **pancreas and ovarian.**

Nutritional information per serving:
Calories: 127.7
Fat: 8.9 g
Saturated fat: 1.3 g
Carbohydrate: 10.1 g
Total sugars: 3.7 g
Protein: 1.8 g
Sodium: 119 mg
Cholesterol: 0 mg
Dietary fiber: 1.7 g

Nutritional information per serving:
Calories: 278.1
Fat: 21.7 g
Saturated fat: 15.5 g
Carbohydrate: 15.5 g
Total sugars: 8.1 g
Protein: 5.2 g
Sodium: 42 mg
Cholesterol: 0 mg
Dietary fiber: 4 g

Nutritional information per serving:
Calories: 310.8
Fat: 3.2 g
Saturated fat: 0.4 g
Carbohydrate: 59.9 g
Total sugars: 5.4 g
Protein: 10.6 g
Sodium: 18 mg
Cholesterol: 0 mg
Dietary fiber: 9.6 g

Maple-Pecan Broccoli

Ingredients:
1 large head of broccoli
4 tablespoons dry sherry
3 tablespoons pure maple syrup
1 tablespoon Dijon mustard
1/2 cup walnut oil
Salt and freshly ground pepper to taste and pinch ground nutmeg
1 cup walnuts, coarsely chopped

Preparation: Cut broccoli into bite-size pieces. Place a large stockpot of water over medium-high heat and bring to a boil. Steam broccoli in boiling water until bright green and crisp but tender; drain and set aside. Whisk together sherry, maple syrup, and Dijon mustard. Gradually whisk in oil. Season with salt, pepper, and nutmeg as desired. Toss broccoli with walnuts and vinaigrette. Serve immediately. Makes 6 servings.

Papaya Black Beans and Rice

This dish could easily be a main course. It is savory and spicy, and the combination of rice and beans makes it a complete protein. Pair it with broiled, light fish such as tilapia or flounder or with some lightly sautéed tofu.

Ingredients:
2 teaspoons olive oil
1 cup red onion, chopped
1/2 cup orange juice
1/4 cup lemon juice
2 tablespoons fresh cilantro, chopped
1/2 teaspoon cayenne pepper
1 cup red bell pepper, finely chopped
1 cup yellow bell pepper, finely chopped
1 medium papaya, peeled, seeded, and diced
2 garlic cloves, peeled and minced
2 cans (15 ounces each) black beans, rinsed and drained
6 cups hot, cooked small- or medium-grain brown rice

Preparation: Heat olive oil in a large skillet over medium heat. Add all ingredients except beans and rice. Cook 5 minutes, stirring occasionally, until onion is translucent and bell peppers are crisp but tender. Stir in beans and cook an additional 6 to 8 minutes, stirring, until cooked through. Serve over brown rice. Makes 8 servings.

Quinoa with Vegetables

*Here is a second recipe from amateur vegan chef Rob Felty
(http://robfelty.com/food).*

Ingredients:
1 tablespoon olive oil
1 large yellow onion, diced
1 green bell pepper, diced
2 garlic cloves, minced
12 ounces assorted fresh mushrooms, washed very well and thinly sliced
1-1/2 teaspoons ground cumin
1 teaspoon ground coriander
1/4 teaspoon ground cayenne pepper (less if you don't like your
    food spicy)
1 can (14 or 14-1/2 ounces) diced tomatoes
1 cup quinoa
2 cups water
1 cube vegetable bouillon
1/4 cup fresh cilantro, chopped
Salt and pepper to taste

Preparation: In a medium saucepan, heat olive oil over
medium-high heat. Add onion and sauté about 1 to 2 minutes.
Add green pepper and garlic; continue sautéing 4 to 6 minutes.
Add mushrooms and cook until liquid is evaporated. Add ground
cumin, ground coriander, cayenne, tomatoes, quinoa, water, and
vegetable bouillon. Bring to a boil; simmer over low heat, covered,
approximately 20 minutes. Add fresh cilantro and season with salt
and pepper as desired. Makes 6 servings.

This recipe's luteolin (green pepper) and fiber (quinoa) may help prevent the following cancers: **ovarian and colon.**

Nutritional information per serving:
Calories: 159.9
Fat: 4.3 g
Saturated fat: 0.5 g
Carbohydrate: 25.2 g
Total sugars: 2.6 g
Protein: 5.1 g
Sodium: 21 mg
Cholesterol: 0 mg
Dietary fiber: 3.1 g

Nutritional information per serving:
Calories: 237.1
Fat: 3.2 g
Saturated fat: 0.2 g
Carbohydrate: 45.9 g
Total sugars: 2.5 g
Protein: 6.2 g
Sodium: 189 mg
Cholesterol: 0 mg
Dietary fiber: 1.8 g

Nutritional information per serving:
Calories: 100.3
Fat: 9.9 g
Saturated fat: 2.7 g
Carbohydrate: 2.0 g
Total sugars: trace
Protein: 0.8 g
Sodium: 308 mg
Cholesterol: 0 mg
Dietary fiber: < 1 g

Rice with Oranges and Almonds

Ingredients:
2 cups reduced-sodium chicken broth
1 cup orange juice
1/4 cup yellow onion, chopped
1-1/2 cups long-grain brown rice, uncooked
1 small navel orange, peeled and sectioned
1/4 cup almonds, sliced
2 tablespoons fresh parsley, chopped
Salt and pepper to taste

Preparation: Place chicken broth and orange juice in a large saucepan and bring to a boil over medium heat. Add onions and rice. Cover, reduce heat, and simmer 20 to 25 minutes or until rice appears tender and liquid is absorbed. Add oranges, almonds and parsley. Stir well. Season with salt and pepper as desired and serve warm. Makes 6 servings.

Sautéed Mushrooms and Shallots in Wine

This dish is a wonderful accompaniment to baked or broiled chicken, lean beef, or pork. Mushrooms have been shown to have immune-boosting properties, meaning that they can help your immune system to function more efficiently (a key to fighting cancer).

Ingredients:
1/4 cup trans-fat–free butter or margarine
2 small shallots, peeled and chopped
2 garlic cloves, finely chopped
1/2 teaspoon salt
1/4 teaspoon dried thyme
1/4 teaspoon marjoram
12 ounces assorted mushrooms (white, crimini, portabella, and shiitake) sliced
1/2 cup Merlot or other dry red wine

Preparation: In 12-inch nonstick skillet, melt butter or margarine over medium heat. Add shallots, garlic, salt, thyme, and marjoram. Cook 2 to 3 minutes until shallots are almost tender, stirring occasionally. Add mushrooms and cook, stirring occasionally, about 15 minutes until mushrooms are golden and tender. Stir in wine; cook an additional 2 minutes. Serve warm. Makes 6 servings.

Sesame Kale

This low-calorie, low-fat side dish maximizes your antioxidant intake of leafy greens, with a delightful honey and sesame flavor. Spinach or Swiss chard can be substituted for the kale for variation. Kale naturally contains a good deal of sodium, so I rarely add salt to this dish.

Ingredients:
1 pound (16 ounces) fresh kale
2 tablespoons reduced-sodium soy sauce or tamari
1 garlic clove, minced
2 teaspoons honey
1 tablespoon red wine vinegar (can substitute white balsamic vinegar)
Pinch of red pepper flakes
2 tablespoons sesame seeds, toasted

Preparation: Separate kale leaves from stems. Chop stems and greens, keeping separate. Steam stems 2 to 3 minutes over about an inch of boiling water, then add greens and steam until just tender, about 3 to 4 minutes more. Drain and allow kale to cool until it can be handled. Squeeze out as much water as possible and place in a serving bowl. In a small mixing bowl, combine soy sauce or tamari, garlic, honey, cider vinegar, and red pepper flakes. Mix with kale in serving bowl and top with sesame seeds. Chill and serve. Makes 6 servings.

This recipe's folate (kale) and allicin (garlic) may help prevent the following cancers: **ovarian and skin.**

Nutritional information per serving:
Calories: 76.9
Fat: 2.1 g
Saturated fat: 0.3 g
Carbohydrate: 10.8 g
Total sugars: 2.0 g
Protein: 3.7 g
Sodium: 368 mg
Cholesterol: 0 mg
Dietary fiber: 1.9 g

Southwest Corn and Black Beans

This is the first of three recipes donated by Pat Eagon, PhD, a biochemist at the University of Pittsburgh and an excellent cook. She notes that this dish is even better the next day.

Ingredients:
6 ears fresh corn (can substitute two 15-ounce cans fresh corn kernels)
2 cans (15 ounces) black beans, drained and rinsed
1 medium red bell pepper, diced
1 medium green bell pepper, diced
3-4 green onions, thinly sliced with green tops
1 small poblano pepper, seeded and diced
3/4 cup cilantro, chopped
Juice and zest of 2 limes
1/4 cup extra-virgin olive oil
1 medium garlic clove, crushed
1/2 teaspoon ground cumin
1 teaspoon sugar
Salt and coarsely ground pepper to taste

Preparation: Place a large pot of salted water over medium-high heat and bring to a boil. Reduce heat and add corn; cook about 10 to 12 minutes, until tender. Remove from heat and let cool. In a large bowl, combine black beans, red and green pepper, green onions, poblano pepper, and cilantro. In a measuring cup, combine lime zest and juice, olive oil, garlic, cumin, and sugar. Cut corn from cobs into bowl with black beans. Pour dressing ingredients in measuring cup over bean-and-corn mixture and season with salt and pepper as desired. Mix well and let sit to enhance flavors if desired. Serve or cover, refrigerate, and serve the next day. Makes 8 servings.

Nutritional information per serving:
Calories: 239.2
Fat: 8.8 g
Saturated fat: 1.2 g
Carbohydrate: 32.0 g
Total sugars: 3.8 g
Protein: 8.0 g
Sodium: 171 mg
Cholesterol: 0 mg
Dietary fiber: 7.2 g

Soy-Nut Rice Pilaf

This rice pilaf is uniquely sweet and nutty. Unlike many other rice dishes, it contains isoflavones that have been shown to protect against some cancers. Plus, it is full of protein and fiber. A perfect complement to a healthy entrée!

Ingredients:
2-1/4 cups water
1 cup long-grain brown rice
1-1/2 cups fresh carrots, thinly sliced
1 cup fresh or thawed frozen broccoli, chopped
3/4 cup sweet red pepper, diced
1/2 cup onion, diced
2 teaspoons fresh ginger, minced
2 garlic cloves, minced
1/3 cup reduced-sodium vegetable broth
1/3 cup soy-nut butter
2-1/2 tablespoons fresh cilantro, chopped
Salt to taste

Preparation: Bring water to a boil in a large saucepan. Stir in rice, carrots, broccoli, red pepper, onion, ginger, and garlic. Reduce heat to low. Cover and simmer 20 minutes or until rice is tender and water has been absorbed. Meanwhile, in a smaller saucepan, combine broth, soy-nut butter, and cilantro and place over medium heat. Cook, stirring constantly, 1 to 2 minutes, until soy-nut butter is smooth. Set aside. When rice has finished cooking, stir in soy-nut–butter mixture and salt as desired. Serve immediately. Makes 4 servings.

This recipe's fiber (brown rice) and isoflavones (soy butter) may help prevent the following cancers: **ovarian and breast.**

Nutritional information per serving:
Calories: 336.6
Fat: 9.0 g
Saturated fat: 1.6 g
Carbohydrate: 52.9 g
Total sugars: 4.6 g
Protein: 11.0 g
Sodium: 172 mg
Cholesterol: 0 mg
Dietary fiber: 5.5 g

Spinach with Cashews and Dried Cherries

You can use any type of chopped nut with this dish, and you may want to try cranberries instead of cherries for a variation.

Ingredients:
3 tablespoons unsweetened dried cherries
1 tablespoon olive oil
9 ounces baby spinach leaves, pre-washed or washed and dried
2 small garlic cloves, minced
2-1/2 tablespoons cashews, chopped
Salt and pepper to taste

Preparation: Place cherries in a small saucepan with enough water to cover. Bring to a boil; remove from heat and let stand 5 minutes, then drain. In a large nonstick skillet, heat olive oil over medium heat. Add baby spinach and garlic to skillet. Sauté, stirring frequently, 5 to 7 minutes or until spinach is tender and wilted. Add cherries and cashews to spinach. Sprinkle with salt and pepper as desired and serve. Makes 4 servings.

Summer Green Beans

Fresh green beans are mixed with rich, cooked mushrooms and topped with hazelnuts and low-fat feta cheese. This is a dish that will get raves and won't hurt your waistline.

Ingredients:
16 ounces (1 pound) fresh green beans, trimmed
1 tablespoon extra-virgin olive oil
2 garlic cloves, peeled and minced
8 ounces fresh mixed mushrooms (any combination of white, crimini, baby portabella, moonlight, shiitake), sliced
1 teaspoon finely grated lemon zest
1/4 cup hazelnuts, chopped
3 tablespoons reduced-fat feta cheese, crumbled
Salt and freshly ground black pepper to taste

Preparation: Cook green beans in a large pot of boiling salted water until crisp-tender, about 5 minutes. Drain into a colander; rinse green beans under cold water to stop cooking; drain well. Place a large nonstick skillet over medium heat and add olive oil. Sauté garlic and mushrooms in olive oil until mushrooms are tender and juices have evaporated, about 8 to 10 minutes. Stir in green beans; heat through. Top with hazelnuts, feta cheese, and season with salt and pepper to taste. Makes 6 servings.

Swiss Chard with Pine Nuts and Breadcrumbs

This is one of my very favorite dishes. I absolutely love it with broiled tilapia or flounder, a baked sweet potato, and a few lemon wedges.

Ingredients:
2-1/4 pounds Swiss chard
Salt
1/4 cup extra virgin olive oil, divided
3 garlic cloves, minced
1/2 cup fine, dry whole-wheat breadcrumbs
1/4 cup pine nuts

Preparation: Place a large bowl of ice water in kitchen working area. Remove ribs from Swiss chard and peel. Bring a large saucepan of salted water to a boil, add Swiss chard ribs, and cook 3 minutes. Add Swiss chard leaves and cook 1 minute. Drain and place Swiss chard into ice water to halt cooking. Drain again. Squeeze dry and chop coarsely. Warm 2 tablespoons olive oil in a medium saucepan over low heat. Add garlic and cook about 3 minutes until translucent. Add Swiss chard; cover and cook 5 minutes, stirring occasionally. Meanwhile, place a small skillet or fry pan over medium heat and add remaining olive oil. Add bread crumbs and sauté, stirring continuously, until golden brown, about 3 minutes. Arrange Swiss chard on 6 individual plates, sprinkle with pine nuts and warm breadcrumbs. Makes 6 servings.

This recipe's lutein (Swiss chard) and allicin (garlic) may help prevent the following cancers: **ovarian and endometrial.**

Nutritional information per serving:
Calories: 98.5
Fat: 3.3 g
Saturated fat: 0.4 g
Carbohydrate: 13.1 g
Total sugars: 2.5 g
Protein: 4.1 g
Sodium: 428 mg
Cholesterol: 0 mg
Dietary fiber: 3.3 g

Nutritional information per serving:
Calories: 154.5
Fat: 9.8 g
Saturated fat: 1.5 g
Carbohydrate: 13.6 g
Total sugars: 2.7 g
Protein: 2.9 g
Sodium: 22 mg
Cholesterol: 0 mg
Dietary fiber: 3 g

Nutritional information per serving:
Calories: 175.1
Fat: 5.9 g
Saturated fat: 0.7 g
Carbohydrate: 23.1 g
Total sugars: 3.5 g
Protein: 7.5 g
Sodium: 58 mg
Cholesterol: 0 mg
Dietary fiber: 6.7 g

Traditional Tabouleh

Ingredients:
1/3 cup bulgur wheat (also called cracked wheat)
5 scallions, finely chopped, white and light green parts only
3 cups flat-leaf parsley leaves, finely chopped
1/2 cup fresh mint leaves, finely chopped
4 medium tomatoes, cored, seeded, and diced
1/2 cup extra virgin olive oil
3 tablespoons fresh lemon juice
Salt (preferably kosher salt) and freshly ground black pepper to taste

Preparation: Soak bulgur wheat in a bowl of warm water about 30 minutes. Strain, squeeze out water, and place in a large bowl. Toss scallions, parsley, and mint with bulgur wheat. Add tomatoes and stir; drizzle in olive oil; toss again. Add lemon juice, salt, and pepper. Toss again; taste and adjust seasoning as desired. Makes 6 servings.

Tuscan-Style Beans

Ingredients:
2 cans (15 ounces each) cannellini beans, rinsed and drained
4 large fresh sage leaves, coarsely chopped (or 2 teaspoons dried sage)
2 garlic cloves, crushed
1 large Vidalia or other sweet onion, quartered
2 tablespoons extra-virgin olive oil, divided
1 cup water
1 medium carrot, finely chopped
1 small celery rib, finely chopped
1 small yellow onion, finely chopped
1 plum tomato, seeded and chopped
Salt and freshly ground black pepper
Garnish: 1/4 cup flat-leaf parsley, chopped

Preparation: Place beans in a deep saucepan. Add sage, garlic, Vidalia onion, and 1 tablespoon olive oil. Pour in water. Simmer, uncovered, 20 to 30 minutes or until most liquid has evaporated and beans are soft but not mushy. Remove onion. Meanwhile, heat remaining oil in a medium skillet over medium-high heat. Sauté carrot, celery, and yellow onion in oil until onion is translucent, about 5 minutes. Add tomato and cook an additional 5 minutes. Stir carrot mixture into bean mixture and season with salt and pepper as desired. Serve warm, garnished with parsley. Makes 6 servings.

SOUPS AND SALADS

Adzuki Bean–Citrus Salad

Adzuki beans are a flavorful bean perfect for soups and stews, as well as salads. This sweet and savory salad contains antioxidants galore and is uniquely satisfying.

Ingredients:
1 cup dried adzuki beans (can substitute black beans or other small beans)
1/4 teaspoon black pepper
2 tablespoons mellow white miso (soy paste)
3 tablespoons orange juice
2 tablespoons lemon juice
2 tablespoons olive oil
1/2 teaspoon fresh ginger, peeled and minced
3 scallions, chopped
2 medium cucumbers, peeled, seeded, and chopped
1 small carrot, chopped
3 tablespoons pecans, chopped
1-1/2 cups baby arugula
1 cup baby romaine-lettuce leaves
1 orange, peeled and divided into sections

Preparation: The night before preparing salad, place beans in a bowl. Add water to cover by 2 inches. Cover and let stand overnight. Rinse and drain beans and place in a medium saucepan. Add water to cover by 2 inches and bring to a boil over high heat. Stir in pepper. Reduce heat to low, cover, and simmer, stirring occasionally, 30 to 40 minutes or until very tender. Drain beans and place in a serving bowl about 10 minutes. Meanwhile, in a large bowl, whisk together miso, orange juice, lemon juice, oil, and ginger. Stir in scallions, cucumbers, carrot, pecans, and adzuki beans. Let stand 10 to 15 minutes to allow flavors to meld. Divide mixed arugula and baby romaine among 4 serving plates. Add 1/4 bean salad to middle of each plate of mixed greens and surround with a few orange slices. Makes 4 servings.

Nutritional information per serving:
Calories: 299.3
Fat: 8.9 g
Saturated fat: 1.3 g
Carbohydrate: 42.7 g
Total sugars: 5.7 g
Protein: 12.1 g
Sodium: 33 mg
Cholesterol: 0 mg
Dietary fiber: 8.7 g

African Pineapple-Peanut Stew

This West-African inspired recipe contains a fantastic combination of sweet and spicy flavors and is high in fiber, vitamin A, and protein. The sweetness of the kale and onions is accentuated by its nutty flavor.

Ingredients:
1 cup Vidalia or other sweet onion, chopped
2 garlic cloves, minced
1 tablespoon olive oil
1 large bunch kale (about 4 to 5 cups)
2 cups canned crushed pineapple, with juice (not drained)
1/2 cup natural peanut butter
1/2 tablespoon Tabasco or other hot sauce
1/4 cup fresh cilantro, chopped
Salt and freshly ground pepper to taste
2 cups cooked brown rice
2-1/2 tablespoons chopped skinless peanuts
1/4 cup chopped scallions

Preparation: Sauté onions and garlic in oil in a covered saucepan over medium heat about 10 minutes, stirring frequently, until onions are lightly browned. While onions and garlic sauté, wash kale and let dry. Remove and discard large stems and blemished kale leaves. Stack kale leaves on a cutting surface and slice cross-wise into 1-inch-wide slices. Add pineapple and its juice to onions and bring to a simmer. Stir in kale; cover and simmer an additional 5 minutes, stirring occasionally, until just tender. Mix in peanut butter, Tabasco sauce, and cilantro and simmer 5 to 6 minutes. Season with salt and pepper as desired and serve over brown rice, topped with chopped peanuts and scallions. Makes 4 servings.

> This recipe's lutein (kale) and vitamin E (peanut butter) may help prevent the following cancers: **colon and skin.**

Nutritional information per serving:
Calories: 442.1
Fat: 22.1 g
Saturated fat: 5.2 g
Carbohydrate: 55.2 g
Total sugars: 22.9 g
Protein: 10.1 g
Sodium: 207 mg
Cholesterol: 0 mg
Dietary fiber: 7.1 g

Barley and Salmon Salad

This salad is a fabulous main-course lunch or dinner entrée and a natural source of omega-3 fatty acids, calcium, and vitamin D. Serve this salad with some hearty, whole-grain bread.

Ingredients:
1 cup barley
3 cups water
Sea salt and freshly ground black pepper
4 scallions, white part only, sliced
1 tablespoon Dijon mustard
2 tablespoons apple-cider vinegar
4 tablespoons extra-virgin olive oil, divided
1 large, ripe mango
1 pint grape tomatoes, cut in half
1 teaspoon honey
1 teaspoon fresh ginger, finely minced
1/4 teaspoon chili powder (more if desired)
Juice and grated zest of 1 lime
1 pound cooked salmon, cut into about 1-inch chunks

Preparation: Rinse barley under cold running water and drain. Bring 3 cups of water to a boil in a medium saucepan. Salt the water and stir in barley. Lower the heat, partially cover and allow barley to cook gently about 50 minutes to 1 hour, or until tender. Drain and let cool. Transfer cooked barley to a serving bowl and season to taste with salt and pepper. Gently stir in scallions. In a small bowl, whisk together mustard and cider vinegar; add 3 tablespoons olive oil and whisk again. Pour this mixture over the barley and combine thoroughly. If time permits, cover and let sit at room temperature about 1 hour. In a separate mixing bowl, gently stir together mango, grape tomatoes, honey, ginger, chili powder, lime juice and zest, and remaining 1 tablespoon olive oil. To serve, divide cooked barley among 6 dinner plates, top with mango salsa, and add salmon chunks. Makes 6 servings.

Nutritional information per serving:
Calories: 388
Fat: 19.1 g
Saturated fat: 3.4 g
Carbohydrate: 33.4 g
Total sugars: 7.9 g
Protein: 21.0 g
Sodium: 113 mg
Cholesterol: 47.6 mg
Dietary fiber: 6.5 g

Blueberry-Coconut Soup with Lime

This was adapted from a recipe that I found in a magazine I read on an airplane, although I make it with light coconut milk which is much lower in saturated fat and calories than regular coconut milk. Blueberries have been all the buzz lately due to their high antioxidant content, and coconut milk contains an immune-boosting fatty acid called lauric acid.

Ingredients:
3 cups blueberries, fresh or frozen
1/3 cup sugar
1/2 cup water
Grated zest of 1 lime
1/4 cup fresh lime juice
1 can (15 ounces) light coconut milk
1/3 cup flaked, toasted, unsweetened coconut

Preparation: In a medium saucepan, combine blueberries, sugar, water, lime zest, and lime juice. Bring to a boil; reduce heat and simmer 10 to 12 minutes. Remove from heat and let cool. Transfer to a large bowl and chill at least 2 hours. In a medium bowl, whisk coconut milk until smooth and light. Stir into chilled blueberry mixture. Divide soup among 6 bowls and serve garnished with toasted coconut. Makes 6 servings.

This recipe's ellagic acid (blueberries) and vitamin C (lime juice) may help prevent the following cancers: **colon and lung.**

Nutritional information per serving:
Calories: 148.8
Fat: 4.4 g
Saturated fat: 3.5 g
Carbohydrate: 25 g
Total sugars: 19.8 g
Protein: 2.3 g
Sodium: 16 mg
Cholesterol: 0 mg
Dietary fiber: 3.5 g

Butternut Squash Soup

This soup contains almost a full day's worth of beta carotene and vitamin C.

Ingredients:
Nonstick cooking spray
1 tablespoon olive oil
2 large leeks, chopped (green and white parts)
1/8 teaspoon each: ground nutmeg and ground cinnamon
4 cups (about 1-1/2 pounds) butternut squash, peeled and cut into cubes
3 small carrots, grated
3 cups reduced-sodium vegetable broth
Salt and pepper

Preparation: Coat a large stockpot with nonstick cooking spray and place over medium-high heat. Add olive oil, then leeks; sauté leeks 6 to 7 minutes, until soft and translucent. Add ground nutmeg and cinnamon and heat until fragrant, about 1 to 1-1/2 minutes. Add squash, carrots, and broth and bring to a boil. Reduce heat and let simmer 20 to 25 minutes, until vegetables are tender. Turn off heat and let cool slightly. Purée in a blender or food processor until mixture is thick and even in consistency. Return to pot; season with salt and pepper as desired and heat gently until warm. Serve immediately. Makes 4 servings.

Nutritional information per serving:
Calories: 204.8
Fat: 3.6 g
Saturated fat: 0.5 g
Carbohydrate: 37.0 g
Total sugars: 12.0 g
Protein: 6.1 g
Sodium: 445 mg
Cholesterol: 0 mg
Dietary fiber: 5.2 g

Chickpea and Spinach Soup

Spinach contains magnesium, calcium, potassium, and tons of vitamins as well as the antioxidant lutein. Combine it with fiber and protein-rich chickpeas and you have one heck of a nutritious soup.

Ingredients:
2 tablespoons olive oil
4 garlic cloves, peeled and minced
1/4 cup shallots, finely chopped
1/3 cup celery, diced
Pinch red pepper flakes
4 cups fat-free, low-sodium vegetable stock
1-1/2 tablespoons fresh rosemary, finely chopped
1 can (15 ounces) garbanzo beans (aka chickpeas), not drained
1-1/4 cups cooked brown rice
1 cup tomatoes, diced (if using canned, do not drain)
Salt and freshly ground black pepper to taste
2 cups fresh spinach, chopped

Preparation: Place a large soup or stock pot over medium heat and add olive oil. Add garlic and shallots and sauté 1-1/2 to 2 minutes. Add celery and red pepper flakes and continue to sauté another 1 to 2 minutes. Add vegetable stock, rosemary, chickpeas, rice, tomatoes, and salt. Cover and bring to a boil. Reduce heat to medium-low and simmer about 30 minutes. Pour about half of soup into a blender or food processor and purée. Return purée to pot. Season with salt and black pepper as desired and add chopped spinach. Simmer on low heat 6 to 7 minutes. Serve hot. Makes 6 servings.

This recipe's folate (spinach) and fiber (garbanzo beans) may help prevent the following cancers: **ovarian and colon.**

Nutritional information per serving:
Calories: 189.0
Fat: 5.8 g
Saturated fat: 0.8 g
Carbohydrate: 23.8 g
Total sugars: 2.4 g
Protein: 5.9 g
Sodium: 148 mg
Cholesterol: 0 mg
Dietary fiber: 4.8 g

Chinese Tofu-Cabbage Soup

This vegan tofu and cabbage soup recipe is reprinted with permission from Vegetarian Soups for All Seasons *by Nava Atlas (Amberwood Press, 2006).*

This recipe's kaempferol (cabbage) and isoflavones (tofu) may help prevent the following cancers: **stomach and prostate.**

Ingredients:
1 tablespoon light olive oil
1 large yellow onion, quartered and thinly sliced
2 cups firmly packed, finely shredded Napa or Savoy cabbage
3/4 cup thinly sliced, small white mushrooms
1 can (6 ounces) sliced water chestnuts, undrained
4 cups (32 ounces) low-sodium, organic vegetable broth
2 tablespoons dry sherry or wine
2 teaspoons reduced-sodium soy sauce
Freshly ground pepper to taste
1 cup fresh snow peas, trimmed and halved
8 ounces firm tofu, cut into 1/2-inch cubes

Preparation: Heat oil in a large soup or stock pot. Add onion and sauté over low heat until golden brown. Add remaining ingredients, except snow peas and tofu. Bring to a rapid simmer, then lower heat. Cover and simmer over low heat 10 minutes. Remove from heat; stir in snow peas and tofu and let soup stand 30 minutes. Return pot to stove; heat through and serve at once. Makes 4 large servings

Nutritional information per serving:
Calories: 194.6
Fat: 8.2 g
Saturated fat: 1.2 g
Carbohydrate: 17.3 g
Total sugars: 6.5 g
Protein: 10.4 g
Sodium: 253 mg
Cholesterol: 0 mg
Dietary fiber: 3.6 g

Fresh Gazpacho

Packed with fresh vegetables, vitamins, and minerals, gazpacho is one of the most nutritious soups. Combined with some hearty bread and your choice of salad, it makes a refreshing and light supper.

Ingredients:
2 cups tomato juice
1/2 small cucumber, peeled and chopped
1 ripe tomato, chopped
2/3 cup yellow pepper, chopped
1 tablespoon onion, minced
1 tablespoon fresh parsley, minced
1 large garlic clove, minced
1 tablespoon fresh basil, minced
2 teaspoons red wine vinegar
1 teaspoon honey
2 teaspoons lime juice
Sea salt to taste
Dash of Tabasco sauce (optional)

Preparation: Place all ingredients in a blender and process until smooth. Work in batches to achieve a uniform consistency. Serve immediately for best flavor. Makes 4 servings.

This recipe's lycopene (tomatoes) and allicin (onion) may help prevent the following cancers: **prostate and stomach.**

Nutritional information per serving:
Calories: 59.2
Fat: 0.2 g
Saturated fat: trace
Carbohydrate: 12.4 g
Total sugars: 1.8 g
Protein: 2.0 g
Sodium: 333 mg
Cholesterol: 0 mg
Dietary fiber: 1.4 g

Hearty Harvest Vegetable Soup

Ingredients:

1 large yellow onion, quartered
3 carrots, trimmed and peeled
1 medium acorn squash, seeded, peeled, and cut into 8 pieces
1 medium Yukon gold or red potato, scrubbed and quartered
6 large garlic cloves, unpeeled
2 teaspoons fresh thyme, chopped
1 tablespoon olive oil
3 cups fat-free, low-sodium vegetable broth, divided
3 cups fresh spinach, chopped
1 tablespoon prepared basil pesto
1 can (15 ounces) Northern White beans, drained and rinsed
Salt and pepper to taste
1 cup (8 ounces) plain nonfat yogurt
2 tablespoons grated Romano or Parmesan cheese, divided

Preparation: Preheat oven to 400°F. Place first 6 ingredients in a 9x13x2-inch baking dish. Drizzle oil over them and toss to coat. Cover with foil and bake 20 minutes. Remove foil; bake an additional 30 minutes. Cool slightly and squeeze garlic cloves into a blender or large food processor. Add remaining vegetables and 2 cups vegetable broth. Purée until smooth and transfer to a large stockpot. Add remaining broth, spinach, pesto, beans, salt, and pepper to stockpot and heat over medium heat. Whisk in yogurt and heat, stirring, until soup is heated through. Ladle into soup bowls. Sprinkle 1 teaspoon grated cheese over each. Makes 6 servings.

Nutritional information per serving:

Calories: 230.9
Fat: 5.3 g
Saturated fat: 1.4 g
Carbohydrate: 36.7 g
Total sugars: 7.0 g
Protein: 9.1 g
Sodium: 251 mg
Cholesterol: 5.7 g
Dietary fiber: 8.2 g

Japanese Udon Vegetable Soup

Udon is a type of thick, wheat-based noodle that is popular in Japanese cuisine. This soup combines Udon in a rich vegetable broth with cabbage, bok choy, carrots, and onions that is complemented with soy sauce and sweet ginger.

Ingredients:
1 tablespoon olive oil
1 small onion, coarsely chopped
1/4 medium cabbage, sliced 1/4-inch thick
6 heads baby Bok Choy, coarsely chopped
3 celery stalks, chopped into 1/4-inch pieces
12 baby carrots, quartered
6 cloves garlic, peeled and coarsely minced
1/2 tablespoon ginger powder
2 tablespoons reduced-sodium soy sauce
Salt and pepper to taste
4 packs (7 ounces each) Udon noodles
6 cups reduced-fat, low-sodium chicken broth
1/2 bunch fresh parsley, coarsely chopped
1 bunch green unions, coarsely chopped

Preparation: Add olive oil, onion, cabbage, bok choy, celery, carrots, garlic, ginger powder, and soy sauce to a large stockpot and place over medium-high heat. Season with salt and pepper as desired. Stir often and cook until vegetables begin to soften or reduce in size by roughly half, approximately 5 to 6 minutes. Add chicken broth; reduce to medium heat and let simmer 5 minutes. Bring soup to a light, rolling boil and add Udon noodles; boil 3 minutes or time indicated by Udon noodle package. When Udon noodles are fully cooked and soft but not mushy, add minced parsley and green onions. Stir until thoroughly combined. Simmer 1 minute and serve. Makes 6 servings.

This recipe's fiber (Udon) and isothiocyanates (bok choy) may help prevent the following cancers: **colon and pancreas.**

Nutritional information per serving:
Calories: 115.2
Fat: 2.5 g
Saturated fat: 0.4 g
Carbohydrate: 17.7 g
Total sugars: 4.6 g
Protein: 5.6 g
Sodium: 367 mg
Cholesterol: 0 mg
Dietary fiber: 3.2 g

Lentil Chili

Legumes such as lentils are a great source of dietary fiber and plant-based compounds that may play a role in reducing colon adenoma formation or growth, thereby decreasing the risk of colorectal cancer. Their phytochemicals are also protective against many other types of cancer.

Ingredients:
3 tablespoons olive oil
1-3/4 cups onions, chopped
2 cups zucchini, diced
2 cups carrots, finely diced
2 cups unpeeled eggplant, finely chopped
1 small jalapeño pepper, seeded and chopped
2 tablespoons garlic, finely chopped
1 tablespoon dried oregano
1-1/2 tablespoons ground cumin
1/2 teaspoon cayenne pepper
1 bay leaf
56 ounces (two 28-ounce cans) diced tomatoes with juice
2-1/2 cups low-sodium vegetable stock
1-1/2 cups red or brown lentils
Salt and pepper to taste
Low-fat sour cream to garnish

Preparation: Heat olive oil in a large saucepan or stockpot over medium heat. Add onions, zucchini, eggplant, carrots, jalapeño, and garlic. Sauté about 4 to 5 minutes, until almost tender. Add oregano, cumin, cayenne, bay leaf; stir a few seconds. Add tomatoes with juice, vegetable stock and lentils; bring to a low boil. Reduce heat and simmer, uncovered, until lentils and vegetables are tender, about 40 minutes. Season with salt and pepper as desired. Pour into 6 bowls or mugs and garnish each with 1 teaspoon low-fat sour cream. Makes 6 servings.

Nutritional information per serving:
Calories: 414.1
Fat: 10.6 g
Saturated fat: 2.5 g
Carbohydrate: 53.2 g
Total sugars: 13.9 g
Protein: 26.5 g
Sodium: 608 mg
Cholesterol: 7.5 mg
Dietary fiber: 13.0 g

Lobster, Mango, and Corn Salad in Watermelon and Grapefruit Vinaigrette

Lobster is low in calories and fat and high in protein. Corn is a great source of the antioxidant lutein, and high intake of lutein-rich foods has been shown to lower the risk of some cancers, as well as cataracts.

This recipe's beta carotene (mango) and lycopene (watermelon) may help prevent the following cancers: **skin and pancreas.**

Lobster Salad Ingredients:
Salt and water as needed
2 (1-1/2 pounds) live Maine lobsters
3 ears fresh sweet corn
1 ripe mango, peeled, pitted, and diced
1/2 cup red bell pepper, diced
1/4 cup red onion, diced
1 large stalk celery, diced
2 tablespoons fresh cilantro, chopped
Salt and white pepper
1 bunch red or green romaine lettuce, washed and torn into pieces

Dressing Ingredients:
1 cup watermelon, seeded and diced
2 tablespoons grapefruit juice
1-1/2 tablespoons apple cider vinegar
1 teaspoon Dijon mustard
3/4 cup extra-virgin olive oil

Preparation: Place a large pot of salted water over medium-high heat and bring to a boil. Add lobsters and reduce heat to medium. Cook lobsters in boiling water 12 to 13 minutes. Let lobsters cool and remove meat from shells. Chop tail and joint meat into 1/2-inch pieces and reserve whole claw meat for garnish. In a medium pot of salted, boiling water, cook corn until tender, about 10 to 15 minutes. Let cool and cut kernels from cobs. Toss lobster meat, corn, mango, red pepper, onion, celery, and cilantro together in a medium mixing bowl and season with salt and pepper. To make dressing, purée watermelon, grapefruit juice, vinegar, and Dijon mustard in a food processor or blender about 1 minute. With motor running, slowly add olive oil. Add about 1/2 cup of dressing to salad mixture and refrigerate 2 hours. (Reserve leftover dressing for another use.) Serve salad over romaine lettuce on individual plates and garnish with a lobster claw. Makes 4 servings.

Nutritional information per serving:
Calories: 282.3
Fat: 2.4 g
Saturated fat: 0.4 g
Carbohydrate: 46.5 g
Total sugars: 19.5 g
Protein: 18.8 g
Sodium: 685 mg
Cholesterol: 71.3 mg
Dietary fiber: 6.4 g

Mango Chicken Salad

This is a super-healthy lunch or dinner entrée salad that is savory and protein-rich. Almonds contain magnesium and vitamin E, which has recently been shown to decrease the rate at which some older individuals suffer memory loss and decline in muscle mass.

Ingredients:
2 cups mixed baby greens
4 skinless, boneless chicken breasts (about 4 ounces each), pre-cooked and chilled
1/4 cup plain low-fat yogurt
3 tablespoons light mayonnaise
3 heaping teaspoons curry paste
Juice of 1/2 lime
1 teaspoon honey
1 teaspoon ginger, minced
1/4 teaspoon salt
1/4 cup red onion, finely chopped
1 ripe but firm mango, chopped
3 tablespoons dried sweet cherries
1/4 cup slivered raw almonds

Preparation: Divide baby greens among 4 large salad or dinner plates. Cube chicken into 1/4- to 1/2-inch sized pieces and set aside. Whisk together yogurt, mayonnaise, curry paste, lime juice, honey, ginger, and salt in a small bowl. Combine chicken, red onion, mango, and dried cherries in a medium bowl. Toss with yogurt-curry dressing. Gently stir in slivered almonds. Place a serving of chicken salad in the center of each plate of greens. Makes 4 servings.

Nutritional information per serving:
Calories: 292.9
Fat: 9.6 g
Saturated fat: 1.8 g
Carbohydrate: 18.3 g
Total sugars: 17.9 g
Protein: 33.3 g
Sodium: 168 mg
Cholesterol: 87.1 mg
Dietary fiber: 2.3 g

Mont Tremblant Red and Green Pepper Soup with Basil

This is the second recipe from Dr. Patricia Eagon, a biochemist and a great cook. She notes, "This recipe is an attempt to duplicate a soup we enjoyed at a little café at Mont Tremblant, Quebec. After skiing in cold weather, this soup was very warming."

This recipe's quercetin (leeks) and luteolin (celery) may help prevent the following cancers: **lung and ovarian.**

Ingredients:
2 tablespoons olive oil
2 medium red bell peppers, chopped
2 medium green bell peppers, chopped
1-1/4 cups leeks, white and light green parts only, chopped
1-1/4 cups celery, some leaves included, chopped
2 medium garlic cloves, minced
1/2 cup dry white wine
1/4 cup tomato paste
2 teaspoons sugar
4 cups low-sodium vegetable or chicken broth
2 medium boiling potatoes, washed and cut into small cubes
1 teaspoon Spike's seasoning (no-salt version)
1/2 teaspoon dried basil
10-12 fresh basil leaves
6-8 sprigs of Italian flat parsley, stems included
6 tablespoons condensed skim milk
Salt and coarsely ground pepper to taste

Preparation: Place a large stockpot over medium heat and add olive oil. Add red and green pepper, leeks, and celery; cook, stirring often, about 7 minutes. Add garlic; cook an additional 3 minutes. Add white wine to deglaze remaining sautéed garlic and vegetable bits. Add tomato paste, sugar, broth, cubed potatoes, Spike's seasoning, and dried basil. Cover and bring to a boil; reduce heat and simmer, partially covered, about 15 minutes until potatoes are tender. Add fresh basil and parsley. Remove from heat and let cool slightly. Transfer soup to a food processor or blender; process until smooth. Return soup to pot; add condensed skim milk and season with salt and pepper as desired. Warm gently and serve. Makes 6 servings.

Nutritional information per serving:
Calories: 164.0
Fat: 5.2 g
Saturated fat: 0.8 g
Carbohydrate: 25.8 g
Total sugars: 8.8 g
Protein: 3.5 g
Sodium: 150 mg
Cholesterol: 2.7 mg
Dietary fiber: 4.7 g

Newport Beach Turkey Pasta Salad

This salad provides a significant amount of your daily fruit and vegetable needs, complex carbohydrates, and protein. It's a perfect meal for a spring or summer evening following a day of activity. You can substitute chicken, shrimp, or even cubes of extra firm tofu for the turkey, for a flavor variation.

Ingredients:
3 cups cooked whole-wheat fusilli or penne, chilled
2 cups roasted skinless turkey breast meat, cubed and chilled
3 stalks celery, finely diced
2 Granny Smith apples, peeled, cored, and chopped
1 cup seedless red or purple grapes, halved
8 ounces fresh pineapple, diced (can substitute canned tidbits—but drain them)
1/4 cup red bell pepper, finely diced
1/4 cup light mayonnaise
1 cup fat-free sour cream
2 tablespoons low-fat milk
1 teaspoon sugar
1/8 teaspoon salt
1/8 teaspoon freshly ground black pepper
1/4 teaspoon ground nutmeg
1 medium head red or green romaine lettuce, washed and torn into pieces

Preparation: In a large bowl, combine pasta, turkey, celery, apples, grapes, pineapple, and bell pepper. In a separate bowl, mix light mayonnaise, sour cream, milk, sugar, salt, pepper, and nutmeg. Combine mayonnaise and chicken mixtures and toss. Divide lettuce among large salad or dinner plates and top with 1/4 chicken-pasta salad mixture. Makes 4 entrée salad servings.

Nutritional information per serving:
Calories: 499.2
Fat: 8.0 g
Saturated fat: 1.2 g
Carbohydrate: 74.9 g
Total sugars: 21.8 g
Protein: 31.9 g
Sodium: 222 mg
Cholesterol: 56.0 mg
Dietary fiber: 5.9 g

Orange-Raspberry Fennel Salad

Fennel, oranges, raspberries, goat cheese, and almonds with romaine lettuce provide a wonderful taste combination. The Citrus Vinaigrette or Balsamic Blueberry Vinaigrette (pages 58 and 53) would be a perfect addition to this salad.

Ingredients:
1 head romaine lettuce, washed and torn into bite-size pieces
1 fresh fennel bulb (about fist size)
1/2 small red onion
1 whole orange, peeled and sectioned
1/4 cup fresh red raspberries
2 ounces goat cheese
1/4 cup almonds, sliced or slivered

Preparation: Place romaine lettuce in a large salad bowl. Slice fennel and red onion into paper-thin strips and add to salad. Add orange slices. Gently toss in berries, goat cheese, almonds, and dressing of choice. Scoop onto 4 large salad bowls or plates. Makes 4 servings.

Nutritional information per serving:
Calories: 175.2
Fat: 9.2 g
Saturated fat: 3.3 g
Carbohydrate: 16.2 g
Total sugars: 6.8 g
Protein: 6.9 g
Sodium: 109 mg
Cholesterol: 11.2 mg
Dietary fiber: 5.9 g

Peanut Butter-Lentil Soup

This creamy lentil and vegetable soup has a combination of antioxidants from onions, carrots, and lentils and a surprisingly savory flavor. This soup is high in protein and is a great source of heart-healthy, unsaturated fat.

This recipe's beta carotene (carrots) and fiber (lentils) may help prevent the following cancers: **liver and colon.**

Ingredients:
2 tablespoons olive oil
3 small carrots, diced
3 small stalks of celery with leaves, diced
3/4 cup yellow onion, chopped
1-1/4 teaspoons dried thyme
1-1/4 teaspoons dried rosemary
2 bay leaves
Salt and pepper to taste
16 ounces dried lentils, rinsed
8 cups low-sodium vegetable stock
1 cup (8 ounces) plain low-fat yogurt
3/4 cup natural peanut butter

Preparation: Place a large stockpot or Dutch oven over medium heat. Add olive oil; heat about 30 seconds. Add carrots, celery, and onion and sauté in olive oil until translucent. Add thyme, rosemary and bay leaves; continue to sauté vegetables and season with salt and pepper as desired. Add lentils and stir together. Add vegetable stock and bring to a boil. Reduce heat and simmer about 1 hour or more, until lentils and vegetables have softened. Meanwhile, stir together yogurt and peanut butter in a small bowl. Remove soup from heat and stir in yogurt and peanut-butter mixture. Remove bay leaves and serve. Makes 8 servings.

Nutritional information per serving:
Calories: 384.5
Fat: 15.7 g
Saturated fat: 3.8 g
Carbohydrate: 40.1 g
Total sugars: 9.0 g
Protein: 20.7 g
Sodium: 304 mg
Cholesterol: 1.8 mg
Dietary fiber: 17.8 g

Perfect Pea Soup

Peas contain folate, vitamin K, and fiber in addition to antioxidants such as phytic acid. This is such a simple soup to make—it will soon become one of your most popular staple dishes.

Ingredients:
1 medium yellow onion, diced
2 garlic cloves, minced
1 tablespoon olive oil
1 bag (10 ounces) frozen peas
3 cups low-sodium vegetable stock or broth
2 bay leaves
1 cup (8 ounces) plain low-fat yogurt
Salt and pepper to taste

Preparation: In a medium-size soup pan or stockpot, brown onion and garlic in olive oil over medium-high heat. Add frozen peas, bay leaves and vegetable stock; bring to a boil. Reduce heat to low and simmer 5 minutes. Remove bay leaves. Being careful not to get burned by the hot liquid, pour contents into a blender. Purée until smooth. Return soup to pot and stir in yogurt, salt, and pepper. Warm gently and serve. Makes 4 servings.

This recipe's folate (peas) and calcium (yogurt) may help prevent the following cancers: **colon and breast.**

Nutritional information per serving:
Calories: 149.5
Fat: 4.7 g
Saturated fat: 1.2 g
Carbohydrate: 19.5 g
Total sugars: 10.0 g
Protein: 7.3 g
Sodium: 228 mg
Cholesterol: 14.8 mg
Dietary fiber: 3.7 g

Pomegranate, Kiwi, Orange, and Papaya Salad

This lightly sweet and spicy fruit salad pairs beautifully with any fish or poultry dish. Pomegranates are a great source of antioxidant polyphenol compounds, as well as vitamin C, potassium, and the B vitamin, pantothenic acid.

Ingredients:
2 teaspoons Champagne or other white wine vinegar
1/8 teaspoon each: salt, pepper, and crushed red pepper flakes
1/4 cup extra-virgin olive oil
4 cups mixed baby greens (such as spinach, arugula, and romaine)
2 oranges, peeled and sectioned
2 medium papayas, peeled and sliced
3 kiwis, peeled and sliced
Seeds from 1 medium pomegranate (about 3/4 cup)

Preparation: Combine vinegar, salt, pepper, and crushed red pepper flakes in a small bowl; whisk in oil until well blended. Toss greens with 2-1/2 tablespoons dressing; arrange on a serving platter. Alternate orange, papaya, and kiwi slices over greens. Drizzle with remaining dressing. Sprinkle salad with pomegranate seeds. Makes 6 servings.

This recipe's ellagic acid (pomegranates) and vitamin C (kiwi) may help prevent the following cancers: **prostate and lung.**

Nutritional information per serving:
Calories: 194.6
Fat: 9.8 g
Saturated fat: 1.4 g
Carbohydrate: 24.5 g
Total sugars: 16.9 g
Protein: 2.1 g
Sodium: 55 mg
Cholesterol: 0 mg
Dietary fiber: 4.3 g

Raspberry-Steak Couscous Salad

This salad is great to serve for guests because it tastes fantastic and looks just lovely on the plate. One word of caution: It takes a fairly long time to prepare.

Ingredients:
1 pound lean boneless top sirloin steak, about 1 inch thick, trimmed of fat
1/2 cup dry red wine
5 tablespoons raspberry or red wine vinegar, divided
2 tablespoons green onions, chopped
2 tablespoons reduced-sodium soy sauce or tamari
2-1/2 teaspoons sugar
2 teaspoons fresh tarragon, chopped (or 1/2 teaspoon dried)
2 tablespoons raspberry all-fruit preserves (preferably seedless)
3/4 cup low-sodium chicken broth
2/3 cup low-fat (1%) milk
1/4 teaspoon ground coriander
1 cup dried couscous (about 6-1/2 ounces)
1 tablespoon olive oil, divided
8 cups spring mix or baby lettuce (or leaf lettuce torn into small pieces)
2 cups fresh raspberries

Preparation: Slice steak across grain into strips about 1/8 inch thick and 3 to 4 inches long. Place steak, wine, 1 tablespoon vinegar, green onions, soy sauce or tamari, 2 teaspoons sugar, and tarragon into a large, heavy-duty resealable plastic bag. Seal and rotate bag numerous times to coat steak. Refrigerate 30 minutes to 1 day, turning occasionally to redistribute contents. When ready to prepare salad, place raspberry preserves in a 2- or 3-quart soup pan or stockpot over low heat and warm until melted, stirring almost constantly. Add chicken broth, milk, and coriander and increase to medium-high heat; bring to a gentle boil. Stir in couscous; cover, remove from heat, and let stand about 5 minutes, until liquid is absorbed. Transfer couscous mixture to a large nonmetal bowl; let cool briefly, fluffing occasionally with a fork. Cover and refrigerate until cool (1 to 2 hours), continuing to fluff occasionally. Meanwhile, heat 1 teaspoon olive oil in a large nonstick skillet or fry pan over medium-high heat. Add steak and its juices and cook, stirring, until browned and to desired doneness (typically 4 to 5 minutes). Transfer steak to a large nonmetal bowl and let cool. Combine remaining 4 tablespoons vinegar, 1 teaspoon sugar, and 2 teaspoons olive oil in a large nonmetal bowl and stir until blended. Add lettuce and stir until coated. Divide lettuce among 4 large salad or dinner plates. Spoon couscous mixture on top of lettuce, then add steak and raspberries. Serve immediately. Makes 4 servings.

Nutritional information per serving:
Calories: 457
Fat: 8.2 g
Saturated fat: 2.0 g
Carbohydrate: 60.2 g
Total sugars: 13.2 g
Protein: 35.6 g
Sodium: 655 mg
Cholesterol: 48.4 mg
Dietary fiber: 8.2 g

Red Onion and Beet Soup

Although they aren't yet a recognized anti-cancer food, beets are loaded with folate, fiber, potassium, and manganese.

Ingredients:
1 tablespoon olive oil
2 medium red onions, sliced
2 garlic cloves, crushed
10 ounces cooked beets (can use canned), cut into sticks
5 cups reduced-sodium vegetable stock
2 ounces cooked whole-grain soup pasta (spirals or small shells work well)
2 tablespoons raspberry vinegar
Salt and freshly ground black pepper
Garnish: Low-fat yogurt and chopped fresh chives

Preparation: Heat olive oil in a flame-proof casserole. Add onions and garlic and cook over low to medium heat about 18 to 20 minutes, until soft and tender. Add beets, vegetable stock, cooked pasta, and vinegar; heat through. Season to taste with salt and pepper. Serve in soup bowls with a spoonful of low-fat yogurt and a sprinkle of fresh chives. Makes 4 servings.

This recipe's quercetin (onion) and fiber (pasta) may help prevent the following cancers: **lung and breast.**

Nutritional information per serving:
Calories: 133.6
Fat: 4.0 g
Saturated fat: 0.7 g
Carbohydrate: 21.0 g
Total sugars: 10.6 g
Protein: 3.4 g
Sodium: 243 mg
Cholesterol: 5.6 mg
Dietary fiber: 3.1 g

Roasted Tomato and Cauliflower Soup

This soup presents beautifully. With a mouth-watering flavor combination of cauliflower and garlicky tomatoes, it is low in calories and high in antioxidants.

Ingredients:
1/2 head cauliflower, pulled apart into bite-size pieces
3/4 teaspoon salt, divided
1/2 teaspoon grated nutmeg
1 tablespoon olive oil
1 medium or 2 small leeks, finely chopped
1/3 cup red or yellow onion, finely chopped
1 can (14 or 14-1/2 ounces) roasted tomatoes, diced
4 cups water
1-1/2 teaspoons fresh rosemary, chopped
1/2 teaspoon ground ginger
2 teaspoons hoisin sauce
Chopped parsley for garnish

Preparation: Preheat oven to 400°F. Spread cauliflower on a non-stick cookie sheet and sprinkle with 1/4 teaspoon salt and nutmeg. Bake 30 minutes until lightly browned; remove from oven and set aside. Place a 4- or 5-quart soup or stockpot over medium heat and drizzle in oil. Add leeks and onions and heat until they just begin to brown, about 8 to 10 minutes. Stir in tomatoes; let simmer and caramelize 5 minutes. Add water, cauliflower, 1/2 teaspoon salt, rosemary, and ginger and bring to a boil. Cover and reduce heat; simmer for 30 minutes. Stir in hoisin sauce and serve in 4 soup bowls garnished with chopped parsley. Makes 4 servings.

This recipe's sulforaphane (cauliflower) and lycopene (tomatoes) may help prevent the following cancers: **breast and pancreas.**

Nutritional information per serving:
Calories: 102.0
Fat: 3.6 g
Saturated fat: trace
Carbohydrate: 14.6 g
Total sugars: 6.6 g
Protein: 2.8 g
Sodium: 735 mg
Cholesterol: 0 mg
Dietary fiber: 3.4 g

Spicy Pumpkin and Yellow Split-Pea Soup

Saffron is an herb that contains disease-fighting substances such as zeaxanthin, lycopene, and various forms of alpha and beta carotene.

This recipe's beta carotene (pumpkin) and fiber (peas) may help prevent the following cancers: **lung and colon.**

Ingredients:
10 cups (2-1/2 quarts) chicken broth
1-1/4 cups dried yellow split peas
1 large yellow onion, chopped
1/4 teaspoon saffron threads
1 tablespoon olive oil
1 teaspoon ground cinnamon
1/4 teaspoon ground ginger
6 cups peeled, seeded, and cubed pumpkin (from a 3- to 4-pound pumpkin)
Salt and pepper
3 tablespoons fresh parsley, minced

Preparation: Bring broth, peas, and onion to a boil in a large soup pot over high heat. Reduce heat to low and simmer, partially covered, 30 to 40 minutes. Meanwhile, in a small pan (or a large metal spoon), heat saffron over low heat about 10 seconds until dry, then grind to a powder with the back of a spoon; steep in 1 tablespoon of boiling water about 1 minute to release flavor. To soup pot, stir in oil, cinnamon, ginger, spoonful of saffron, and pumpkin. Bring to a boil, then reduce to low and simmer, partially covered, stirring occasionally, about 1 hour. The soup is done when the pumpkin begins to fall apart and the peas are tender. Season with salt and pepper as desired and sprinkle with parsley before ladling into bowls. Makes 6 servings.

Nutritional information per serving:
Calories: 247.3
Fat: 4.1 g
Saturated fat: 0.4 g
Carbohydrate: 38.8 g
Total sugars: 2.7 g
Protein: 13.8 g
Sodium: 16 mg
Cholesterol: 8.3 mg
Dietary fiber: 10.9 g

Spinach Salad with Garlicky Croutons

This vitamin- and antioxidant-rich salad goes great with a tall glass of lemonade or some iced green tea.

Ingredients:
1-1/2 pounds spinach or baby spinach
1 large red onion, thinly sliced and separated into rings
8 ounces white or crimini mushrooms, thinly sliced
1 large red bell pepper, stemmed, seeded, and thinly sliced
2 ounces reduced-fat feta cheese, crumbled
1/2 cup lemon juice
4 teaspoons olive oil
1/2 teaspoon dry oregano
2 garlic cloves, whole but peeled
1 small whole-wheat French bread baguette, cut into approximately 1/2-inch slices

Preparation: If using regular spinach, remove stems and tear into bite-size pieces. Place spinach, red onion, mushrooms, and bell pepper in a large bowl and set aside. In a blender, whirl cheese, lemon juice, olive oil, oregano, and one clove of garlic until blended smoothly. Set aside. Place baguette slices in single layer on nonstick baking sheet and broil about 5 inches below heat, turning once, until golden on both sides (about 3 to 4 minutes). Let slices cool briefly and rub remaining garlic clove evenly over top of each toasted slice. Discard garlic clove. Pour dressing over salad and mix until evenly coated. Spoon salad onto individual plates and distribute toasted bread slices onto each individual salad. Makes 4 servings.

Strawberry-Peach Yogurt Soup (Chilled)

This soup can be a main course, side dish, or dessert. It pairs nicely with a chunky fresh-fruit salad or a pita sandwich.

Ingredients:
2 cups fresh peaches, sliced
2 cups (16 ounces) vanilla low-fat yogurt
1 cup strawberries, hulled and sliced
1 cup orange juice (calcium-fortified, preferably)
1 tablespoon honey
Garnish: 4 sliced strawberries

Preparation: Combine all ingredients in a blender or food processor. Purée until smooth. Cover and chill 2 to 3 hours before serving. Serve garnished with a sliced strawberry. Makes 4 servings.

This recipe's quercetin (onion) and lutein (spinach) may help prevent the following cancers: **endometrial and skin.**

Nutritional information per serving:
Calories: 305
Fat: 7.0 g
Saturated fat: 1.7 g
Carbohydrate: 38.0 g
Total sugars: 6.1 g
Protein: 10.5 g
Sodium: 553 mg
Cholesterol: 2.5 mg
Dietary fiber: 7.5 g

This recipe's calcium (yogurt) and vitamin C (strawberries) may help prevent the following cancers: **colon and bladder.**

Nutritional information per serving:
Calories: 217.6
Fat: 2.0 g
Saturated fat: 1.0 g
Carbohydrate: 39.8 g
Total sugars: 35.8 g
Protein: 7.6 g
Sodium: 82 mg
Cholesterol: 6.1 mg
Dietary fiber: 2.5 g

The Anti-Cancer Cookbook

Turkey Escarole Soup

When you've run out of ideas of what to do with leftover turkey after the holidays, here is a healthy and delicious turkey soup recipe that is unlike any that you have had in the past.

Ingredients:
1 tablespoon olive oil
2 cups carrots, grated
1 small onion, diced
3 small garlic cloves, minced
5-1/4 cups low-sodium chicken broth (or 3 cans, 14 or 14-1/2 ounce each)
2 cups water
2 heads (1-1/2 pounds) escarole, cut into 1-inch pieces
1/2 cup whole wheat orzo
2 cups cooked turkey breast meat
1/8 teaspoon coarsely ground pepper

Preparation: In a 5-1/2 or 6 quart Dutch oven, heat oil over medium-high heat. Add carrots, onion, and garlic; cook about 4 minutes or until onion softens, stirring often. Stir in chicken broth and water and bring to a boil. Stir in escarole and orzo; heat until boiling. Reduce heat to medium-low and simmer, uncovered, 6 minutes or until escarole and orzo are tender. Add turkey and ground pepper and stir. Reduce heat to low and simmer 3 to 4 minutes until turkey is heated through, stirring occasionally. Makes 6 servings.

This recipe's kaempferol (escarole) and beta carotene (carrots) may help prevent the following cancers: **endometrial and lung.**

Nutritional information per serving:
Calories: 194.2
Fat: 4.2 g
Saturated fat: 0.6 g
Carbohydrate: 20.4 g
Total sugars: 2.2 g
Protein: 18.7 g
Sodium: 473 mg
Cholesterol: 32 mg
Dietary fiber: 4.4 g

Warm Blackened-Tuna Salad

Tuna steaks are loaded with protein and omega-3 fatty acids, which have anti-inflammatory and immune-boosting properties. Red cabbage has a level of antioxidants superior to any other cabbage.

Ingredients:
Nonstick cooking spray
5 cups romaine lettuce, torn into pieces
2 cups red cabbage, coarsely shredded
2 medium orange bell peppers, cut into thin strips
1-1/2 cups zucchini, sliced (unpeeled)
1 teaspoon onion powder
1/2 teaspoon each: garlic powder, ground red pepper, dried thyme, and ground black pepper
3/4 pound fresh or thawed tuna steaks, cut 1-inch thick
1/3 cup water
3/4 cup onion, thinly sliced
2 tablespoons balsamic vinegar
1-1/2 teaspoons Dijon mustard
1 teaspoon canola oil
1/2 teaspoon chicken bouillon granules

Preparation: Preheat broiler. Spray broiler pan with nonstick cooking spray. Combine romaine lettuce, cabbage, peppers, and zucchini in large bowl; set aside. Combine onion powder and remaining spices in small bowl. Rub spice mixture onto both sides of tuna. Place tuna on broiler pan. Broil 4 inches from heat about 10 minutes or until desired doneness, turning halfway through broiling time. Cover and set aside. For dressing, bring water to a boil in small saucepan over high heat. Add onion slices; reduce heat to medium-low. Simmer, covered, about 5 minutes until onion is tender. Add vinegar, mustard, oil, and bouillon granules; cook and stir until heated through. Place romaine mixture on 4 salad plates; slice tuna and arrange on top. Drizzle with dressing. Serve warm. Makes 4 servings.

Nutritional information per serving:
Calories: 227.5
Fat: 3.1 g
Saturated fat: trace
Carbohydrate: 15.3 g
Total sugars: 5.6 g
Protein: 24.6 g
Sodium: 221 mg
Cholesterol: 21.6 mg
Dietary fiber: 3.5 g

White Turkey Chili

Ingredients:
3/4 pound lean ground turkey (or chopped, cooked turkey)
1 tablespoon olive oil
1 medium yellow onion, chopped
2 garlic cloves, minced
1/4 cup green pepper, diced
Salt and pepper
1 can (15-1/2 ounces) cannellini beans, drained and rinsed
1 can (15 ounces) yellow corn kernels
1 jar (16 ounces) mild tomato salsa
1 pound fresh ripe tomatoes, seeded and diced

Preparation: If using ground turkey, brown in a small-medium nonstick skillet. Drain and blot meat with paper towels to absorb excess grease. In a skillet, heat olive oil over medium-high heat. Add onion, garlic, and green pepper and cook until translucent, about 3 to 4 minutes. Add turkey and heat, stirring occasionally; season with salt and pepper as desired. Add beans, corn, salsa, and tomatoes and heat, stirring occasionally, until bubbly and heated through. Makes 4 servings.

This recipe's luteolin (green pepper) and fiber (beans) may help prevent the following cancers: **ovarian and colon.**

Nutritional information per serving:
Calories: 228.5
Fat: 7.3 g
Saturated fat: 0.4 g
Carbohydrate: 23.8 g
Total sugars: 8.2 g
Protein: 16.9 g
Sodium: 309 mg
Cholesterol: 32.5 mg
Dietary fiber: 6.3 g

Nutritional information per serving:
Calories: 313.5
Fat: 6.7 g
Saturated fat: 1.1 g
Carbohydrate: 29.8 g
Total sugars: 12.1 g
Protein: 33.5 g
Sodium: 164 mg
Cholesterol: 75.7 mg
Dietary fiber: 1.4 g

Nutritional information per serving:
Calories: 137.7
Fat: 0.5 g
Saturated fat: 0 g
Carbohydrate: 33.8 g
Total sugars: 24.6 g
Protein: 1.4 g
Sodium: 6 mg
Cholesterol: 0 mg
Dietary fiber: 4.6 g

Whole-Grain Chicken Noodle Soup

Recent research has shown that chicken soup really might be able to fight the common cold. This soup has even more health benefits!

Ingredients:
2 tablespoons olive oil
2 cups celery, diced
2 cups button mushrooms, sliced
2 cups yellow onion, chopped
4 skinless, boneless chicken breasts, roasted or grilled (or skinless meat from 1 rotisserie chicken)
2-1/2 tablespoons garlic, minced
Freshly ground black pepper
3 cups cooked whole-wheat blend penne or fusilli
8 cups low-sodium chicken broth
1 tablespoon fresh parsley, chopped
1 tablespoon fresh oregano, chopped

Preparation: Add olive oil to large nonstick saucepan and heat over medium-high heat. Add celery, mushrooms, and onion and sauté until vegetables are lightly browned, about 5 minutes. Stir in shredded chicken, garlic, and black pepper as desired, and stir to blend well. Add pasta, chicken broth, parsley, and oregano and bring to a gentle boil. Reduce heat to simmer, cover pot, and let simmer about 10 to 15 minutes. Makes 8 servings

Wine Berry Soup

You can serve this soup warm or chilled; it is delicious both ways.

Ingredients:
1 cup 100% cranberry juice
1 cup fresh strawberries, hulled and sliced
1 cup fresh raspberries
1/2 cup fresh blueberries
1/4 cup pure maple syrup
1 cinnamon stick
Pinch of ground cloves
1/4 cup fruity red wine (such as Zinfandel)
For garnish: 1 lemon, thinly sliced

Preparation: Combine cranberry juice, berries, maple syrup, cinnamon stick, and ground cloves in a medium saucepan and place over medium-high heat. Bring to a boil; remove from heat and let cool until warm. Discard cinnamon stick and stir in wine. Serve immediately or refrigerate in a covered container at least 2 hours, until chilled, before serving. Pour into 4 soup bowls and garnish with lemon slices. Makes 4 servings.

CASUAL DINING: SANDWICHES, BURRITOS, PIZZA, AND MORE

Black-Bean Cakes with Mango Salsa

A recent article published in the Journal of Agriculture and Food Chemistry *noted that black beans are as rich in antioxidant compounds called anthocyanins as grapes and cranberries. Additionally, black beans are high in protein and contain plenty of cholesterol-lowering fiber.*

This recipe's saponins (beans) and quercetin (onion) may help prevent the following cancers: **pancreas and lung.**

Mango Salsa Ingredients:
2 cups mango, peeled and diced
1/3 cup red pepper, diced
1/4 cup red onion, finely diced
1 Serrano pepper, seeded and minced
2 tablespoons fresh cilantro, coarsely chopped
2 teaspoons fresh ginger root, minced
1 tablespoon fresh lime juice

Black-Bean Cakes Ingredients:
2 cans (15 ounces each) black beans, drained and rinsed
1/3 cup chopped fresh cilantro
1/4 red onion, finely chopped
1 egg white, lightly beaten
1 teaspoon ground cumin
1 teaspoon garlic, minced
1/2 teaspoon ground allspice
1/8 teaspoon cayenne pepper
1/3 cup whole-wheat breadcrumbs (toasted whole-wheat bread works well)
Nonstick cooking spray
1 tablespoon olive oil
Garnish: chopped fresh cilantro, sliced tomatoes, and lime wedges

Preparation: Combine all mango salsa ingredients in a mixing bowl; stir and set aside. In a large bowl, mash black beans with a fork until they stick together. Add cilantro, onion, egg white, cumin, garlic, allspice, and cayenne pepper; mix well until blended. Divide bean mixture into 8 equal parts. Shape into 1/2-inch-thick patties and coat with breadcrumbs. Spray each side of patties with nonstick cooking spray. In a medium skillet, heat oil over medium heat. Add bean cakes and fry until golden brown on both sides, turning once, about 8 to 10 minutes total. Serve warm with mango salsa and garnish with cilantro, tomatoes, and lime wedges. Makes 4 servings, 2 patties each.

Nutritional information per serving:
Calories: 335.2
Fat: 6.0 g
Saturated fat: 0.4 g
Carbohydrate: 55.2 g
Total sugars: 14.2 g
Protein: 15.1 g
Sodium: 109 mg
Cholesterol: 0 mg
Dietary fiber: 13.0 g

Mini Vegetable-Bean Burgers

Ingredients:
1 tablespoon canola oil, divided
1/4 cup of each diced vegetable: onion, red pepper, yellow pepper, carrots and celery
2/3 cup canned white cannellini beans, rinsed and drained
1 egg, lightly beaten
1/3 cup seasoned breadcrumbs
4 small whole-wheat buns
1 cup romaine lettuce leaves, torn into small pieces
2 plum tomatoes, sliced
1/2 cup broccoli sprouts
1/2 red onion, sliced into rings.
Grainy mustard and ketchup

Preparation: In an 8-inch nonstick skillet, heat one teaspoon of oil. Add all of the vegetables (each 1/4 cup) and cook over medium heat, stirring occasionally, until moisture has evaporated and vegetables become soft. Set aside and allow to cool slightly. In a medium mixing bowl, mash cannellini beans with a fork. Stir in egg, then breadcrumbs, and finally heated mixed vegetables. Mix thoroughly. Shape mixture into 4 approximately equal-size patties. Set patties on a plate, cover, and refrigerate at least 20 minutes. When veggie patties have cooled, toast buns and heat 1 teaspoon of remaining oil in skillet over medium heat. Add 2 patties. Cook, turning once or twice, until lightly brown on both sides. Repeat with remaining 2 patties. Serve each patty on whole-wheat toasted buns, with lettuce, tomato, onion, sprouts, and grainy mustard and ketchup or your other favorite condiments. Makes 4 servings, 1 mini burger each.

This recipe's phytic acid (beans) and sulforaphane (broccoli sprouts) may help prevent the following cancers: **breast and bladder.**

Nutritional information per serving:
Calories: 246.6
Fat: 7.0 g
Saturated fat: 0.7 g
Carbohydrate: 36.6 g
Total sugars: 3.3 g
Protein: 9.3 g
Sodium: 484 mg
Cholesterol: 53 mg
Dietary fiber: 5.2 g

Falafel Pita Sandwich

Falafel is a popular Middle Eastern dish that is made of ground, uncooked fava or garbanzo beans, onions, parsley, and spices. Unlike in this recipe, however, it is usually deep fried. These high-fiber falafel patties can also be served simply atop greens as a salad.

Ingredients:
2/3 cup ripe plum tomatoes, diced
1/2 cup cucumber, peeled and chopped
1/3 cup plain nonfat yogurt
Salt and pepper as desired
1 can (15 ounces) garbanzo beans
1 medium red or yellow onion, coarsely chopped
1/4 cup packed parsley leaves
2 garlic cloves, minced
1/2 teaspoon ground cumin
1/2 teaspoon dried oregano
2 teaspoons lemon juice
Salt and pepper to taste
1 cup fine whole-grain breadcrumbs, divided
1 egg yolk
Nonstick cooking spray
2 cups mixed greens
4 sandwich-size pita breads, top 1/3 cut off

Preparation: Combine tomato, cucumber, and yogurt in a small bowl. Season to taste with salt and pepper. Set aside. In a blender or food processor, process garbanzo beans, onion, parsley, garlic, cumin, and oregano until smooth. Stir in lemon juice and season to taste with salt and pepper if desired. Stir in 1/2 cup bread-crumbs and egg yolk. Form bean mixture into 16 small patties, using about 1-1/2 tablespoons of bean mixture for each patty. Coat patties with remaining 1/2 cup of bread crumbs. Spray a large skillet with nonstick cooking spray and place over medium heat until hot. Cook falafel patties over medium heat until golden brown on the bottom, 2 to 3 minutes. Spray tops of falafel with cooking spray and turn; cook an additional 2 to 3 minutes. Arrange 1/2 cup mixed greens into each pita and place 4 falafel patties on top of greens in each pita; serve with tomato-cucumber relish. Makes 4 servings, 1 sandwich each.

Nutritional information per serving:
Calories: 385.1
Fat: 4.7 g
Saturated fat: 0.9 g
Carbohydrate: 68.7 g
Total sugars: 18.6 g
Protein: 17.0 g
Sodium: 501 mg
Cholesterol: 52.8 mg
Dietary fiber: 10.7 g

Fish Tacos

There are dozens of fish taco recipes out there, but this is one of my favorites. Obesity is linked to many forms of cancer, and this filling, low-calorie dish will help you keep the pounds in check.

Ingredients:
1 pound white flaky fish, such as tilapia or mahi mahi
1/4 cup canola oil, plus more for grill
1 lime, juiced
2 teaspoons chili powder
1 jalapeño pepper, seeded and coarsely chopped
1/4 cup fresh cilantro leaves, chopped
8 flour tortillas

Garnish:
1-1/2 cup white cabbage, shredded
1/2 cup romaine lettuce, chopped
1/2 cup salsa
1/2 cup low-fat sour cream

Preparation: Preheat indoor or outdoor grill to medium-high heat and brush with canola oil if necessary. Place fish in a medium-size dish. Whisk together the oil, lime juice, chili powder, jalapeño, and cilantro; pour mixture over fish and allow to marinate 15 to 20 minutes. Remove fish from marinade and place onto hot grill, flesh side down. Grill fish 4 minutes on first side and then flip; grill 30 seconds and remove. Wait 5 minutes for fish to cool a bit and flake with a fork. Place tortillas on grill and grill about 20 to 30 seconds. Divide fish among tortillas and garnish with about 1/4 of the cabbage, lettuce, salsa, and sour cream. Makes 4 servings, 2 fish tacos each.

> This recipe's monounsaturated fat (canola oil) and sulforaphane (cabbage) may help prevent the following cancers: **breast and lung.**

Nutritional information per serving, with garnishes:
Calories: 268.2
Fat: 10.2 g
Saturated fat: 2.1 g
Carbohydrate: 28.6 g
Total sugars: 1.3 g
Protein: 15.5 g
Sodium: 348 mg
Cholesterol: 31.6 mg
Dietary fiber: 2.1 g

Grilled Vegetable Pizza

This recipe's calcium (mozzarella) and lycopene (tomatoes) may help prevent the following cancers: **colon and pancreas.**

Ingredients:
2 cups zucchini, sliced about 1/4 inch thick
1 cup eggplant, sliced about 1/4 inch thick
1 cup yellow squash, sliced about 1/4 inch thick
Salt as needed
2 tablespoons olive oil plus more if needed
1 pre-made (10-ounce) whole-wheat pizza crust
1 cup shredded part-skim mozzarella cheese, divided
1/4 cup roasted red pepper (from jar, in water, drained), thinly sliced
2 plum tomatoes, seeded and coarsely chopped
2 tablespoons fresh basil leaves, chopped

Preparation: Prepare and preheat outdoor grill. Lightly salt zucchini, eggplant, and squash, then brush with oil. Grill on both sides until vegetables are tender. Sprinkle crust with about 1/4 cup mozzarella cheese. Top with grilled vegetables, roasted peppers, tomatoes, basil, and remaining cheese. Place crust on grill 5 inches from coals. Cover and grill for 3 to 4 minutes until cheese is melted. Makes 4 servings, 1/4 pizza each.

Nutritional information per serving:
Calories: 374.4
Fat: 12.0 g
Saturated fat: 3.4 g
Carbohydrate: 56.1 g
Total sugars: 12.8 g
Protein: 10.5 g
Sodium: 705 mg
Cholesterol: 3.1 mg
Dietary fiber: 4.7 g

Healthier Chicken Nuggets with Raspberry Dipping Sauce

This is a kid-friendly dinner option that is baked, not fried, and skinless. It contains less fat than most chicken nuggets but still has loads of flavor. You can substitute dried cranberries for the raspberries in the dipping sauce to get a different flavor.

This recipe's fiber (bran flakes) and calcium (yogurt) may help prevent the following cancers: **colon and breast.**

Ingredients:
1/3 cup bran flakes, crushed
1/3 cup corn flakes, crushed
1 teaspoon paprika
1/2 teaspoon dried oregano
1/2 teaspoon garlic powder
1/4 teaspoon ground pepper
2 egg whites, slightly beaten
1 pound (16 ounces) skinless, boneless chicken breast halves, cut into 1-inch pieces
1 cup (8 ounces) plain low-fat yogurt
1/4 cup fresh or thawed frozen raspberries

Preparation: Preheat oven to 450°F. In a large zip-lock plastic bag, combine crushed bran flakes, corn flakes, paprika, oregano, garlic powder, and pepper; shake to combine well. Place egg whites in a small bowl. Dip chicken pieces into egg whites and allow excess to drain off. Add chicken pieces, a few at a time, to crushed cereal mixture; shake to coat well. Place chicken pieces in a single layer in a shallow baking pan. Bake 8 to 10 minutes or until chicken is no longer pink. Meanwhile, place yogurt and raspberries in a blender or food processor and blend about 20 seconds. Divide chicken among 4 plates and serve with about 1/4 cup raspberry dipping sauce. Makes 4 servings.

Nutritional information per serving:
Calories: 185.3
Fat: 2.9 g
Saturated fat: 1.0 g
Carbohydrate: 9.9 g
Total sugars: 5.8 g
Protein: 29.9 g
Sodium: 127 mg
Cholesterol: 66.3 mg
Dietary fiber: < 1 g

Herb and Goat-Cheese Pizza

This aromatic herb pizza combines the earthy and piney flavors of sage and thyme with fresh rosemary and oregano. Premade, trans-fat–free pizza crusts can typically be found in the refrigerated section of your local grocery store.

This recipe's quercetin (onion) and lycopene (tomatoes) may help prevent the following cancers: **skin and prostate.**

Ingredients:
1 (10-ounce) whole-wheat pizza crust
1 tablespoon extra-virgin olive oil
1 medium red onion, thinly sliced into rings
3 medium Roma tomatoes, sliced
4 ounces goat cheese, crumbled
10 fresh sage leaves, sliced into 1/4-inch pieces
1 tablespoon fresh thyme leaves, chopped
1 tablespoon fresh oregano, finely chopped
1 tablespoon snipped fresh rosemary, finely chopped

Preparation: Preheat oven to 450°F. Place pizza crust on a non-stick baking sheet. Place a large skillet over medium heat and add olive oil. Sauté red onion in oil 5 to 7 minutes, until translucent and tender. Spread onion evenly over pizza crust and top with tomato slices, spreading evenly to crust edges. Top with cheese. Bake 5 minutes, then sprinkle sage, thyme, rosemary, and oregano evenly over pizza. Return to oven and bake 6 or 7 minutes more, or until tomatoes are hot and cheese has melted. Makes 4 servings, 1/4 pizza each.

Nutritional information per serving:
Calories: 372.4
Fat: 11.6 g
Saturated fat: 6.1 g
Carbohydrate: 58.1 g
Total sugars: 3.1 g
Protein: 8.9 g
Sodium: 552 mg
Cholesterol: 22.3 mg
Dietary fiber: 3.6 g

Mexican Chicken Sandwich

Saturated fat is associated with many diseases, including heart disease and some cancers. Aim instead for unsaturated fats—such as olive or canola oil and avocados—which are a healthy complement to this lean and spicy chicken sandwich.

This recipe's monounsaturated fat (avocado) and naringenin (lime zest) may help prevent the following cancers: **breast and lung.**

Ingredients:
4 chicken-breast cutlets
1/2 teaspoon chili powder
1/4 teaspoon salt
1/4 teaspoon ground cumin
1/8 teaspoon cayenne pepper
1 tablespoon olive or canola oil
4 large whole-wheat rolls, split
1/4 cup reduced-fat mayonnaise
3/4 teaspoon grated lime peel
1 tablespoon fresh chives, diced
1/8 teaspoon freshly ground pepper
4 leaves of green-leaf or butter lettuce
1 medium ripe tomato, thinly sliced
1 avocado, peeled, pitted, and sliced

Preparation: Pound chicken cutlets between wax paper or plastic wrap to 1/4-inch thick. In a small cup, combine chili powder, salt, cumin, and cayenne pepper. Sprinkle over both sides of chicken. In large skillet, heat oil over medium-high heat. Cook chicken 1-1/2 to 2 minutes per side, until cooked thoroughly. Set aside. Toast rolls. In a small bowl, combine mayonnaise, lime peel, chives, and pepper. Spread herb mayonnaise on cut sides of rolls. Place lettuce, chicken, tomato slices, and avocado slices on bottom of rolls; replace tops. Makes 4 servings, 1 sandwich each.

Nutritional information per sandwich:
Calories: 359.1
Fat: 18.7 g
Saturated fat: 2.8 g
Carbohydrate: 25.8 g
Total sugars: 4.4 g
Protein: 21.9 g
Sodium: 372 mg
Cholesterol: 192 mg
Dietary fiber: 5.2 g

Mozzarella and Basil Turkey Burgers with Grilled Vegetables

This is a much more nutritious version of an American favorite than the typical burger and fries. You can easily double the quantities if you are having a party and need to feed a crowd.

Ingredients:
1/3 cup reduced-fat mayonnaise
2 teaspoons fresh chives, minced
1/2 teaspoon dried oregano
1/8 teaspoon garlic powder
1-1/2 pounds lean ground turkey
3 tablespoons fresh basil, shredded
1 small yellow onion, minced
1 large egg plus 2 large egg whites, lightly beaten
2 tablespoons Parmesan cheese, grated
1-1/2 tablespoons balsamic vinegar
1 cup coarse whole-wheat breadcrumbs
1/4 teaspoon each: salt and freshly ground black pepper, divided
2 small eggplants, peeled and thinly sliced
2 small zucchini, thinly sliced on the diagonal
6 ounces fresh mozzarella cheese, sliced into 6 medium slices
6 butter-lettuce leaves, washed and dried
12 thin slices red, ripe tomato
6 whole-grain rolls

Preparation: To make herb mayo, stir together low-fat mayonnaise, chives, oregano, and garlic powder in a small mixing bowl. Cover and chill in refrigerator. Thoroughly (and gently) combine ground turkey, basil, onion, egg/egg whites, Parmesan cheese, vinegar, bread crumbs, and 1/8 teaspoon each salt and black pepper. Form mixture into six patties. Cover and reserve in refrigerator. In a mixing bowl, toss sliced vegetables with oil and 1/8 teaspoon each salt and pepper. Prepare a charcoal or indoor grill to medium heat. Place sliced vegetables on grill and cook both sides until tender; set aside. Grill turkey burgers on grill, turning once until internal temperature reaches 165°F and to desired doneness. Remove to an oven-proof dish. Assemble grilled eggplant and zucchini on top of turkey burgers. Top each burger with slice of fresh mozzarella. Melt in preheated broiler. Toast whole grain rolls on grill or in toaster. Remove to plates and assemble burgers with lettuce and tomato slices. Serve with herb mayo on side. Makes 6 turkey burgers.

Nutritional information per burger:
Calories: 437.8
Fat: 16.2 g
Saturated fat: 4.5 g
Carbohydrate: 42.0 g
Total sugars: 9.6 g
Protein: 30.9 g
Sodium: 546 mg
Cholesterol: 122.8 mg
Dietary fiber: 8.2 g

Portobello Tofu Tacos

There is a Mexican restaurant near my home that makes great tacos and burritos—and I always order a combination filling of tofu and portobello mushrooms. Then I thought, "Hey! I can make these at home." These tacos are a delicious way to incorporate soy into your diet.

Ingredients:
1-1/2 tablespoons olive or canola oil
1 small yellow onion, chopped
3 garlic cloves, crushed
1 red bell pepper, diced (optional)
6 baby portobello mushroom caps (or 2 to 3 large portobello caps), sliced
1 package (12 ounces) firm tofu, crumbled (about 1-1/2 cups)
1 tablespoon chili powder
1/4 teaspoon cumin
1/4 teaspoon dried oregano
1-1/2 tablespoons soy sauce or tamari
1/3 cup tomato sauce
8 corn tortillas
Garnish: lettuce, onions, tomatoes, and salsa

Preparation: Place a large skillet over medium heat and add oil. Sauté onion, garlic, bell pepper, and mushrooms in oil 2 to 3 minutes. Add tofu, chili powder, cumin, oregano, and soy sauce and heat 3 minutes. Add tomato sauce and simmer over low heat until mixture is fairly dry. Heat tortillas in a heavy, ungreased skillet, turning each from side to side until soft and pliable. Place a small amount of tofu mixture in the center of each tortilla, fold in half, and garnish, if desired. Makes 4 servings, 2 tacos each.

This recipe's isoflavones (tofu) and lycopene (tomato sauce) may help prevent the following cancers: **prostate and pancreas.**

Nutritional information per 2-taco serving:
Calories: 347.5
Fat: 15.1 g
Saturated fat: 1.8 g
Carbohydrate: 33.2 g
Total sugars: 5.7 g
Protein: 19.7 g
Sodium: 472 mg
Cholesterol: 0 mg
Dietary fiber: 6.1 g

Power Crunch Pita Pockets

This recipe's isoflavones (tofu) and lutein (spinach) may help prevent the following cancers: **prostate and ovarian.**

Ingredients:
1 cup (8 ounces) plain nonfat yogurt
2 tablespoons sesame tahini (pre-mix with a spoon if oil has separated)
1 teaspoon lemon juice
2 small garlic cloves, crushed
4 large whole-wheat pita breads
8 ounces extra firm silken tofu
1 cup fresh spinach leaves, torn into bite-size pieces (about 1 inch each)
3 tablespoons red onion, finely diced
4 plum tomatoes, chopped
1 cup mixed sprouts: broccoli and alfalfa
1 large avocado, halved, pitted, peeled, and cut into thin wedges

Preparation: In a small bowl, combine yogurt, tahini, lemon juice, and garlic and mix well. Set aside. Slice an edge from each pita bread and carefully open pockets. In a medium bowl, combine tofu, spinach, red onion, and tomatoes. Add 1/4 cup of yogurt-tahini sauce and toss gently to mix. Spoon mixture into each pocket. Add some sprouts and avocado to each pita; drizzle each with 1 tablespoon tahini sauce and serve. Makes 4 sandwiches.

Nutritional information per pita sandwich:
Calories: 395.7
Fat: 13.7 g
Saturated fat: 2.2 g
Carbohydrate: 50.7 g
Total sugars: 7.8 g
Protein: 17.4 g
Sodium: 42 mg
Cholesterol: 1.2 mg
Dietary fiber: 9.5 g

Pumpkin Burritos

These burritos are positively scrumptious. The pumpkin provides a healthy dose of iron, vitamins A and C, and, like beans, is loaded with dietary fiber.

Ingredients:
6 large whole-wheat tortillas
1 tablespoon olive oil
1 cup zucchini, chopped (unpeeled)
1/2 cup corn kernels
1/3 cup yellow onion, diced
2 tablespoons chipotle pepper (jarred jalapeño pepper), chopped
1 can (15 ounces) solid-pack 100% pumpkin
1 can (15-1/2 ounces) navy beans, rinsed and drained
1/4 cup water
1 teaspoon chili powder
1/2 teaspoon dried oregano
Toppings: 1-1/2 cups romaine lettuce, shredded
3 ripe tomatoes, diced
3 tablespoons nonfat sour cream

Preparation: Preheat oven to 200°F. Wrap tortillas in aluminum foil and warm in oven about 5 minutes. While they warm, place a large skillet over medium heat and add oil. When oil is hot, add zucchini, corn, onion, and pepper; cook, stirring, until tender, about 4 to 5 minutes. Add pumpkin, beans, water, chili powder, and oregano and cook, stirring occasionally, about 4 minutes until heated through. Spoon about 1/2 cup of pumpkin mixture into each tortilla and roll each up, folding sides to enclose. Place each on a separate dinner plate and garnish with 1/4 cup lettuce, tomatoes, and 1-1/2 tablespoons sour cream. Makes 6 servings, 1 burrito each.

> This recipe's fiber (navy beans) and beta carotene (pumpkin) may help prevent the following cancers: **colon and liver.**

Nutritional information per serving:
Calories: 374.7
Fat: 7.5 g
Saturated fat: 1.6 g
Carbohydrate: 64.1 g
Total sugars: 5.7 g
Protein: 12.7 g
Sodium: 370 mg
Cholesterol: < 1 mg
Dietary fiber: 10.5 g

Roasted Tomato Quesadillas

These might be the most nutritious and flavorful quesadillas that you have ever made.

Ingredients:
1 can (14-1/2 ounces) roasted diced tomatoes, drained
2/3 cup fresh or thawed frozen corn kernels
3/4 cup canned black beans, rinsed and drained
1/3 cup yellow onion, diced
2-1/2 tablespoons fresh cilantro, finely chopped
1/4 teaspoon salt (preferably kosher salt)
1/4 teaspoon each: garlic powder, onion powder, and ground cumin
1/8 teaspoon cayenne pepper
1 teaspoon lime juice
6 whole-wheat flour tortillas (8-inch size)
2 cups shredded reduced-fat Monterey Jack cheese
Nonstick cooking spray
2 limes cut into wedges
1/4 cup low-fat sour cream

Preparation: Place diced tomatoes in a large bowl and use a fork to mash them into smaller pieces. Add corn, black beans, onion, cilantro, salt, garlic, onion powder, ground cumin, cayenne pepper, and lime juice and stir until well-blended. Lay tortillas out on working area and sprinkle one half of each tortilla with 1/3 cup Monterey Jack cheese. Top cheese with 1/4 cup tomato mixture, reserving remainder. Fold each tortilla in half and set aside. Spray a large nonstick skillet with cooking spray and place over medium heat; cook each quesadilla about 2-1/2 to 3 minutes per side, until lightly brown (cheese will be melting). Cut each quesadilla into 3 wedges and serve with remaining tomato-bean salsa, lime, and 2 teaspoons low-fat sour cream. Makes 6 servings, 1 quesadilla each.

This recipe's lycopene (tomatoes) and anthocyanins (black beans) may help prevent the following cancers: **prostate and pancreas.**

Nutritional information per serving:
Calories: 332.0
Fat: 10.0 g
Saturated fat: 5.3 g
Carbohydrate: 42.5 g
Total sugars: 4.2 g
Protein: 18.0 g
Sodium: 516 mg
Cholesterol: 25 mg
Dietary fiber: 5.3 g

Roasted Vegetable Panini

These scrumptious, veggie-laden Italian sandwiches contain vitamins A and C, fiber, calcium, iron, and folate.

Ingredients:
Nonstick cooking spray
6 cups sliced mixed vegetables (zucchini, mushrooms, yellow
  onions, red or orange bell peppers, eggplant)
1 tablespoon garlic, minced
1 tablespoon extra-virgin olive oil
1 tablespoon fresh rosemary, chopped
1 teaspoon oregano
Salt and pepper to taste
8 slices whole-grain sourdough or peasant's bread
1 cup baby arugula (can substitute baby spinach)
4 ounces thin-sliced smoked mozzarella or provolone cheese
Nonstick cooking spray

Preparation: Preheat oven to 400°F. Coat a 9x13-inch baking dish or cookie sheet with nonstick cooking spray. Place vegetables and garlic in baking dish and drizzle with olive oil. Sprinkle with chopped rosemary, oregano, and salt and pepper. Roast vegetables in oven 30 to 35 minutes, or until tender, stirring occasionally (about every 5 to 10 minutes). Spoon vegetable mix onto four bread slices, and top with arugula and cheese. Place another slice of bread on top. Coat a skillet with nonstick cooking spray and cook each side of sandwich 2 to 3 minutes, until lightly browned. Serve hot. (Sandwich grill can also be used instead of skillet.) Makes 4 panini sandwiches.

This recipe's folate (arugula) and allicin (garlic) may help prevent the following cancers: **colon and stomach.**

Nutritional information per sandwich:
Calories: 253.3
Fat: 9.7 g
Saturated fat: 3.5 g
Carbohydrate: 29.0 g
Total sugars: 4.3 g
Protein: 12.5 g
Sodium: 416 mg
Cholesterol: 18.0 mg
Dietary fiber: 3.3 g

Salmon BLTs with Herb Dressing

You can grill the salmon indoors on a stovetop or stand-alone grill, with equally tasty results. Grilling covered allows the fish to heat by convection and decreases carcinogen exposure.

Ingredients:
Nonstick cooking spray, olive-oil flavor
2-1/2 tablespoons low-fat sour cream
2 tablespoons plain low-fat yogurt
2 teaspoons chives, snipped
1 teaspoon garlic, minced
4 salmon fillets, with skin, about 1-inch thick (about 5 ounces each)
8 slices whole-grain bread
4 large romaine or butter-lettuce leaves
2 ripe but firm medium tomatoes
6 slices fully cooked turkey bacon, each slice broken in half

Preparation: Spray grill rack with nonstick spray and prepare outdoor grill for covered, direct grilling over medium heat. Stir sour cream, yogurt, chives, and garlic together in a small bowl until well blended; set aside. Sprinkle salmon with salt and pepper as desired. Place salmon, skin side facing down, on heated grill rack; cook covered about 11 to 12 minutes, until salmon is opaque, but do not turn. Slide thin metal spatula or pancake turner between skin and salmon meat and transfer salmon to a plate (discard skin). Toast bread on grill rack about 1 minute per side. Spread herb dressing on 1 side of each of 4 toasted bread slides. Top with 1 folded lettuce leaf, 1 salmon fillet, 2 or 3 slices of tomato, and 3 half-pieces turkey bacon. Place top toasted bread slice on each sandwich and serve. Makes 4 salmon BLTs.

Nutritional information per serving:
Calories: 458.2
Fat: 21.8 g
Saturated fat: 5.1 g
Carbohydrate: 30.5 g
Total sugars: 14.0 g
Protein: 35.0 g
Sodium: 676 mg
Cholesterol: 103.2 mg
Dietary fiber: 4.8 g

Vegan Tofu Patties

If you cannot get extra-firm tofu, use firm tofu and cut it into strips, set wax paper or a tea towel on top of it and a cutting board and set a dictionary or heavy book on top for about 10 minutes to press the water out. These tofu patties are perfect with the Creamy Tahini Sauce (page 60).

Ingredients:
1 pound (16 ounces) extra-firm tofu or pressed firm tofu
2 tablespoons extra-virgin olive oil
1/2 cup red pepper, finely chopped
1/3 cup zucchini, grated
1/4 cup celery, minced
3 garlic cloves, minced
1/2 cup fresh basil leaves, finely chopped
1 cup cooked brown rice
1/4 cup quick oats
1 tablespoon jalapeño pepper, minced
1 tablespoon fresh ginger, minced
1 cup fresh or frozen corn kernels
1/2 teaspoon turmeric
2 teaspoons paprika
1-1/2 teaspoons ground coriander
1 teaspoon ground cumin
1/4 teaspoon each: salt and ground black pepper
1 cup fine whole-wheat breadcrumbs (you can toast 2 pieces of wheat bread and finely chop them)
2 cups mixed baby greens
1 cup grape tomatoes, halved

Preparation: Preheat oven to 375°F. Cut tofu into chunks, and mash with a potato masher or process in a blender or food processor about 30 to 40 seconds. Place tofu in a large bowl. Place a large skillet or nonstick fry pan over medium-high heat and add olive oil. Add red pepper, zucchini, celery, garlic, basil, brown rice, oats, jalapeño, and ginger to skillet and sauté 8 to 10 minutes. Add corn and all spices and sauté an additional 1 to 2 minutes. Remove from heat and let cool about 4 or 5 minutes. Add vegetable-spice mixture to tofu; mix well by hand or on low in a food processor, just until mixture forms clumps. Form mixture into a dozen balls, flatten to 3/4-inch thickness, coat with breadcrumbs, and place on a nonstick baking sheet. Bake 25 minutes until outside is crisp and browned. Divide baby greens and tomatoes among 4 dinner plates, add 3 tofu patties to each, and serve with condiments or dressing of choice. Makes 4 servings, 3 patties each.

Nutritional information per serving:
Calories: 358.1
Fat: 16.1 g
Saturated fat: 1.9 g
Carbohydrate: 36.0 g
Total sugars: 7.0 g
Protein: 17.3 g
Sodium: 98 mg
Cholesterol: 0 mg
Dietary fiber: 5.0 g

Nutritional information per fajita:
Calories: 247.6
Fat: 7.6 g
Saturated fat: 1.3 g
Carbohydrate: 30.0 g
Total sugars: 1.8 g
Protein: 14.8 g
Sodium: 354 mg
Cholesterol: 25.4 mg
Dietary fiber: 2.5 g

Nutritional information per serving:
Calories: 348.6
Fat: 11.4 g
Saturated fat: 5.9 g
Carbohydrate: 43.1 g
Total sugars: 7.0 g
Protein: 18.4 g
Sodium: 702 mg
Cholesterol: 368 mg
Dietary fiber: 2.6 g

Whole-Grain Turkey Fajitas

Ingredients:
8 whole-wheat flour tortillas (7-inch diameter)
2 teaspoons chili powder
1/2 teaspoon dried oregano
12 ounces lean turkey-breast cutlets
2 teaspoons canola oil, divided
1 red bell pepper, thinly sliced
1 yellow bell pepper, thinly sliced
1/2 medium sweet yellow onion, sliced into rings
8 butter-lettuce leaves, washed and dried
3/4 cup salsa of choice

Preparation: Preheat oven to 200°F. Wrap tortillas in foil and place in oven while making fajita filling. Mix chili powder and oregano on waxed paper and rub spice mixture into turkey cutlets. In a large skillet, heat 1 teaspoon oil. Add bell-pepper slices and onion and cook over medium-high heat 4 to 6 minutes, stirring often, until lightly browned and tender-crisp. Remove to a bowl, using a slotted spoon. Heat remaining oil in same skillet. Add cutlets and cook over medium-high heat 4 to 6 minutes, turning once, until browned and no longer pink in center when tested with knife. Cut turkey crosswise into narrow strips. Top each warm tortilla with a lettuce leaf and arrange turkey and bell-pepper strips down middle. Serve with salsa. Makes 8 fajitas.

Washington Apple Pizza

Ingredients:
1/2 cup low-fat ricotta cheese
3 tablespoons red onion, minced
1/4 cup green bell pepper, diced
1/4 cup orange bell pepper, diced
1 (16-ounce) pre-cooked whole-wheat pizza crust
1 Fuji, Jonagold, or Golden Delicious apple, cored and thinly sliced
1/2 cup jarred sweet red pepper, thinly sliced
3/4 cup shredded part-skim mozzarella cheese

Preparation: Preheat oven to 425°F. In a small bowl, combine ricotta cheese, onion, green and orange pepper; mix well. Spread on pizza crust. Layer apple and red pepper on top of ricotta mixture. Sprinkle with mozzarella. Bake about 9 to 11 minutes or until cheese melts and pizza is heated through. Makes 4 servings.

Wild Mushroom Quesadillas with Warm Black-Bean Salsa

A friend sent me this recipe that she found in a Rachael Ray *magazine (Rachael Ray has some fantastic recipes, by the way). I made a few changes so that it is a bit lower in fat and calories.*

Ingredients:

3 tablespoons extra-virgin olive oil, divided
16 crimini mushroom caps, thinly sliced
12 shiitake mushroom caps, thinly sliced
1/2 teaspoon each: salt and coarsely ground black pepper
1 tablespoon fresh thyme leaves, chopped
1/2 cup yellow onion, finely chopped
2 garlic cloves, chopped
1 jalapeño pepper, seeded and chopped
1 can (15 ounces) black beans, drained and rinsed
1 cup frozen corn kernels
1/2 cup sun-dried tomatoes, reconstituted in water and finely chopped
1/2 cup barbecue sauce
Salt and freshly ground black pepper
Nonstick cooking spray, olive-oil flavor
4 (12-inch) whole-wheat flour tortillas
2 cups shredded reduced-fat Monterey jack cheese

Preparation: Place a medium nonstick skillet over medium heat. Add 2 tablespoons olive oil and sliced mushrooms to hot skillet. Season mushrooms with salt, black pepper, and thyme. Sauté mushrooms 10 minutes or until dark and tender; remove from heat. Transfer mushrooms to a dish; return skillet to stove and place over medium heat. Add remaining tablespoon olive oil to skillet; add onions, garlic, and jalapeño pepper and sauté 2 to 3 minutes, then add beans and corn to the pan. Stir in chopped tomatoes and barbecue sauce and season with salt and pepper as desired. Transfer warm salsa to a serving dish. Place a griddle pan or large nonstick skillet over medium heat and spray with nonstick cooking spray. Add 1 flour tortilla. Cook tortilla 1 minute, then turn. Sprinkle 1/2 cup cheese over 1/2 of tortilla. Cover cheese with 1/4 cooked sliced mushrooms. Fold plain tortilla half over filling and gently press down with a spatula. Cook filled quesadilla 30 seconds to 1 minute on each side until lightly brown and crisp and cheese has melted. Remove quesadilla to a large cutting board or transfer to a warm oven to hold; repeat with remaining quesadilla ingredients. Cut each quesadilla into wedges and serve with warm salsa for topping. Makes 8 servings.

Nutritional information per serving:
Calories: 396.8
Fat: 15.4 g
Saturated fat: 5.4 g
Carbohydrate: 50.5
Total sugars: 9.7 g
Protein: 16.6 g
Sodium: 735 mg
Cholesterol: 18.4 mg
Dietary fiber: 6.5 g

MAIN
COURSES

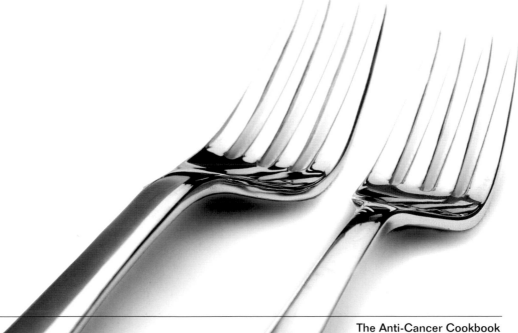

The Anti-Cancer Cookbook

Baked Lean Lemon Sole

Fish and seafood are healthy and nutritious and should be a part of the American diet. In this quick and easy sole recipe, it is best to use thicker fillets and cook them a bit longer, because the thinner ones do not turn out as nicely.

This recipe's lutein (watercress) and folate (arugula) may help prevent the following cancers: **ovarian and breast.**

Ingredients:
Small bunch each: baby arugula and watercress sprigs, washed and dried
3/4 cup fine whole-wheat breadcrumbs
4 sole fillets (about 1-1/2 to 2 pounds total)
2 teaspoons olive oil (preferably garlic- or rosemary-infused)
1/4 cup lemon juice
Salt and freshly ground black pepper
2 tablespoons parsley, chopped
4 lemon wedges

Preparation: Preheat oven to 450°F. Divide arugula and watercress among 4 dinner plates. Place breadcrumbs in a small bowl and roll each fish fillet to cover both sides. Place fish skin-side down in a shallow baking pan. Brush fish with olive oil. Bake about 7 to 15 minutes, depending on thickness of fillets. If fillets are very thin, check for doneness after 3 to 4 minutes. If fish hasn't darkened in color, it may be broiled for about 40 seconds. Do not overcook. Use a spatula and place each piece of fish onto dinner plate on top of greens. Pour any pan juices over fish and sprinkle with lemon juice, salt, pepper, and chopped parsley. Garnish with lemon wedges. Makes 4 servings.

Nutritional information per serving:
Calories: 275.6
Fat: 8.4 g
Saturated fat: 1.3 g
Carbohydrate: 16.1 g
Total sugars: 1.7 g
Protein: 33.9 g
Sodium: 285 mg
Cholesterol: 78.2 mg
Dietary fiber: 1.1 g

Balsamic Chicken with Pears

This is a wonderful way to prepare chicken with a rich and unique flavor. The red onion and cherries provide some valuable antioxidant nutrients, and the pears contain fiber and vitamin C.

This recipe's anthocyanins (cherries) and quercetin (onion) may help prevent the following cancers: **breast and lung.**

Ingredients:
6 skinless and boneless chicken breasts (about 3 to 4 ounces each)
Salt and freshly ground black pepper
1 tablespoon extra-virgin olive oil
1/4 cup red onion, minced
2 medium Bosc or Bartlett pears, peeled, cored, and sliced
1 cup low-sodium chicken broth or stock
1/4 cup balsamic vinegar
1 tablespoon plus 1 teaspoon sugar
2 teaspoons cornstarch
1/4 cup dried tart cherries

Preparation: Pat chicken dry with paper towels. Place each chicken breast between two sheets of plastic wrap. Using a meat mallet, carefully pound chicken breasts to a uniform thickness of about 1/2 inch. Season both sides with salt and pepper. Heat olive oil in a large nonstick skillet over medium heat; add chicken and sauté, turning once, 3 to 4 minutes on each side, until golden brown. Remove from heat and transfer to a platter; cover and keep warm. To same pan, add onion and sauté over medium-high heat 2 minutes or until soft; decrease heat to medium and add pears. Continue sautéing, stirring occasionally, 3 to 4 minutes, until pears are soft and golden brown. To prepare sauce, combine chicken broth, balsamic vinegar, sugar, and cornstarch in a small bowl. Pour over pear mixture and add cherries. Increase heat to high and simmer, stirring frequently, 6 to 8 minutes or until sauce thickens slightly. Return chicken and any juices to pan. Bring mixture back to a simmer and decrease heat to medium. Cook 10 minutes or until a meat thermometer registers an internal temperature of 165°F (juices will run clear when cut with the tip of a knife). Taste and adjust seasonings if necessary. Remove chicken from heat and place on individual serving plates or on a large platter. Using a slotted spoon, mound fruit over top. Spoon sauce over fruit and around chicken. Serve immediately. Makes 6 servings.

Nutritional information per serving:
Calories: 208.4
Fat: 3.6 g
Saturated fat: 0.4 g
Carbohydrate: 21.5 g
Total sugars: 15.2 g
Protein: 22.5 g
Sodium: 137 mg
Cholesterol: 54.9 mg
Dietary fiber: 2.1 g

The Anti-Cancer Cookbook

Balsamic Tilapia with Cabbage Salad

This light and healthy dish can stand alone, serve as sandwich filler, or even be used to make fish tacos. Any flaky white fish can be substituted for the tilapia. The cabbage salad is most flavorful if made ahead of time and brought to room temperature before serving.

Ingredients:
1/2 cup orange juice
1/4 cup balsamic vinegar
2 tablespoons sugar, divided
Juice of 2 limes
1 head cabbage, shredded or coarsely chopped
1/2 small yellow onion, minced
1 large cucumber, coarsely chopped
1/3 cup fresh cilantro, chopped
Nonstick cooking spray
1 pound tilapia fillets
Salt and pepper to taste

Preparation: Place orange juice, vinegar, and 1 tablespoon sugar in a small saucepan over medium heat and warm until reduced to a syrupy consistency, about 10 minutes. In a small bowl, combine remaining tablespoon sugar and lime juice. Place cabbage, onion, cucumber, and cilantro in a large bowl and toss with lime-juice mixture. Heat a broiler. Spray broiler pan with nonstick cooking spray and broil tilapia approximately 2 minutes per side or just until fish is lightly browned and flakes easily. Try not to overcook. Divide cabbage mixture among 4 dinner plates. Brush fish generously with vinegar reduction and serve on top of cabbage salad. You can also use a fork to flake the fish into pieces and toss with vinegar reduction. Makes 4 generous servings.

Nutritional information per serving:
Calories: 284.2
Fat: 7.0 g
Saturated fat: 1.1 g
Carbohydrate: 29.5 g
Total sugars: 21.6 g
Protein: 25.8 g
Sodium: 102 mg
Cholesterol: 68 mg
Dietary fiber: 5.9 g

Barbecued Vegetarian Shish Kebabs

You can substitute chunks of meat, tofu, or seafood (such as scallops or shrimp) for the tempeh in this recipe for variation. Feel free to experiment with other veggies such as shallots, red onions, various colored peppers, mushrooms, and even sugar snap peas.

Ingredients:
1/2 cup plain spaghetti sauce
1 tablespoon brown mustard
2 tablespoons barley malt syrup
2 tablespoons pure maple syrup
2 tablespoons extra-virgin olive oil
2 teaspoons reduced-sodium tamari or soy sauce
1 tablespoon brown rice vinegar
1 tablespoon freshly squeezed lime juice
3 garlic cloves, minced
1/4 cup onion, minced
1/4 teaspoon dried basil
1 pound organic tempeh, cut into 1-inch cubes and steamed 15 minutes
1 cup cherry tomatoes
8 medium button mushrooms, stemmed and washed
1 small red bell pepper, sliced into thick strips
1 medium yellow onion, sliced into wide wedges
1 medium zucchini, sliced into thick rounds
1 medium yellow squash, sliced into thick rounds
8 bamboo shish kebab sticks or metal skewers

Preparation: To prepare barbecue sauce, place spaghetti sauce, mustard, barley malt syrup, maple syrup, tamari or soy sauce, olive oil, brown rice vinegar, lime juice, garlic, minced onion, and basil in a blender. Purée several seconds. Attractively arrange tempeh cubes and pieces of each vegetable on shish kebab sticks, alternating different colored vegetables with tempeh. Baste with barbecue sauce and grill, turning and basting to prevent vegetables from drying out or burning. Grill until vegetables are tender, about 7 to 10 minutes. Makes 8 servings, 1 kebab each.

This recipe's lycopene (tomatoes) and quercetin (onions) may help prevent the following cancers: **pancreas and lung.**

Nutritional information per serving:
Calories: 199.9
Fat: 6.7 g
Saturated fat: 1.1 g
Carbohydrate: 22.2 g
Total sugars: 10.2 g
Protein: 12.7 g
Sodium: 97 mg
Cholesterol: 0 mg
Dietary fiber: 7.6 g

Broccoli and Scallop Linguini

Scallops are high in protein and low in fat and calories. Pair them with broccoli, tomatoes, and onions and some whole-wheat pasta and you have a really nutritious and attractive dinner.

Ingredients:
3/4 pound uncooked fresh scallops
2 medium yellow onions, cut in half lengthwise and sliced
1 cup apple juice
2 tablespoons dry white wine
2 garlic cloves, minced
1 teaspoon each: dried marjoram, dried basil, and dried oregano
1/4 teaspoon ground black pepper
3 cups broccoli florets
1/4 cup water
1 tablespoon plus 1 teaspoon cornstarch
1-1/2 cups fresh tomatoes, seeded and chopped
1/4 cup grated Parmesan cheese
4 cups hot cooked whole-wheat linguine

Preparation: Cut larger scallops into quarters or 1-inch pieces. Combine onions, apple juice, wine, garlic, marjoram, basil, oregano, and pepper in a large skillet; bring to a boil over high heat. Add broccoli; return to a boil. Reduce heat to medium-low. Cover and simmer 7 minutes; add scallops. Return to a boil and reduce heat. Cover and simmer 1 to 2 minutes or until scallops are opaque. Remove scallops and vegetables; set aside. Combine water and cornstarch in a small bowl; stir into mixture in skillet. Cook, stirring, over medium heat until mixture boils and thickens. Once boiling, cook and stir 2 minutes more. Stir in tomatoes and cheese; heat through. Return scallops and vegetables to skillet; heat through. Toss mixture with linguine. Makes 4 servings, about 2 cups each.

> This recipe's isothiocyanates (broccoli) and lycopene (tomatoes) may help prevent the following cancers: **ovarian and prostate.**

Nutritional information per serving:
Calories: 421.1
Fat: 4.3 g
Saturated fat: 1.2 g
Carbohydrate: 53.5 g
Total sugars: 12.0 g
Protein: 42.0 g
Sodium: 431 mg
Cholesterol: 78.8 mg
Dietary fiber: 8.0 g

Broccoli and Tomato Halibut

This recipe was adapted from one that I found years ago in Easy Home Cooking *magazine. Few vegetables rival broccoli and tomatoes in nutritional value. If you are watching your sugar and carbohydrate intake, this dish is perfect for you because it contains fewer than 10 grams of carbohydrates per serving.*

This recipe's allicin (garlic) and lycopene (tomatoes) may help prevent the following cancers: **colon and prostate.**

Ingredients:
2 tablespoons extra-virgin olive oil
2 cups fresh broccoli florets, chopped
2-1/2 cups fresh ripe tomatoes, diced
2 tablespoons lemon juice
1-1/2 tablespoons garlic, minced
1 teaspoon dried tarragon
1/2 teaspoon sugar
1/4 teaspoon each: salt and freshly ground black pepper
4 halibut steaks (about 5 to 6 ounces each)

Preparation: Heat oil in a large skillet over medium heat about 1 minute. Add broccoli and heat 5 minutes. Add all remaining ingredients except halibut; cook 5 minutes, stirring occasionally. Add halibut; cover and cook about 5 minutes on each side. Divide halibut and vegetables among 4 dinner plates. Makes 4 servings.

Nutritional information per serving:
Calories: 218.0
Fat: 7.6 g
Saturated fat: 1.0 g
Carbohydrate: 8.5 g
Total sugars: 3.6 g
Protein: 28.9 g
Sodium: 85 mg
Cholesterol: 40.8 mg
Dietary fiber: 1.5 g

Cheesy Brown Rice and Lentil Casserole

This dish is flavorful and savory, not at all like those bland casseroles that you may have had in the past. As a side dish, the recipe makes about twice as many servings. For a vegan option, use your favorite soy cheese instead of the cheddar.

Ingredients:
1/2 cup dry red wine
1-1/2 cups reduced-sodium vegetable broth
1/2 cup dried lentils
1/2 cup uncooked brown rice
1 cup diced tomatoes, mashed with a potato masher
1 medium yellow onion, minced
3 small garlic cloves, minced
1/4 teaspoon dried thyme
1 bay leaf
Sea salt and ground pepper to taste
1/4 teaspoon dried basil
1/2 cup shredded reduced-fat cheddar cheese (or soy cheese)

Preparation: Preheat oven to 350°F. In a 6-cup casserole dish, combine all ingredients except cheese. Mix thoroughly and cover with a tight-fitting lid or foil. Bake 90 to 100 minutes, or until lentils are tender and liquid is absorbed, stirring 2 or 3 times during baking. Take off foil or lid, remove the bay leaf, and top with shredded cheese. Return to oven, uncovered, and heat 3 to 4 minutes, until cheese melts. Makes 4 large servings.

This recipe's saponins (lentils) and resveratrol (red wine) may help prevent the following cancers: **pancreas and kidney.**

Nutritional information per serving:
Calories: 230.9
Fat: 2.1 g
Saturated fat: 0.9 g
Carbohydrate: 39.5 g
Total sugars: 4.1 g
Protein: 13.5 g
Sodium: 163 mg
Cholesterol: 3.5 mg
Dietary fiber: 9.1 g

Citrus-Barbecued Tofu

This is the ideal soy-based main dish for a spring or summer evening. It goes perfectly with a small mixed green salad and some crusty, whole-grain bread.

Ingredients:
1 package (14 ounces) extra-firm tofu
Juice of 2 lemons
1/4 cup orange juice
1 tablespoon pure maple syrup
2 tablespoons apple cider vinegar
1 tablespoon extra-virgin olive oil
1-1/2 teaspoons fresh rosemary, chopped (or 1/2 teaspoon dried rosemary)
3 garlic cloves, crushed
1-1/2 teaspoons tamari or soy sauce
Dash of black pepper

Preparation: Cut tofu into 6 thick slices and set aside. In a ceramic bowl, whisk together all remaining ingredients to make marinade. Place tofu slices in a large, flat dish and generously pour marinade over them. Reserve a portion of marinade in the refrigerator for when you do the actual cooking. Cover tofu and refrigerate at least 8 hours—preferably overnight to attain best flavor. Preheat grill to medium heat and brush lightly with olive oil. Grill tofu slices, brushing with extra marinade while cooking, about 5 minutes on each side. Makes 3 servings, 2 tofu slices each.

Nutritional information per serving:
Calories: 260.0
Fat: 14.0 g
Saturated fat: 1.9 g
Carbohydrate: 15.7 g
Total sugars: 7.5 g
Protein: 17.8 g
Sodium: 177 mg
Cholesterol: 0 mg
Dietary fiber: 1.8 g

Corn-Crusted Yogurt Fish

This is a scrumptious, light fish recipe containing low-fat dairy products and monounsaturated fats. It would be complemented nicely by the Heirloom Tomato and Olive Salad (page 85) and some freshly grilled eggplant or zucchini.

This recipe's lutein (arugula) and vitamin D (yogurt) may help prevent the following cancers: **stomach and breast.**

Ingredients:
1 cup plain low-fat yogurt
1 teaspoon Tabasco or other hot sauce
1 cup cornmeal
4 tilapia or flounder fillets (about 6 to 8 ounces each)
1 tablespoon olive oil and more as needed, to prevent sticking
1 cup baby arugula
1 lemon, cut in wedges.

Preparation: Combine yogurt and hot sauce in a baking dish. Add fish fillets and marinate 15 minutes. Drain fish and dredge each side of fish with cornmeal. Place a large skillet over medium heat. Add olive oil and pan-fry fish 3 to 4 minutes on each side. Divide arugula among 4 dinner plates. Serve fish on top of arugula with lemon wedges. Makes 4 servings.

Nutritional information per serving:
Calories: 339.0
Fat: 6.6 g
Saturated fat: 2.0 g
Carbohydrate: 22.0 g
Total sugars: 4.6 g
Protein: 47.9 g
Sodium: 242 mg
Cholesterol: 123.5 mg
Dietary fiber: 2.3 g

Crispy Tofu and Vegetables

This recipe's quercetin (onions) and isoflavones (tofu) may help prevent the following cancers: **lung and prostate.**

Ingredients:
2 cups fresh sugar snap peas (about 8 ounces)
1 package (14 ounces) light, extra-firm tub-style tofu, drained
3 tablespoons reduced-sodium soy sauce or tamari, divided
1/4 cup yellow cornmeal
1/8 teaspoon ground red pepper
2 teaspoons toasted sesame oil, divided
1 medium red bell pepper, cut into thin strips
1 medium yellow bell pepper, cut into thin strips
6-8 green onions, cut into approximately 2-inch pieces
2 teaspoons canola oil
1 tablespoon sesame seeds, toasted

Preparation: Remove strings and tips from pea pods; cut in half and set aside. Cut tofu crosswise into eight 1/2-inch thick slices. Drain on paper towels if necessary. Arrange slices in a single layer in a 2-quart rectangular baking dish. Pour 2 tablespoons soy sauce or tamari over tofu; turn slices to coat. Let stand at room temperature 15 minutes. In a shallow dish, combine cornmeal and ground red pepper. Drain tofu, discarding marinade. Carefully dip tofu slices in cornmeal mixture; press gently to coat both sides. Set tofu slices aside. Pour 1 teaspoon sesame oil into a large nonstick skillet and place over medium-high heat. Stir-fry red and yellow pepper about 2 minutes. Add pea pods and green onions; stir-fry 2 to 3 minutes until crisp-tender. Remove skillet from heat; stir in remaining 1 tablespoon soy sauce or tamari. Transfer vegetables to serving platter; cover and keep warm. Wipe skillet clean. In same skillet, heat remaining sesame oil and canola oil over medium heat. Cook coated tofu slices 2 to 3 minutes on each side or until crisp and golden brown. Divide vegetable mixture between 4 dinner plates. Serve tofu slices over vegetable mixture and sprinkle with sesame seeds. Makes 4 servings.

Nutritional information per serving:
Calories: 297.8
Fat: 16.6 g
Saturated fat: 2.3 g
Carbohydrate: 18.9 g
Total sugars: 2.1 g
Protein: 18.2 g
Sodium: 769 mg
Cholesterol: 0 mg
Dietary fiber: 4.5 g

Curried Apple Vegetable Chicken

This is another great recipe courtesy of Dr. Patricia Eagon (biochemist at the University of Pittsburgh). She recommends serving it over basmati rice with some plain yogurt. I think it would also be delicious with brown rice or couscous.

Ingredients:
4 skinless, boneless chicken breasts, about 1-1/2 pounds, cut into 3/4-inch cubes.
1 tablespoon each: cornstarch, reduced-sodium soy sauce, and dry sherry
1 teaspoon sugar
2 tablespoons extra-virgin olive oil, divided
1 medium to large yellow onion, chopped
1 cup carrots, chopped
1 medium red pepper, chopped
1 tablespoon mustard seed
3 cloves garlic, minced
2 tablespoons ginger, minced or freshly grated
1 tablespoon curry powder (more or less to preference)
1 can (14 ounces) low-sodium chicken broth
1 very large or 2 medium sweet potatoes or yams (about 1 pound), peeled and cut into 3/4-inch cubes
1 bay leaf
1 large Granny Smith or other tart apple, cored and chopped
5 ounces fresh baby spinach leaves (half a large bag)
Cilantro, chopped

Preparation: Place chicken in a large bowl. Add cornstarch, soy sauce, dry sherry, and sugar; stir to coat chicken. Set aside. Place a large skillet or wok over medium-high heat; add 2 teaspoons olive oil and heat. Add onion and carrots; sauté about 5 minutes, until somewhat soft. Add red pepper; sauté an additional 3 minutes. Remove vegetables to a bowl; set aside. Add 1 teaspoon oil to same skillet and heat to medium high; add mustard seed, stirring, until seeds begin to pop. Lower heat to medium and add garlic; sauté 2 minutes. Add ginger and sauté another 2 minutes. Add curry powder and let mixture cook 1 to 2 minutes, making sure not to burn seeds and spices. Add remaining tablespoon olive oil to skillet. Stir chicken mixture in bowl and add to skillet, continuing to stir. Cook chicken about 4 to 5 minutes, stirring frequently, until lightly browned. Add chicken broth, reserved vegetables, sweet potatoes (or yams), and bay leaf. Cook, covered, about 8 minutes, or until sweet potatoes are nearly soft. Add apples to mixture and stir; cook, covered, 3 to 4 minutes, until apples soften slightly. Add spinach and stir; cook, covered, 1 to 2 minutes, until spinach is wilted. If desired, thicken mixture with a little cornstarch mixed with water. Garnish with chopped cilantro and serve. Makes 6 servings.

This recipe's beta carotene (sweet potatoes) and folate (spinach) may help prevent the following cancers: **skin and pancreas.**

Nutritional information per serving:
Calories: 283.5
Fat: 7.1 g
Saturated fat: 1.2 g
Carbohydrate: 24.3 g
Total sugars: 9.1 g
Protein: 30.6 g
Sodium: 257 mg
Cholesterol: 68.3 mg
Dietary fiber: 4.6 g

Dijon Tofu with Sweet Potatoes and Kale

This recipe was adapted from one that I originally found in Bon Appétit *magazine. It contains healthy soy isoflavones and one of the most nutritious leafy green vegetables known, kale.*

Ingredients:
1 package (14 ounces) extra-firm tofu
1/2 cup whole-grain Dijon mustard
4 tablespoons canola oil, divided
1/2 medium onion, sliced
1 tablespoon fresh ginger, peeled and minced
1 bunch kale, stem cut from each leaf, leaves thinly sliced crosswise (about 8 cups)
1 small sweet potato, peeled, halved lengthwise, thinly sliced crosswise
2 tablespoons fresh lime juice

Preparation: Cut tofu into eight 1/2-inch-thick slices. Arrange on paper towels and let drain 10 minutes. Spread both sides of each slice with mustard. Heat 2 tablespoons of canola oil in a large non-stick skillet over medium-high heat. Add onion and ginger; sauté 1 minute. Add kale, sweet potato, and lime juice. Cover, reduce heat to low, and cook until potato is tender and kale is wilted, about 10 to 15 minutes. Meanwhile, heat remaining 2 tablespoons oil in another large nonstick skillet over medium heat. Add tofu; cover and cook until heated through and crisp, about 2 minutes per side. (Some mustard seeds will fall off tofu.) Arrange kale and sweet-potato mixture on a platter or 4 separate dinner plates. Overlap tofu slices atop vegetables and serve. Makes 4 servings.

Nutritional information per serving:
Calories: 286.8
Fat: 27.0 g
Saturated fat: 5.3 g
Carbohydrate: 24.4 g
Total sugars: 2.0 g
Protein: 20.3 g
Sodium: 648 mg
Cholesterol: 0 mg
Dietary fiber: 5.0 g

Greek Turkey Meatloaf

Use lean turkey meat in this recipe for the highest protein-to-fat ratio. I really like to eat this meatloaf on the second day, warmed and crumbled over a big salad of mixed baby greens and sliced grape tomatoes.

Ingredients:
Nonstick cooking spray, olive-oil flavor
2 garlic cloves, minced
1 large red onion, chopped
1/2 of a 16-ounce package frozen flat-leaf spinach—thawed, drained, and squeezed dry
1 teaspoon dried oregano
4 ounces reduced-fat feta cheese, crumbled
1/2 cup quick-cooking oats
1 pound ground turkey breast
1 tablespoon poultry seasoning
Salt and pepper to taste

Preparation: Preheat oven to 350°F. Spray a large fry pan or skillet with nonstick cooking spray and place over medium-high heat. Add garlic and onion and sauté until onion is translucent. Add remaining ingredients; heat gently and mix well. Spray a loaf pan with nonstick cooking spray (or use a nonstick loaf pan). Add turkey mixture and bake 55 to 60 minutes. Let cool 5 minutes and serve. Can be refrigerated and reheated, or served cold or at room temperature. Makes 6 servings.

This recipe's lutein (spinach) and quercetin (onion) may help prevent the following cancers: **ovarian and lung.**

Nutritional information per serving:
Calories: 203.5
Fat: 9.5 g
Saturated fat: 1.6 g
Carbohydrate: 9.8 g
Total sugars: 1.6 g
Protein: 19.7 g
Sodium: 239 mg
Cholesterol: 46.7 g
Dietary fiber: 2.7 g

Grilled Chicken with Avocado Salsa

Ingredients:
4 ripe plum tomatoes, chopped, or 12 cherry tomatoes, halved
1/2 small red onion, finely chopped
1 jalapeño pepper, seeded and diced
2 tablespoons fresh cilantro, chopped
1/4 cup fresh lime juice, divided
1/2 avocado, peeled
1/2 cup plain nonfat yogurt
1/2 small red onion, coarsely chopped
1/4 cup fresh lime juice
1/4 cup fresh cilantro
4 boneless, skinless chicken breasts (about 5 to 6 ounces each)
Salt and freshly ground black pepper

Preparation: To make the salsa, combine tomatoes, red onion, pepper, and cilantro in a small bowl. Chop avocado and sprinkle with 2 tablespoons of lime juice to keep from browning. Add avocado and remaining lime juice to bowl and toss to combine. (This can be made in advance and stored in the refrigerator for up to 1 day.) In a small food processor, purée yogurt, red onion, lime juice, and cilantro to make a yogurt marinade. Transfer marinade to a shallow bowl or a plastic bag. Add chicken and coat well with marinade. Refrigerate from 1 hour up to 8 hours. Preheat a grill to medium-high heat. Remove chicken from marinade; discard remaining marinade and season chicken with salt and pepper as desired. Grill chicken on both sides until cooked through, about 6 minutes per side. Serve each chicken breast with avocado salsa. Makes 4 servings.

Nutritional information per serving:
Calories: 286.6
Fat: 5.0 g
Saturated fat: 0.5 g
Carbohydrate: 11.4 g
Total sugars: 5.4 g
Protein: 49.0 g
Sodium: 145 mg
Cholesterol: 95.6 mg
Dietary fiber: 2.7 g

Grilled Garden Pasta

I adapted this recipe from one that I found in Better Homes and Gardens *magazine a few years ago. To make this delicious dish, you grill some vegetables, chop them into bite-size pieces, and toss them with pasta.*

Ingredients:
6 ounces whole-wheat spaghetti or vermicelli
1/2 cup small fresh basil leaves
1/3 cup reduced-fat feta cheese, crumbled
2 tablespoons pine nuts
2 medium garlic cloves, minced
1 jalapeño pepper, seeded and minced
2 teaspoons lemon peel, finely grated
5 tablespoons extra-virgin olive oil, divided
1/4 cup lemon juice
1/4 teaspoon salt
1 yellow onion, cut into 3/4-inch slices
1 small zucchini, peeled or unpeeled, cut into 3/4-inch slices
1 small eggplant, peeled or unpeeled, cut into 3/4-inch slices
2 ripe but firm medium tomatoes, sliced 3/4-inch thick

Preparation: Prepare spaghetti or vermicelli according to package directions (typically cook in a large pot of boiling water until tender). While it cooks, combine basil, feta cheese, pine nuts, garlic, jalapeño pepper, and lemon peel in a small bowl; set aside. Drain pasta and toss with 1/4 cup olive oil, lemon juice, and salt. Cover and keep warm. Place a nonstick grill on stovetop and heat over medium heat until hot. Brush vegetables with remaining olive oil. Add half the onion, zucchini, eggplant, and tomatoes and grill until brown and tender, about 5 minutes per side. Remove from grill and repeat with remaining vegetables. Let vegetables cool slightly, and then cut into bite-size chunks. Divide pasta among 4 dinner plates and swirl into individual nests. Add 1/4 vegetables to each and 1/4 basil-feta mixture. Makes 4 servings.

Nutritional information per serving:
Calories: 395.6
Fat: 19.2 g
Saturated fat: 3.9 g
Carbohydrate: 43.4 g
Total sugars: 4.9 g
Protein: 12.3 g
Sodium: 315 mg
Cholesterol: 3.3 mg
Dietary fiber: 3.2 g

Lemon Broiled Salmon with Ginger and Fennel

Fennel has some phytoestrogen-like properties, similar to soy, and has been used medicinally to help alleviate symptoms such as chills, cramps, and abdominal pain. Some people claim that fennel is useful during chemotherapy or radiation treatment to alleviate side effects, such as nausea and indigestion.

Ingredients:
2 medium-size fennel bulbs, stalks removed
1/2 cup lemon juice (fresh or bottled)
3 tablespoons ginger, peeled and minced
2 tablespoons extra virgin olive oil
2 shallots, peeled and minced
Salt and freshly ground pepper
4 medium salmon fillets (6 to 8 ounces each)
Nonstick cooking spray, olive oil style

Preparation: Preheat oven to 400°F. Trim fennel bulbs in half from top to bottom, lay flat and cut into thin strips horizontally. In a medium mixing bowl, combine fennel, lemon juice, ginger, olive oil, and shallots. Mix well and season with salt and pepper as desired. Lay each salmon fillet on a board and season with salt and pepper. Spray a baking pan or sheet with nonstick cooking spray and place salmon fillets on top. Bake salmon 13 to 15 minutes, until lightly browned on edges and flaky. To serve, mound fennel salad into 4 large bowls, place a salmon fillet on each, and pour 1/4 of remaining pan juices onto each fillet. Makes 4 servings.

Nutritional information per serving:
Calories: 262.8
Fat: 15.2 g
Saturated fat: 2.4 g
Carbohydrate: 12.9 g
Total sugars: 0.7 g
Protein: 18.6 g
Sodium: 113 mg
Cholesterol: 50.2 mg
Dietary fiber: 3.8 g

Mahi Mahi with Citrus Sauce and Black Beans

Ingredients:
Citrus Sauce Ingredients:
Zest and juice of 4 Florida grapefruit
Zest and juice of 2 limes
1 small yellow onion, finely chopped
1 teaspoon garlic, chopped
1-1/2 tablespoons cider vinegar
5 tablespoons olive oil
1/4 teaspoon cracked black pepper
Salt to taste
4 Mahi Mahi fillets (about 8 ounces each)

Black Bean Purée Ingredients:
Nonstick cooking spray
1 garlic clove, minced
1 small onion, chopped
1 jalapeño pepper, seeded and chopped
1 cup cooked black beans (or canned, drained and rinsed)
1 cup fat-free, low-sodium chicken stock
Salt and pepper to taste

1-1/2 tablespoons canola oil

Preparation: Combine all citrus sauce ingredients in a small bowl and mix. Place fish in a square baking or serving dish. Ladle enough sauce over fish to cover, reserving remainder. Marinate for two hours. To make black-bean purée, spray a large skillet with nonstick cooking spray and sauté garlic, onion, and jalapeño until soft. Add beans and chicken stock. Cook 15 minutes. Place in blender and process until smooth; season with salt and pepper as desired. Heat canola oil in sauté pan until very hot. Place fish in skillet and cook approximately 2 minutes on each side. Ladle black-bean purée on serving plate and set fillets on top. Ladle a little of remaining citrus sauce over fish. Makes 4 servings.

This recipe's pectin (citrus zest) and fiber (beans) may help prevent the following cancers: **esophageal and pancreas.**

Nutritional information per serving:
Calories: 380.8
Fat: 18 g
Saturated fat: 2.1 g
Carbohydrate: 14.4 g
Total sugars: 2.1 g
Protein: 40.3 g
Sodium: 139 mg
Cholesterol: 204 mg
Dietary fiber: 4.4 g

Orange-Broccoli Beef

Broccoli is one of the healthiest foods you can eat. It is loaded with fiber and antioxidants such as vitamin C, carotenoids, and sulforaphane, which studies have shown to be associated with a lower risk of developing many types of cancer.

Ingredients:
1 boneless beef top sirloin steak (about 1 pound)
1/2 cup orange juice
1 teaspoon sugar
2 teaspoons reduced-sodium soy sauce
3 teaspoons canola oil, divided
3/4 pound broccoli florets, coarsely chopped
1 cup medium-size carrots, sliced on the diagonal
1 medium red bell pepper, seeded and thinly sliced
2 small green onions, sliced on the diagonal
1 garlic clove, minced
3/4 cup cold water
2 teaspoons cornstarch
1 tablespoon grated orange peel
8 ounces whole-wheat fettuccini

Preparation: Slice beef lengthwise in half, then crosswise into 1/8-inch slices; place beef in nonmetallic bowl. Add orange juice, sugar, and soy sauce. Toss to coat evenly. Let marinate 30 minutes, or cover and refrigerate overnight. Heat 2 teaspoons canola oil in large nonstick skillet or wok over medium-high heat until hot. Add broccoli, carrots, bell pepper, and green onion; cook and stir 2 minutes. Remove vegetables to large bowl. Drain beef; reserve marinade. Heat remaining 1 teaspoon oil in same skillet over medium-high heat until hot. Add beef to skillet; cook 1 to 2 minutes or until no longer pink. Add vegetables and reserved marinade to skillet; bring to a boil. Stir water into cornstarch until smooth; add to skillet. Cook until thickened, stirring constantly. Sprinkle with grated orange peel. Cook noodles according to package directions, omitting salt; drain. Spoon beef mixture over noodles and serve immediately. Makes 4 servings.

Nutritional information per serving:
Calories: 471.9
Fat: 15.1 g
Saturated fat: 2.5 g
Carbohydrate: 47.3 g
Total sugars: 6.4 g
Protein: 36.7 g
Sodium: 210 mg
Cholesterol: 69 mg
Dietary fiber: 7.8 g

Pacific Spinach, Shrimp, and Scallop Stir-Fry

If you don't own a wok, a large skillet will do just fine to prepare this dish.

Ingredients:
2 tablespoons extra-virgin olive oil, divided
3 tablespoons pine nuts
1 pound uncooked medium shrimp, cleaned, shelled, and deveined
1 pound fresh scallops, cut into quarters if large
2 teaspoons fresh ginger, peeled and grated
3 small garlic cloves, finely chopped
1 cup red bell pepper, cut into 1-inch diagonal pieces
8 ounces fresh spinach, stemmed, washed, and shredded
4 green onions, cut into 1/2-inch diagonal pieces
1/4 cup reduced-sodium chicken stock
1/4 cup reduced-sodium soy sauce or tamari
1/4 cup dry sherry (can substitute rice wine)
1 tablespoon cornstarch

Preparation: Add 1 tablespoon olive oil to a wok and place over medium heat. When oil is hot, add pine nuts and reduce heat to low. Cook, stirring continuously, until pine nuts are lightly browned. Remove with a finely slotted or draining spoon and place on paper towels to drain. Add remaining oil to wok and heat over medium heat; add shrimp and scallops until shrimp are pink and scallops are opaque. Add ginger, garlic, and red pepper; cook about 3 to 4 minutes over medium-high heat, stirring occasionally. Add spinach and onion; heat, stirring, for about 1 minute. In a small bowl, combine chicken stock, soy sauce or tamari, sherry, and cornstarch; pour into wok. Raise heat to high and bring liquid to a boil, stirring constantly. The liquid will thicken and clear; once thickened, stir in pine nuts and serve. Makes 4 servings.

This recipe's folate (spinach) and quercetin (onions) may help prevent the following cancers: **colon and endometrial.**

Nutritional information per serving:
Calories: 362.3
Fat: 13.5 g
Saturated fat: 1.6 g
Carbohydrate: 13.2 g
Total sugars: 2.2 g
Protein: 47.0 g
Sodium: 1023 mg
Cholesterol: 210 mg
Dietary fiber: 2.6 g

Pan-Cooked Bok Choy Salmon

This is a sweet and savory salmon dish that is loaded with antioxidants and takes just minutes to prepare. Bok choy is the Chinese form of cabbage. An easy way to pre-cook the salmon for this dish is to wrap each fillet separately in tin foil and heat for about 20 minutes in a 325°F preheated oven.

This recipe's kaempferol (cabbage) and vitamin D (salmon) may help prevent the following cancers: **breast and colon.**

Ingredients:
1-1/2 pounds bok choy or Napa cabbage, chopped
2 cups broccoli slaw
2 tablespoons olive oil
2 teaspoons sesame seeds
1 pound cooked wild salmon, divided into 4 fillets
Salt and freshly ground black pepper

Preparation: Place cabbage and broccoli slaw in colander; rinse and drain. Place olive oil and sesame seeds in a large skillet over medium heat. When oil is hot, add cabbage and broccoli slaw. Cook, stirring, 5 to 6 minutes; reduce heat to low and add salmon. Cook salmon and vegetables about 4 minutes, until fragrant and heated through. Season with salt and freshly ground black pepper as desired and divide among 4 dinner plates. Makes 4 servings.

Nutritional information per serving:
Calories: 284.1
Fat: 12.1 g
Saturated fat: 1.4 g
Carbohydrate: 10.0 g
Total sugars: 4.6 g
Protein: 33.8 g
Sodium: 286 mg
Cholesterol: 76 mg
Dietary fiber: 5.2 g

Pan-Seared Salmon with Orange Vinaigrette

This delicious and tangy dish contains valuable disease-fighting nutrients, such as vitamin C, omega-3 fatty acids, and vitamin D.

Ingredients:
2 cups orange juice
3 tablespoons red onion, finely chopped
3 tablespoons lime juice (preferably fresh)
2 teaspoons honey-Dijon mustard
2 teaspoons chili powder
1 cup fat-free Italian salad dressing
8 Alaska salmon fillets or steaks (6 to 8 ounces each), thawed if frozen
Salt and freshly ground black pepper to taste
1 tablespoon olive oil
3 tablespoons fresh cilantro or parsley, chopped

Preparation: Sauce: Heat orange juice in a small saucepan over medium-high heat until it reduces to the consistency of syrup (makes about 1/4 cup). Let cool slightly. Place onion, lime juice, mustard, and chili powder in a blender; add cooled orange-juice syrup. Blend 30 seconds; with blender running, slowly drizzle in Italian salad dressing so that mixture emulsifies.

Salmon: Preheat oven to 400°F. Lightly season salmon with salt and pepper. Heat an oven-proof sauté pan 2 minutes over medium-high heat, then add olive oil. Sear salmon on one side 2 to 3 minutes. Turn salmon over and place entire pan into oven. Bake 4 to 8 minutes, or until fish flakes easily when tested with a fork. Divide orange vinaigrette sauce evenly among plates and make a pool of sauce in the center of each serving plate. Top with a salmon fillet and garnish with cilantro or parsley. Makes 8 servings.

This recipe's quercetin (onion) and pectin (lime juice) may help prevent the following cancers: **lung and prostate.**

Nutritional information per serving:
Calories: 318.6
Fat: 10.2 g
Saturated fat: 1.3 g
Carbohydrate: 12.1 g
Total sugars: 7.8 g
Protein: 44.6 g
Sodium: 593 mg
Cholesterol: 120.4 mg
Dietary fiber: 0.4 g

Pasta with Chicken and Seasoned Italian Tomatoes

A number of studies have shown that Americans do not consume enough whole grains or get the recommended number of servings of fruits or vegetables each day. This dish provides plenty of whole grain and vegetable nutrients as well as lean protein that will leave you feeling satisfied.

Ingredients:
Nonstick cooking spray
1 medium yellow onion, diced
3 small garlic cloves, minced
1-1/2 cups fresh button mushrooms
1 pound uncooked chicken breast, cut into 1-inch pieces
2 cans (14 or 14-1/2 ounces) diced tomatoes, drained
1/3 cup balsamic vinegar
1 teaspoon each: dried basil and dried oregano
1/2 teaspoon each: dried thyme and dried rosemary
1/4 cup tomato paste
2-2/3 cups cooked whole-wheat linguini or angel hair pasta

Preparation: Spray a large skillet with nonstick cooking spray. Add onion, garlic, and mushrooms to skillet and sauté 5 minutes over low heat. Add chicken pieces and cook over medium-high heat until chicken is no longer pink. Once cooked, add diced tomatoes, tomato paste, balsamic vinegar, and spices to chicken mixture. Mix together well and simmer over medium-low heat about 20 minutes. Toss 1 cup sauce with 2/3 cup cooked pasta for each serving. Makes 4 servings.

Nutritional information per serving:
Calories: 455.2
Fat: 2.8 g
Saturated fat: 1.7 g
Carbohydrate: 66.5 g
Total sugars: 14.6 g
Protein: 41.0 g
Sodium: 182 mg
Cholesterol: 68.5 mg
Dietary fiber: 7.1 g

Pecan Orange Roughy with Cranberry Compote

Ingredients for cranberry compote:

1 package (6 ounces) dried cranberries
1/3 cup orange juice
2/3 cup water
1/4 teaspoon each: ground cinnamon, ground ginger, ground cloves, and ground nutmeg

Ingredients for orange roughy:

1-1/2 cup pecans
2 tablespoons flour
1 egg plus 1 egg white
2 tablespoons water
6 orange roughy filets (about 1-3/4 to 2 pounds)
1 teaspoon trans-fat–free butter, cut into tiny pieces

Preparation: Cranberry compote: Place all compote ingredients in a medium skillet and heat over medium-high heat, stirring frequently. Heat about 10 minutes, until liquid boils off and mixture is of a sauce consistency. Let cool and refrigerate.

Orange roughy: Preheat oven to 425°F. Place pecans and flour in bowl of food processor or blender; pulse or mix until just finely chopped. Do not overprocess (if nut liquid is forming, you have overprocessed). Place pecan mixture in a shallow dish or plate. In another shallow dish, whisk egg, egg white, and water. Dip each fish fillet first in egg mixture, then in pecan mixture, pressing to make pecan coating stick. Spray a 13x9-inch pan or baking dish large enough to hold all the fish with nonstick cooking spray. Place fillets in single layer in pan. Dot with butter. Bake 15 to 20 minutes, or until fish begins to flake with a fork. Serve with cranberry compote on top or on the side. Makes 6 servings.

Nutritional information per serving:
Calories: 390.1
Fat: 18.5 g
Saturated fat: 2.2 g
Carbohydrate: 29.9 g
Total sugars: 20.2 g
Protein: 26.0 g
Sodium: 117 mg
Cholesterol: 62.5 mg
Dietary fiber: 3.6 g

Pork Chops with Cherry Sauce

Pork is one of those protein sources of which you should limit your consumption. However, when you choose to eat pork chops, preparing them with recipes such as this low-calorie one will maximize your antioxidant intake. This is one of my parents' favorite dishes.

Ingredients:
4 (about 3/4 pound total weight) boneless center-cut pork loin chops, medium thickness
1/2 cup bottled reduced-fat balsamic vinaigrette
Nonstick cooking spray, olive-oil flavor
1/2 cup shallots, thinly sliced
1/2 cup low-sodium chicken broth
1/2 cup dried cherries
Salt and freshly ground pepper

Preparation: Place pork and vinaigrette in shallow baking dish and turn once to coat; marinate 10 to 15 minutes. Spray a medium skillet with nonstick cooking spray and place over medium heat. Lift pork, shake off excess marinade, and transfer to skillet, reserving marinade in dish. Sauté pork chops until brown, about 3 to 4 minutes per side. Transfer chops to a plate. Add shallots to skillet and stir until softened, about 1 minute. Add chicken broth, cherries, and reserved marinade. Bring to a low boil. Return chops to skillet and simmer until pork is cooked thoroughly, cherries are tender, and the sauce has slightly reduced—about 3 minutes per side. Season with salt and pepper as desired. Serve chops on dinner plates, topped with cherry sauce. Makes 4 servings.

This recipe's allicin (shallots) and anthocyanins (cherries) may help prevent the following cancers: **lung and breast.**

Nutritional information per serving:
Calories: 248.9
Fat: 9.3 g
Saturated fat: 2.5 g
Carbohydrate: 20.9 g
Total sugars: 15.0 g
Protein: 20.4 g
Sodium: 568 mg
Cholesterol: 48.4 mg
Dietary fiber: 1.0 g

Raspberry-Mango Tilapia

This low-fat dish has the tropical flavors of mangos and carries the sweet antioxidant punch of delicious raspberries. Pair it with the Orange-Almond Rice (page 88) and some steamed broccoli for a perfect meal.

Ingredients:
4 medium tilapia fillets (about 1-1/2 pounds total)
1 cup fresh raspberries
1 mango, peeled and diced
1 jalapeño pepper, seeded and chopped
1 tablespoon fresh cilantro, chopped

Preparation: Heat oven to 450°F. Place tilapia fillets on a non-stick baking sheet or baking sheet lined with foil and lightly sprayed with nonstick cooking spray. Bake 10 minutes or until fish flakes easily with fork. Meanwhile, combine remaining ingredients in a medium nonmetallic bowl. Divide fish among 4 dinner plates and top with raspberry mango salsa. Makes 4 servings.

This recipe's vitamin C (raspberries) and beta carotene (mango) may help prevent the following cancers: **pancreas and lung.**

Nutritional information per serving:
Calories: 270.2
Fat: 5.4 g
Saturated fat: 1.0 g
Carbohydrate: 12.7 g
Total sugars: 9.1 g
Protein: 42.7 g
Sodium: 121 mg
Cholesterol: 110 mg
Dietary fiber: 3.1 g

Red Snapper with Ginger Cabbage and Apples

This recipe's kaempferol (cabbage) and quercetin (apple) may help prevent the following cancers: **ovarian and breast.**

Chemicals in cabbage called indoles may be able to prevent certain tumors by triggering the body to make enzymes that block new cancer-cell growth.

Ingredients:
Nonstick cooking spray
2 tablespoons fresh ginger, peeled and thinly sliced
4 cups packed red cabbage, shredded or thinly sliced
1/2 teaspoon salt, divided
1 tablespoon cider vinegar
1 teaspoon sugar
1 Granny Smith apple, cored and sliced
4 red snapper fillets (about 6 ounces each)
1 cup nonfat (skim) milk
1 cup fine whole-grain breadcrumbs
1 tablespoon fresh parsley, finely chopped

Preparation: Place a large skillet or fry pan over medium heat and spray with nonstick cooking spray. Add ginger and sauté about 2 minutes. Add cabbage and 1/4 teaspoon salt. Reduce heat to low, cover and cook, stirring occasionally, 20 minutes. Stir in vinegar and sugar; transfer to bowl to cool. Place sliced apple in a microwave-safe dish, cover with waxed paper and microwave on high for 1 minute or until softened. Set aside. Cut each snapper fillet crosswise diagonally into 3 strips; soak fish strips in milk. In a shallow bowl, combine breadcrumbs, parsley, and remaining 1/4 teaspoon salt. Wipe out skillet, spray with nonstick cooking spray, and place over medium-high heat. Dip fish strips into breadcrumb mixture to coat; place in skillet and sauté 6 to 8 minutes, turning to brown evenly and cook through. To serve, toss apple slices with cabbage; mound mixture in center of each of 4 dinner plates. Arrange fish strips around each mound of apple mixture. Makes 4 servings.

Nutritional information per serving:
Calories: 342.3
Fat: 3.9 g
Saturated fat: 1.0 g
Carbohydrate: 34.8 g
Total sugars: 6.4 g
Protein: 42.0 g
Sodium: 652 mg
Cholesterol: 64.2 mg
Dietary fiber: 3.4 g

Roasted Mediterranean Shrimp and Orzo

My friend, Angela Razo, is a fantastic cook, and this is one of her very own recipes. She likes it best when refrigerated and served chilled.

Ingredients:
8 ounces (1/2 pound) dry whole-wheat orzo pasta
1/3 cup lemon juice (preferably freshly squeezed)
1/3 cup extra-virgin olive oil, plus 2 teaspoons for drizzling
1/2 teaspoon salt, plus more for seasoning
1 teaspoon pepper, plus more for seasoning
1-1/2 pounds large fresh shrimp, shelled and deveined
2/3 cup scallions, minced
1/3 cup fresh dill, chopped
1/2 cup fresh parsley, chopped
1 medium cucumber, peeled and finely diced
1/3 cup red onion, finely diced
6 ounces reduced-fat feta cheese, crumbled

Preparation: Preheat oven to 400°F. Place a large stockpot of water over medium-high heat and bring to a boil. Add orzo; reduce heat to medium and cook 9 to 11 minutes, until tender. Meanwhile, combine lemon juice, 1/3 cup olive oil, 1/2 teaspoon salt, and teaspoon pepper in a small bowl. Drain orzo and place in a large bowl. Add lemon-juice–oil mixture and stir. Place cleaned shrimp on nonstick baking sheet; drizzle with remaining olive oil and season with salt and pepper, if desired. Roast in oven 5 to 6 minutes, until cooked through. Add shrimp, scallions, dill, parsley, cucumber, onion, and feta to orzo and stir. Serve immediately or refrigerate and serve. Makes 6 servings.

This recipe's vitamin C (lemon juice) and allicin (onions) may help prevent the following cancers: **lung and stomach.**

Nutritional information per serving:
Calories: 333.9
Fat: 17.1 g
Saturated fat: 4.2 g
Carbohydrate: 32.4 g
Total sugars: 2.1 g
Protein: 12.6 g
Sodium: 396 mg
Cholesterol: 20.4mg
Dietary fiber: 2.9 g

Seared Asian Tuna

Tuna is low in fat, but rich in healthy omega-3 and omega-6 fatty acids. Like salmon, it is also one of few natural sources of vitamin D. I often serve this dish on a bed of baby greens or wilted spinach.

Ingredients:
3 tablespoons light soy sauce
1 teaspoon sugar
1/8 teaspoon crushed red pepper flakes
1/2 cup fat-free, reduced-sodium chicken broth
1 teaspoon sesame oil
1 green onion, chopped (white and green parts)
2 large garlic cloves, minced
4 tuna steaks, about 1 inch thick, approximately 4 to 5 ounces each
Salt and freshly ground black pepper
1 tablespoon extra-virgin olive oil

Preparation: In a small bowl, stir together soy sauce, sugar, red pepper flakes, and chicken broth until blended. In a small saucepan, heat sesame oil. Stir in green onion and garlic and cook, stirring, about 1 minute. Add soy-sauce mixture; simmer until it reduces to approximately 1/3 cup. Meanwhile, sprinkle fish with salt and black pepper. Heat olive oil in a large pan over moderately high heat. Add the tuna and cook until brown, about 3 minutes. Turn and cook tuna until done to your taste. Many people prefer tuna slightly pink in the center. When done, cut tuna into slices and serve with sauce. Makes 4 servings.

This recipe's allicin (garlic) and vitamin D (tuna) may help prevent the following cancers: **stomach and kidney.**

Nutritional information per serving:
Calories: 177.5
Fat: 5.5 g
Saturated fat: 0.9 g
Carbohydrate: 3.0 g
Total sugars: 1.4 g
Protein: 29.0 g
Sodium: 554 mg
Cholesterol: 60 mg
Dietary fiber: < 1 g

Seared Scallops with Tropical Orange Salsa

Orange-colored fruits, like the sweet and juicy mangos and papaya in this recipe, contain beta-carotene and lycopene, two antioxidants that have been shown to decrease free-radical damage that can contribute to the development of some cancers.

This recipe's beta carotene (mango) and vitamin C (orange juice) may help prevent the following cancers: **skin and lung.**

Ingredients:
3 cups orange juice
1/3 cup red onion, minced
2/3 cup fresh mango, diced into small pieces
1/2 cup fresh papaya, diced into small pieces
1/3 cup fresh pineapple, diced into small pieces (or canned tidbits, drained)
1 jalapeño pepper, seeded and minced
2 teaspoons fresh cilantro, chopped
3/4 teaspoon salt, divided
24 medium sea scallops (about 3/4 pound), muscle tabs removed
1/2 teaspoon black pepper
1 tablespoon olive oil

Preparation: In a saucepan over medium-high heat, place orange juice and heat about 20 to 25 minutes, until it reduces to about 2/3 cup. Combine onion, mango, papaya, pineapple, jalapeño pepper, cilantro, and 1/4 teaspoon salt in a bowl and toss. Add 2 tablespoons reduced orange juice and toss again. Season scallops with remaining salt and the pepper. In a non-stick skillet over medium heat, heat olive oil and add scallops. Sear first side 2 to 3 minutes until golden brown; turn and heat second side again 2 to 3 minutes until cooked through. On 4 separate dinner plates, mound 1/4 of the salsa in middle, surround with 6 scallops in a circle, and divide and pour remaining orange-juice reduction over scallops. Makes 4 servings.

Nutritional information per serving:
Calories: 255.8
Fat: 5.0 g
Saturated fat: 0.4 g
Carbohydrate: 28.9 g
Total sugars: 22.6 g
Protein: 23.8 g
Sodium: 520 mg
Cholesterol: 55 mg
Dietary fiber: 1.7 g

Spa Chicken with Watercress and Sun-Dried Tomatoes

This dish is so incredibly delicious that you will never realize how low in fat and healthy it is. It presents beautifully, so try it for a dinner party sometime.

Ingredients:
1 tablespoon olive oil
2 tablespoons shallots, finely chopped
1 cup white wine
2 tablespoons fresh lemon juice
2 tablespoons fresh tarragon, chopped
1/2 cup sun-dried tomatoes, rehydrated and chopped
4 boneless, skinless chicken breasts (about 5 to 6 ounces each)
Salt and freshly ground pepper to taste
1-1/2 cups water or more to cook the chicken
1 bunch watercress, washed and stemmed

Preparation: Heat olive oil in a large soup pot over medium heat. Add shallots and cook 3 minutes. Increase heat to high; add wine, lemon juice, tarragon, and sun-dried tomatoes; simmer 1 minute. Season chicken breasts with salt and pepper as desired and add them to pan with enough water to cover them. Bring liquid to a boil and adjust heat so that mixture simmers. Cook 10 to 12 minutes, until chicken is just cooked through. Remove chicken from pan and set aside. Continue to simmer cooking liquid until it has reduced by half. Divide watercress among 4 plates. Place chicken on top of watercress, garnish with sun-dried tomatoes, and drizzle hot reduction over chicken. Makes 4 servings.

Nutritional information per serving:
Calories: 261. 6
Fat: 5.2 g
Saturated fat: 0.3 g
Carbohydrate: 6.2 g
Total sugars: 2.7 g
Protein: 47.5 g
Sodium: 263 mg
Cholesterol: 95 mg
Dietary fiber: 0.9 g

Spaghetti Squash with Lamb and Brown Rice

Most lamb dishes contain lots of meat and little else, except perhaps a rich sauce. This dish is made with a savory vegetable and whole-grain base and flavored with lean lamb meat, keeping it healthy and relatively low in calories and fat.

Ingredients:
1 spaghetti squash (about 3 to 4 pounds)
1/2 pound lean ground lamb
1/3 cup celery, chopped
1/2 cup red onions, chopped
3 garlic cloves, minced
2 tablespoons fresh basil, coarsely chopped
2 tablespoons fresh rosemary
8 ounces thick tomato sauce
1/3 cup cooked brown rice
3 tablespoons crumbled reduced-fat feta cheese

Preparation: Preheat oven to 350°F. Cut spaghetti squash in half and place in baking dish, flesh side down. Add about 1/2 inch of water and bake approximately 1 hour or until squash is tender. While squash is cooking, begin browning meat in a large nonstick skillet. Add celery, onion, and garlic. When meat is cooked through and vegetables are tender, add fresh basil and rosemary; cook 2 to 3 minutes. Gradually stir in tomato sauce and cooked rice. Serve spaghetti squash topped with sauce and crumbled, reduced-fat feta cheese. Makes 6 servings.

This recipe's luteolin (celery) and lycopene (tomato paste) may help prevent the following cancers: **ovarian and pancreas.**

Nutritional information per serving:
Calories: 205.2
Fat: 7.2 g
Saturated fat: 4.0 g
Carbohydrate: 25.4 g
Total sugars: 2.4 g
Protein: 9.7 g
Sodium: 214 mg
Cholesterol: 25.6 mg
Dietary fiber: 1.4 g

Spice-rubbed Filet Mignon with Grilled Tomatoes

These filets are great if you top them with a few tablespoons of the Blueberry Bourbon Sauce (page 54). You can work out the timing of this dish so that both the tomatoes and filet finish cooking at the same time, or cook the tomatoes first and then grill the steak. For the healthiest diet, only eat grilled red meat occasionally.

Grilled Tomatoes Ingredients:
4 large, ripe but firm tomatoes
Kosher or sea salt as needed
1 tablespoon red wine vinegar
2-1/2 tablespoons extra-virgin olive oil, divided
2 small garlic cloves, minced
1 small shallot, minced
Salt and freshly ground black pepper
1/2 tablespoon fresh parsley, chopped
1/2 tablespoon fresh basil, chopped

Filet Mignon Ingredients:
1 tablespoon extra-virgin olive oil
1 tablespoon fresh thyme, chopped
1/2 teaspoon chili powder
1/2 teaspoon salt
1/2 teaspoon coarsely ground black pepper
1 pound filet mignon, 1-1/2 to 2 inches thick, trimmed of fat and cut into 4 portions

Preparation: Preheat gas grill to high or prepare a medium-hot charcoal fire. Remove green stems from tomatoes, but do not core. Cut each tomato horizontally in half, turn over and gently remove seeds. Sprinkle cut side with kosher or sea salt. Set cut side down on a wire rack and let drain 30 minutes. In a small bowl, whisk together vinegar, 2 tablespoons olive oil, garlic, and minced shallot. Season as desired with salt and pepper. Lightly oil drained tomatoes with remaining 1/2 tablespoon olive oil. Arrange tomatoes cut side down on grate; grill, turning halfway through grilling, until skin begins to soften and blister, about 7 to 9 minutes. Add chopped parsley and basil to vinaigrette, transfer tomatoes to serving platter, and drizzle with vinaigrette. (Tomatoes can be served warm or at room temperature.) Combine oil, thyme, chili powder, salt, and pepper in a small bowl. Rub mixture on all sides of steaks. Grill steaks 4 to 5 minutes per side for medium-rare doneness. Let steaks stand 5 minutes before serving. Serve each filet mignon with 2 thick grilled tomato slices. Makes 4 servings of 1 steak plus 2 grilled tomato halves.

Nutritional information per serving:
Calories: 332.6
Fat: 21.8 g
Saturated fat: 5.9 g
Carbohydrate: 8.7 g
Total sugars: 4.8 g
Protein: 25.4 g
Sodium: 365 mg
Cholesterol: 70.2 mg
Dietary fiber: 2.5 g

Sweet Potato and Peanut Stew

This delightful, satisfying stew contains almost half of your daily fiber requirements. You can serve the stew alone or over couscous or cooked brown rice.

Ingredients:
1 tablespoon extra-virgin olive oil
1 large yellow onion, chopped
1 medium red bell pepper, seeded and chopped
2 garlic cloves, minced
2 teaspoons light brown sugar
1 teaspoon fresh ginger, peeled and grated
1/2 teaspoon ground cumin
1/2 teaspoon ground cinnamon
1/4 teaspoon cayenne pepper
1-1/2 pounds sweet potatoes, peeled and diced into 1/2-inch chunks
1 can (14-1/2 ounces) diced tomatoes
1-1/2 cups low-sodium vegetable stock
1 cup canned red kidney beans, drained and rinsed
1 cup garbanzo beans, drained and rinsed
2 tablespoons smooth natural peanut butter
1/2 cup chopped raw or dry-roasted peanuts

Preparation: Heat olive oil in a large saucepan over medium heat. Add onion and cook until soft and translucent, about 5 minutes. Add bell pepper and garlic; cover and cook until softened, about 5 minutes. Stir in brown sugar, ginger, cumin, cinnamon, and cayenne and cook, stirring, about 30 seconds. Add sweet potatoes and stir until coated with onion-spice mixture. Stir in tomatoes and stock. Bring to a boil; reduce heat to low, and simmer until vegetables are soft, about 30 minutes. About 10 minutes before end of cooking time, add kidney beans, garbanzo beans, and peanut butter and stir until evenly distributed; simmer until heated through. If a thicker consistency is desired, purée 1 cup of stew in a blender or food processor, then stir back into pot. Sprinkle with chopped peanuts and serve. Makes 4 large servings.

This recipe's beta carotene (sweet potatoes) and folate (garbanzo beans) may help prevent the following cancers: **lung and colon.**

Nutritional information per serving:
Calories: 432.2
Fat: 12.2 g
Saturated fat: 1.9 g
Carbohydrate: 62.7 g
Total sugars: 13.9 g
Protein: 17.9 g
Sodium: 382 mg
Cholesterol: 0 mg
Dietary fiber: 18.2 g

Swordfish with Grapefruit and Tequila Salsa

Ingredients:
4 large ruby red grapefruit
2 limes
1/2 green chile, seeded and thinly sliced
1 green onion, finely chopped
2 tablespoons fresh coriander, chopped
1 tablespoon sugar
3 tablespoons tequila
4 large swordfish steaks
2 tablespoons extra-virgin olive oil
Salt and freshly ground black pepper to taste

Preparation: Use a zester or paring knife to remove zest from grapefruits and 1 lime. Remove all the pith from grapefruits and divide each into segments. Squeeze or juice zested lime and place lime juice in a small bowl. Mix grapefruit, citrus zest, chile, onion, coriander, sugar, and tequila with lime juice; set aside. Preheat a broiler. Juice second lime; combine lime juice with olive oil, salt, and pepper as desired and brush both sides of fish with mixture. Place swordfish about 4 inches beneath pre-heated broiler and cook about 4 to 5 minutes on each side. Serve each swordfish fillet with grapefruit-tequila salsa. Makes 4 servings.

Nutritional information per serving:
Calories: 304.0
Fat: 10.8 g
Saturated fat: 1.9 g
Carbohydrate: 32.8 g
Total sugars: 21.0 g
Protein: 18.9 g
Sodium: 78 mg
Cholesterol: 33.2 mg
Dietary fiber: 5.1 g

Tilapia with Warm Cherry Tomatoes and Olives

Tilapia is a wonderful, healthy fish that is inexpensive and incredibly easy to cook. The fish is low in fat, high in protein, and mild in flavor. Although this attractive dish tastes fantastic, it only takes about 15 minutes to prepare from start to finish.

Ingredients:
2 tablespoons olive oil
1-1/2 pounds tilapia fillets
Salt and pepper to taste
2 cups (1 pint) cherry tomatoes, halved
1/4 cup fresh parsley, chopped
1/3 cup pitted kalamata olives, halved
Juice of 1 lemon (or 1 tablespoon bottled lemon juice)
1 tablespoon grated Parmesan cheese

Preparation: In a large heavy skillet, heat oil over medium-high heat. Add fish and season with salt and pepper; sauté, turning once, until fish turns white throughout and flakes easily, about 3 minutes per side. Transfer fish to a dish or platter with sides. In same skillet, add tomatoes, parsley, and olives; sauté for several minutes until tomatoes are soft. Season sauce with salt, pepper, and lemon juice. Pour sauce over fish, and top with a sprinkle of Parmesan cheese. Serve immediately. Makes 4 servings.

This recipe's lycopene (tomatoes) and vitamin C (lemon juice) may help prevent the following cancers: **prostate and esophageal.**

Nutritional information per serving:
Calories: 289.4
Fat: 13.4 g
Saturated fat: 1.8 g
Carbohydrate: 6.7 g
Total sugars: 2.3 g
Protein: 35.5 g
Sodium: 444 mg
Cholesterol: 86.4 mg
Dietary fiber: 1.1 g

Tofu-Stuffed Eggplant

Even carnivores will love this dish. It is a great way to include some soy isoflavones and healthy whole grains in your diet. Many health experts recommend foregoing red meat from time to time and eating more plant-based main dishes.

Ingredients:
3 medium eggplants
3 tablespoons olive oil
8 ounces white mushrooms, washed very well and chopped
1 medium red bell pepper, seeded and chopped
4 garlic cloves, finely chopped
2 cups yellow onion, finely chopped
1/2 cup extra-firm tofu
2 cups cooked brown rice
1/4 teaspoon dried oregano
Pinch of salt and pepper
1/4 cup shredded part-skim provolone cheese (soy cheese can be substituted)

Preparation: Preheat oven to 375°F. Cut eggplants in half lengthwise and scoop out the insides with a spoon. Leave a layer of eggplant about 1 inch thick so that each eggplant half becomes a bowl. Chop removed eggplant into small pieces. Place a large nonstick skillet over medium heat and add olive oil. Add mushrooms, pepper, and garlic and heat, stirring occasionally, about 5 minutes. Add chopped eggplant and heat 10 minutes. Add tofu and continue to cook over medium heat 5 minutes. Mix rice into the cooked vegetable mixture and season with oregano, salt, and pepper. Place eggplant on a large baking sheet or dish. Scoop the mixture into the eggplant bowls and bake 25 minutes on center rack. Sprinkle cheese evenly on top of each eggplant bowl and bake another 5 to 7 minutes. Makes 6 servings, 1/2 eggplant each.

Nutritional information per serving:
Calories: 264.5
Fat: 5.7 g
Saturated fat: 2.4 g
Carbohydrate: 40.5 g
Total sugars: 10.3 g
Protein: 12.8 g
Sodium: 140 mg
Cholesterol: 10.2 mg
Dietary fiber: 12.1 g

Vegan Tofu and Kale 'Quiche'

Full-fat tofu makes this a very tasty dish, although the low-fat variety can be substituted. If you are not vegan and enjoy dairy products, feel free to substitute some shredded provolone or reduced-fat cheddar for the soy cheese.

Ingredients:
1 teaspoon canola oil
1/2 cup green onions, white and green parts, chopped
8 ounces firm tofu, crumbled
8 ounces soft tofu, crumbled
1 cup kale, leaves and stems, finely chopped
1 cup grated soy cheese, any flavor
1/2 cup red bell pepper, diced
1/8 teaspoon salt
1/2 teaspoon turmeric
9-inch whole-wheat prepared pie shell

Preparation: Preheat oven to 350°F. Place a medium fry pan or skillet over medium heat and add canola oil. Add green onions and sauté about 3 minutes. Add all remaining ingredients (except pie shell) and sauté until kale begins to wilt and cheese starts to melt, about 4 to 5 minutes. Place pie shell on a nonstick baking sheet. Transfer skillet ingredients to pie shell and bake 40 to 45 minutes. Let stand at least 10 minutes before serving. Makes 6 servings.

This recipe's isoflavones (tofu) and lutein (kale) may help prevent the following cancers: **breast and ovarian.**

Nutritional information per serving:
Calories: 315.6
Fat: 18.4 g
Saturated fat: 1.9 g
Carbohydrate: 18.0 g
Total sugars: 1.0 g
Protein: 19.5 g
Sodium: 457 mg
Cholesterol: 0 mg
Dietary fiber: 3.3 g

Whole-Grain Spaghetti and Turkey Meatballs

This is a great family meal that even kids will love, and they won't even realize how healthy it is. You can add any vegetables that you like to the sauce, such as broccoli and peppers, depending on your personal taste.

Ingredients:
1 pound lean ground turkey
3 tablespoons red onion, minced
3 tablespoons fine whole-wheat breadcrumbs
3 small garlic cloves, minced
2 tablespoons fresh parsley, chopped
1/4 teaspoon each: salt and pepper
Nonstick cooking spray
1/4 cup baby carrots, diced
1/4 cup white mushrooms, thinly sliced
1/4 cup yellow onion, diced
2 cups tomato sauce (preferably a jarred organic brand)
8 ounces whole-wheat angel hair or vermicelli
2 tablespoons reduced-fat feta cheese, divided

Preparation: Combine turkey, onion, breadcrumbs, garlic, parsley, salt, and pepper in a large bowl and stir until evenly and well distributed. Form mixture into 12 medium-size meatballs. Place a medium nonstick skillet over medium heat and spray with nonstick cooking spray. Add baby carrots, mushrooms, and onion; heat, stirring, about 3 to 4 minutes, until mushrooms have softened and onion is translucent. (Alternatively, on a microwaveable plate or dish, microwave baby carrots, mushrooms, and sweet onion for about 35 to 45 seconds until somewhat soft.) Place a large saucepan over medium heat and add tomato sauce and warm vegetables. Bring to a boil and add turkey meatballs. Lower heat and cover; cook about 12 to 15 minutes. Meanwhile, cook pasta as directed by package; drain and place on 4 dinner plates. Add sauce and 3 meatballs to each plate and sprinkle with 1/2 tablespoon feta cheese. Makes 4 servings.

Nutritional information per serving:
Calories: 427.7
Fat: 10.5 g
Saturated fat: 2.9 g
Carbohydrate: 51.0 g
Total sugars: 7.2 g
Protein: 32.3 g
Sodium: 808 mg
Cholesterol: 81.3 mg
Dietary fiber: 8.3 g

Whole-Wheat Penne with Lemon-Garlic Chicken

This is a perfect warm- or cold-weather healthy dinner. Serve it with a salad of mixed baby greens, sliced strawberries, and a light balsamic or citrus vinaigrette.

Ingredients:
8 ounces dry whole-wheat penne
1 pound boneless skinless chicken breasts, cut into strips
Chili powder as needed
1 tablespoon extra-virgin olive oil
1 small yellow onion, chopped
2 garlic cloves, minced
1/4 cup lemon juice
2 medium tomatoes, seeded and chopped
1/4 cup water
Pinch of red pepper flakes
Salt and freshly ground pepper

Preparation: In a large stockpot, cook dry pasta according to package directions. Drain and set aside. Meanwhile, sprinkle strips of chicken with chili powder and place a large skillet over medium heat. Add oil and cook onion, garlic, and chicken; turn chicken until both sides are browned. Add lemon juice, tomatoes, water, and red pepper flakes; cook 2 to 3 minutes. Add cooked penne; heat through. Season with salt and pepper as desired. Divide among 4 dinner plates. Serve hot. The whole dish or leftovers can also be refrigerated and served cold or at room temperature. Makes 4 servings.

> This recipe's selenium (penne) and quercetin (onion) may help prevent the following cancers: **endometrial and colon.**

Nutritional information per serving:
Calories: 375.7
Fat: 6.1 g
Saturated fat: 0.3 g
Carbohydrate: 47 g
Total sugars: 3.1 g
Protein: 33.2 g
Sodium: 247 mg
Cholesterol: 60.8 mg
Dietary fiber: 7.2 g

BEVERAGES

This section includes recipes for drinks that are both delicious and good for you. Any dairy ingredient can be substituted with a soy version, and vice versa. If you are using frozen fruit rather than fresh, allow fruit to thaw a bit before preparing the beverage to achieve the best consistency and flavor. When using soy milk, choose a brand of soy milk that is fortified with calcium and vitamin D to get the greatest health benefits.

Banana-Berry Breakfast Shake

The night before preparing this shake, wrap sliced banana in plastic wrap or place in a freezer storage bag and freeze.

Ingredients:
1 medium banana, sliced into chunks and frozen
1/4 cup fresh or frozen unsweetened blueberries
1/4 cup fresh or frozen unsweetened raspberries
1-1/2 cups low-fat (1%) milk
1/2 teaspoon vanilla extract
1/4 teaspoon almond extract
Pinch of ground cinnamon

Preparation: In a blender, combine all ingredients except cinnamon. Blend 20 seconds or more until smooth. Pour into glasses and garnish with a sprinkle of ground cinnamon. Makes 2 servings.

> This recipe's anthocyanins (berries) and calcium (milk) may help prevent the following cancers: **colon and breast.**

Nutritional information per serving:
Calories: 176.8
Fat: 3.2 g
Saturated fat: 2.0 g
Carbohydrate: 28.2 g
Total sugars: 24.0 g
Protein: 8.8 g
Sodium: 125 mg
Cholesterol: 10 mg
Dietary fiber: 1.5 g

Citrus Shake

Ingredients:
12 ounces (1-1/2 cups) calcium-enriched orange juice
2 small ripe bananas
1/2 cup low-fat vanilla yogurt
1-1/2 teaspoons vanilla extract

Preparation: Combine all ingredients in blender until smooth. Pour into glass and serve immediately. Makes 2 servings.

> This recipe's vitamin C (orange juice) and calcium (yogurt) may help prevent the following cancers: **prostate and colon.**

Nutritional information per serving:
Calories: 234.4
Fat: 0.8 g
Saturated fat: 0.5 g
Carbohydrate: 51.7 g
Total sugars: 32.9 g
Protein: 5.1 g
Sodium: 38 mg
Cholesterol: 2.8 mg
Dietary fiber: 2.6 g

Cranberry Cocktail

Ingredients:
2 cups 100% cranberry juice, chilled
1 cup unsweetened apple juice, chilled
4 tablespoons fresh lime juice, chilled
2 tablespoons sugar
1 cup unsweetened pink grapefruit juice, chilled
Fresh lime slices

Preparation: Combine all ingredients in a pitcher, stirring well. Serve over ice and garnish with fresh lime slices. Makes 4 servings.

Nutritional information per serving:
Calories: 109.2
Fat: 0 g
Saturated fat: 0 g
Carbohydrate: 27.0 g
Total sugars: 22.8 g
Protein: 0.3 g
Sodium: 8 mg
Cholesterol: 0 mg
Dietary fiber: 0 g

Dairy-free Chocolate-Almond-Banana Shake

This recipe's isoflavones (soy milk) and epicatechins (cocoa) may help prevent the following cancers: **breast and colon.**

Ingredients:
4 cups frozen ripe bananas, cut into chunks
1 cup regular soy milk
3 tablespoons unsweetened cocoa powder
3 packets Splenda® or other low-calorie sweetener
1 teaspoon almond extract

Preparation: Remove frozen banana chunks from the freezer and allow them to thaw 5 to 10 minutes to soften slightly. Place banana chunks in a blender along with remaining ingredients, and process 2 to 3 minutes to thoroughly purée and blend flavors. Serve immediately. Makes 4 servings.

Nutritional information per serving:
Calories: 200.3
Fat: 3.1 g
Saturated fat: 0.3 g
Carbohydrate: 39.0 g
Total sugars: 36.0 g
Protein: 4.1 g
Sodium: 10 mg
Cholesterol: 0 mg
Dietary fiber: 4.0 g

Georgia Peach Cooler

Ingredients:
4 cups silken tofu, drained
2 cups fresh or frozen peaches, sliced or chopped
1 cup apple juice, chilled
1 ripe banana, cut into chunks
Juice of 1 lime

Preparation: Place all ingredients in a blender and process until smooth. Serve immediately in tall glasses. Makes 4 servings.

This recipe's quercetin (apple juice) and isoflavones (tofu) may help prevent the following cancers: **lung and breast.**

Nutritional information per serving:
Calories: 186.6
Fat: 5.0 g
Saturated fat: trace
Carbohydrate: 24.7 g
Total sugars: 14.5 g
Protein: 10.2 g
Sodium: <1 mg
Cholesterol: 0 mg
Dietary fiber: 3.3 g

Ginger-Lemon Iced Green Tea

Ingredients:
2 cups water
1 cup sugar or Splenda® low-calorie sweetener
1 teaspoon ground ginger
1-1/2 teaspoons grated lemon peel
6 green-tea bags
4 teaspoons fresh lemon juice
Sparkling or seltzer water as needed

Preparation: Add water, sugar or Splenda®, ground ginger, and lemon peel to medium saucepan and bring to boil over medium heat. Reduce heat to where it sustains a gentle boil and cook about 7 to 8 minutes. Remove from heat and add green-tea bags. Steep tea mixture 10 minutes, stirring or dunking tea bags frequently. Remove tea bags and stir lemon juice into tea liquid. Cover and refrigerate (lasts for up to 2 weeks). To make a cup of iced tea, pour 1/4 cup of concentrated tea mixture into a tall glass and stir in 3/4 cup of sparkling or seltzer water. Add ice cubes and serve. Makes 1-1/2 cups of syrup (enough for about 6 glasses of iced tea).

Nutritional information per serving prepared with Splenda® or other low-calorie sweetener:
Calories: 2, Fat: 0 g, Saturated fat: 0 g, Carbohydrate: 0.6 g, Total sugars: 0 g, Protein: 0 g, Sodium: 0 mg, Cholesterol: 0 mg, Dietary fiber: 0.1 g

This recipe's catechins (green tea) and pectin (lemon peel) may help prevent the following cancers: **breast and lung.**

Nutritional information per serving:
Calories: 126
Fat: 0 g
Saturated fat: 0 g
Carbohydrate: 32.0 g
Total sugars: 31.2 g
Protein: 0 g
Sodium: 0 mg
Cholesterol: 0 mg
Dietary fiber: 0 g

Mocha Shake

If you do not like low-calorie sweeteners, simply substitute 2 teaspoons of sugar.

Ingredients:
4 teaspoons unsweetened cocoa powder
2 packets Splenda® or other low-calorie sweetener
2 teaspoons instant coffee
1/2 cup low-fat milk
2/3 cup low-fat vanilla frozen yogurt
4 ice cubes, crushed

Preparation: In a small bowl, combine cocoa, Splenda® (or sugar) and instant coffee. Add milk and stir until smooth. Transfer to a blender, and add frozen yogurt and crushed ice cubes. Blend for about 1 minute or until frothy. Makes 2 servings.

This recipe's calcium (milk) and catechins (cocoa) may help prevent the following cancers: **colon and breast.**

Nutritional information per serving, prepared with Splenda®:
Calories: 137.5
Fat: 4.7 g
Saturated fat: 3.0 g
Carbohydrate: 17.8 g
Total sugars: 15.0 g
Protein: 6.0 g
Sodium: 51 mg
Cholesterol: 12.5 mg
Dietary fiber: 0 g

Orange Snow Frost

Ingredients:
2-1/2 cups calcium-fortified orange juice
1 cup low-fat vanilla frozen yogurt
8 ice cubes
1/4 teaspoon ground cinnamon
1/2 teaspoon almond extract
4 long strips of orange peel for garnish

Preparation: In a blender, combine orange juice, frozen yogurt, ice cubes, cinnamon, and almond extract, and process on low-medium speed until smooth. Pour into 4 martini glasses or low tumblers and garnish with orange peel. Makes 4 servings.

This recipe's vitamin C (orange juice) and calcium (frozen yogurt) may help prevent the following cancers: **lung and breast.**

Nutritional information per serving:
Calories: 131.0
Fat: 1.4 g
Saturated fat: 0.8 g
Carbohydrate: 26.2 g
Total sugars: 2.5 g
Protein: 3.4 g
Sodium: 32 mg
Cholesterol: 5.0 mg
Dietary fiber: 1.0 g

Peppermint Hot Chocolate

Ingredients:
3 tablespoons unsweetened cocoa powder
2 tablespoons plus 2 teaspoons Splenda®
2 cups low-fat milk
1/4 teaspoon peppermint extract

Preparation: In a small saucepan, whisk together cocoa and Splenda®. Gradually add milk to cocoa mixture and whisk until well blended. Cook over medium-low heat until thoroughly heated, stirring occasionally. Stir in peppermint extract and serve immediately. Makes 2 servings.

> This recipe's catechins (cocoa) and vitamin D (milk) may help prevent the following cancers: **prostate and colon.**

Nutritional information per serving:
Calories: 153
Fat: 5.0 g
Saturated fat: 1.0 g
Carbohydrate: 17.5 g
Total sugars: 14 g
Protein: 9.5 g
Sodium: 0 mg
Cholesterol: 10 mg
Dietary fiber: 0 g

Vanilla-Almond Soy Nog

Ingredients:
1 quart light vanilla-flavored soy milk, chilled
6 ounces silken-style tofu, extra firm
3 tablespoons honey
1 teaspoon vanilla extract
2 teaspoons almond extract
1-1/2 teaspoons cinnamon
1/4 teaspoon nutmeg

Preparation: In a blender, combine all ingredients and blend until smooth. Chill before serving. Makes 6 servings.

> This recipe's calcium (soy milk) and isoflavones (tofu) may help prevent the following cancers: **breast and prostate.**

Nutritional information per serving:
Calories: 98.6
Fat: 3.8 g
Saturated fat: 1.0 g
Carbohydrate: 10.2 g
Total sugars: 6.6 g
Protein: 5.9 g
Sodium: 23 mg
Cholesterol: 0 mg
Dietary fiber: 0 g

Watermelon Lemonade

Watermelon is packed with the antioxidant lycopene, and lemons contain plenty of vitamin C. Add some berries and you have one healthy drink!

Ingredients:
8 cups seeded watermelon cut into 1-inch chunks
1 cup fresh strawberries, hulled and quartered
1 cup granulated sugar
1/2 cup freshly squeezed lemon juice (about 3 lemons)
Approximately 2 cups water
Thin watermelon wedges with the rind for garnish

Preparation: In a food processor fitted with a steel blade or a blender, pulse watermelon, strawberries, and sugar until blended and smooth. Strain through a fine-mesh strainer into a 2-quart container, pushing down on the solids to get all the juice. Add lemon juice and enough water to make 1-1/2 quarts. Chill until very cold. Serve over ice with a wedge of watermelon. Makes about 1-1/2 quarts or 6 servings, 8 ounces each.

This recipe's lycopene (watermelon) and anthocyanins (berries) may help prevent the following cancers: **prostate and esophageal.**

Nutritional information per serving:
Calories: 217.3
Fat: 1.7 g
Saturated fat: 0 g
Carbohydrate: 48.5 g
Total sugars: 44.3 g
Protein: 2 g
Sodium: 7 mg
Cholesterol: 0 mg
Dietary fiber: 2.3 g

SMOOTHIES

Nutritional information per serving:
Calories: 189.4
Fat: 1.0 g
Saturated fat: < 1g
Carbohydrate: 34.1 g
Total sugars: 29.0 g
Protein: 11.0 g
Sodium: 15 mg
Cholesterol: 11 mg
Dietary fiber: 2 g

Nutritional information per serving:
Calories: 136.5
Fat: 2.5 g
Saturated fat: 0.5 g
Carbohydrate: 24.3 g
Total sugars: 18.5 g
Protein: 4.2 g
Sodium: 15 mg
Cholesterol: 0 mg
Dietary fiber: 1.6 g

Lemon-Strawberry Yogurt Smoothie

Ingredients:
1 teaspoon lemon zest
2 teaspoons lemon juice
1 cup fresh or frozen strawberries
1 cup orange juice
12 ounces (two 6-ounce containers or 1-1/2 cups) low-fat vanilla yogurt
1 cup crushed ice (or 8 ice-cubes)

Preparation: Place all ingredients in the blender. Blend for approximately 30 seconds until smooth and serve. Makes 2 servings.

Breakfast Blast Smoothie

This breakfast drink is loaded with vitamins, fiber, and healthy phytoestrogens. I sometimes add a banana or some almond butter to this drink for variation.

Ingredients:
1 apple, peeled, cored, and diced
1 peach, pitted and sliced
1 tablespoon rolled oats
Handful of fresh mint leaves
1 tablespoon honey
1 teaspoon vanilla extract
8 ounces vanilla soy milk

Preparation: Blend all ingredients together until smooth. Serve chilled. Makes 2 servings.

Kiwi-Pear Fusion Smoothie

Ingredients:
2 kiwi fruit, peeled and diced
2 bananas, sliced
1 pear, diced
12 ounces (1-1/2 cups) low-fat lemon yogurt

Preparation: Place yogurt in blender and add fruit. Blend for about 30 to 45 seconds, until desired thickness. You may need both a spoon and a straw to drink. Makes 2 servings.

> This recipe's vitamin D (yogurt) and fiber (pear) may help prevent the following cancers: **breast and colon.**

Nutritional information per serving:
Calories: 329
Fat: 9 g
Saturated fat: 0 g
Carbohydrate: 68.5 g
Total sugars: 59.4 g
Protein: 10.5 g
Sodium: 86 mg
Cholesterol: 10 mg
Dietary fiber: 8 g

Apple-Cherry Pie Smoothie

Ingredients:
1 cup fresh sweet cherries, pitted
1 apple, cored and diced
1 medium ripe banana
1 kiwi, peeled and diced
1/4 cup blueberries
1/4 cup chilled apple juice or apple cider

Preparation: Place all fruit into a blender and blend about 30 seconds. Add apple juice or cider and blend another 20 seconds, or until well mixed. Makes 2 servings.

> This recipe's anthocyanins (cherries) and quercetin (apple) may help prevent the following cancers: **bladder and lung.**

Nutritional information per serving:
Calories: 198.8
Fat: 0.6 g
Saturated fat: 0
Carbohydrate: 47.0 g
Total sugars: 39.4 g
Protein: 1.6 g
Sodium: 4 mg
Cholesterol: 0 mg
Dietary fiber: 4 g

Mango Ginger Smoothie

Ingredients:
2 ripe mangos, peeled and chopped into small chunks
2 pieces crystallized ginger (approximately 1 ounce)
1 cup nonfat buttermilk
1 cup (8 ounces) nonfat vanilla yogurt
1/2 cup crushed ice or 4 ice cubes

Preparation: In a blender, purée mangos and ginger, scraping down sides as necessary. Add buttermilk, yogurt, and ice; purée until smooth and frothy. Serve immediately. Makes 4 servings.

This recipe's beta carotene (mango) and calcium (yogurt) may help prevent the following cancers: **lung and breast.**

Nutritional information per serving:
Calories: 220.3
Fat: 3.5 g
Saturated fat: 1.5 g
Carbohydrate: 41.2 g
Total sugars: 31.4 g
Protein: 6 g
Sodium: 230 mg
Cholesterol: 9.8 mg
Dietary fiber: 0 g

Apricot-Apple Smoothie

Ingredients:
1 apple, peeled, cored, and chopped into small pieces
4 ounces apricot halves (from a can), chopped
1 cup (8 ounces) plain or vanilla low-fat yogurt
1 teaspoon lime juice
3 ice cubes
1/2 teaspoon vanilla extract
2 tablespoons honey

Preparation: Place all ingredients into a blender and blend approximately 30 seconds or until smooth. Serve immediately. Makes 2 servings.

This recipe's beta carotene (apricots) and calcium (yogurt) may help prevent the following cancers: **liver and colon.**

Nutritional information per serving:
Calories: 155.4
Fat: 2.1 g
Saturated fat: 0 g
Carbohydrate: 27.8 g
Total sugars: 21.7 g
Protein: 6.5 g
Sodium: 86 mg
Cholesterol: 7 mg
Dietary fiber: 1 g

Banana and Peanut Butter Smoothie

Ingredients:
1 large frozen banana, cut into chunks
1-1/2 cups (12 ounces) vanilla or regular soy milk
2 tablespoons natural peanut butter
Pinch of cinnamon

Preparation: Place all ingredients into a blender and blend until thick and smooth. Serve immediately. Makes 2 servings.

This recipe's vitamin E (peanut butter) and isoflavones (soy milk) may help prevent the following cancers: **stomach and prostate.**

Nutritional information per serving:
Calories: 217.8
Fat: 10.6 g
Saturated fat: 2.5 g
Carbohydrate: 21.2 g
Total sugars: 10.8 g
Protein: 9.4 g
Sodium: 98 mg
Cholesterol: 0 mg
Dietary fiber: 2.9 g

Blissful Berry Smoothie

Ingredients:
1 cup fresh or frozen unsweetened raspberries
1 cup fresh or frozen unsweetened strawberries
1 medium ripe banana
2 cups orange juice

Preparation: Place all fruit and juice into a blender and blend until smooth. Makes 2 servings.

This recipe's anthocyanins (berries) and vitamin C (orange juice) may help prevent the following cancers: **colon and prostate.**

Nutritional information per serving:
Calories: 232
Fat: 2 g
Saturated fat: 0 g
Carbohydrate: 51.0 g
Total sugars: 34.2 g
Protein: 2.5 g
Sodium: 4 mg
Cholesterol: 0 mg
Dietary fiber: 3.5 g

Strawberry, Mango, and Orange Smoothie

Ingredients:
1/2 cup fresh or frozen strawberries
1 large mango, sliced or in chunks
12 ounces pure orange juice
4 ice cubes

Preparation: Place all ingredients into a blender and blend until smooth. If desired, place mixture in the refrigerator for 5 to 10 minutes, and then serve. Makes 4 servings.

This recipe's vitamin C (orange juice) and beta carotene (mango) may help prevent the following cancers: **lung and liver.**

Nutritional information per serving:
Calories: 88.8
Fat: 0.8 g
Saturated fat: 0 g
Carbohydrate: 19.4 g
Total sugars: 16.0 g
Protein: 1.1 g
Sodium: 2 mg
Cholesterol: 0 mg
Dietary fiber: 1 g

Watermelon Wave Smoothie

This smoothie is the perfect afternoon pick-me-up on a warm summer day.

Ingredients:
2 cups fresh seedless watermelon chunks, cubed
1 cup fresh or frozen unsweetened raspberries
2 scoops nonfat vanilla frozen yogurt

Preparation: Blend watermelon and raspberries about 30 seconds. Add frozen yogurt to blender and blend approximately 20 more seconds or until smooth. Makes 2 servings.

This recipe's lycopene (watermelon) and vitamin D (yogurt) may help prevent the following cancers: **pancreas and breast.**

Nutritional information per serving:
Calories: 233.5
Fat: 1.5 g
Saturated fat: 0 g
Carbohydrate: 43.0 g
Total sugars: 31.5 g
Protein: 7.5 g
Sodium: 48 mg
Cholesterol: 4 mg
Dietary fiber: 1 g

Tropical Blue Smoothie

Ingredients:
1/4 cup vanilla or regular soy milk
1/2 cup pineapple juice
1/4 cup fresh or frozen unsweetened blueberries
1 cup pineapple chunks, fresh or frozen
1 ripe banana, peeled
2 teaspoons flaxseed oil
1 tablespoon wheat germ

Preparation: Using a blender, blend together soy milk, pineapple juice, pineapple chunks, blueberries, banana, wheat germ, and oil, in succession, until smooth. Makes 2 servings.

This recipe's lignans (flax oil) and vitamin E (wheat germ) may help prevent the following cancers: **prostate and colon.**

Nutritional information per serving:
Calories: 205.1
Fat: 5.1 g
Saturated fat: 0.5 g
Carbohydrate: 36.5 g
Total sugars: 23.7 g
Protein: 3.3 g
Sodium: 6 mg
Cholesterol: 0 mg
Dietary fiber: 3 g

Peachy Orange Soy Smoothie

Ingredients:
6 ounces vanilla cultured soy yogurt (Stonyfield makes a great soy yogurt)
1-1/4 cups fresh or frozen peach slices
1 teaspoon fresh lime juice
1/2 cup orange juice
1 teaspoon honey

Preparation: Using a blender, blend all ingredients until smooth and serve. Makes 2 servings.

This recipe's isoflavones (soy yogurt) and vitamin C (peaches) may help prevent the following cancers: **prostate and esophageal.**

Nutritional information per serving:
Calories: 165.6
Fat: 1.2 g
Saturated fat: 0 g
Carbohydrate: 34.1 g
Total sugars: 27.1 g
Protein: 4.6 g
Sodium: 21 mg
Cholesterol: 0 mg
Dietary fiber: 2 g

Strawberry, Nectarine, and Watermelon Smoothie

Ingredients:
3 cups (24 ounces) low-fat strawberry yogurt
2 cups seedless watermelon, cubed
2 cups nectarines, cubed
1/2 cup fresh strawberries, sliced

Preparation: Combine ingredients in a blender and blend until smooth, about 1 minute. Makes 4 servings.

This recipe's calcium (yogurt) and lycopene (watermelon) may help prevent the following cancers: **colon and pancreas.**

Nutritional information per serving:
Calories: 140
Fat: 1.5 g
Saturated fat: 0.5 g
Carbohydrate: 26 g
Total sugars: 23 g
Protein: 4.5 g
Sodium: 70 mg
Cholesterol: 5 mg
Dietary fiber: 3 g

Banana-Almond Smoothie

I love the flavor combination of almonds and bananas. This smoothie is protein-rich, filling, and packed with calcium—which may ward off colon cancer, as well as the extra pounds. You can easily divide the ingredient quantities in half to make a single serving.

Ingredients:
2 small frozen bananas
2 cups vanilla, calcium-enriched soy milk
4 tablespoons low-fat vanilla yogurt (or use vanilla cultured soy yogurt)
2 tablespoons almond butter
2 tablespoons whey protein

Preparation: Ahead of time: peel ripe bananas and wrap in saran wrap. Freeze for at least 2 hours, overnight preferably. Place frozen bananas and all other ingredients in blender and purée to desired consistency. Makes 2 servings.

This recipe's calcium (soy milk) and vitamin E (almond butter) may help prevent the following cancers: **breast and colon.**

Nutritional information per serving:
Calories: 239.0
Fat: 15.4 g
Saturated fat: 2.3 g
Carbohydrate: 13.9 g
Total sugars: 2.5 g
Protein: 11.2 g
Sodium: 29 mg
Cholesterol: 1.4 mg
Dietary fiber: 2.3 g

The Anti-Cancer Cookbook

DESSERTS

Apple-Cherry Oat-Nut cookies

These whole-grain cookies contain natural ingredients, are low in calories, and have almost no saturated fat. This recipe was adapted from one by vegan chef, Beverly Lynn Bennett, author of the great new cookbook, Vegan Bites: Recipes for Singles.

This recipe's quercetin (apples) and anthocyanins (cherries) may help prevent the following cancers: **lung and breast.**

Ingredients:
1-3/4 cups whole-wheat pastry flour
1-2/3 cups rolled oats
1-1/4 cups oat bran
1 teaspoon cinnamon
1/2 teaspoon baking powder
1/4 teaspoon nutmeg
1-1/2 cups apples of choice, peeled, sliced, and divided
1/2 cup frozen apple juice concentrate, thawed
1/2 cup maple syrup
1/3 cup canola oil
1 teaspoon vanilla
1/2 teaspoon almond extract
2/3 cup dried tart cherries
1/2 cup pecans or walnuts, chopped

Preparation: Preheat oven to 350°F. In a large bowl, place flour, oats, oat bran, cinnamon, baking powder, and nutmeg; stir until well combined. Finely dice 1/2 cup sliced apples and set aside. Place remaining sliced apples in a blender or food processor and purée. Add apple-juice concentrate, maple syrup, oil, vanilla, and almond extract, and blend 1 minute. Add apple purée mixture to dry ingredients and stir well to combine. Fold in reserved apple, cherries, and pecans. Drop batter by rounded tablespoonfuls onto two nonstick cookie sheets. Bake 12 to 15 minutes or until cookies are lightly brown around edges and on bottom. Allow cookies to cool on cookie sheets about 3 minutes before transferring to a rack to cool completely. Store in an airtight container. Makes 24 cookies.

Nutritional information per cookie:
Calories: 161.2
Fat: 5.6 g
Saturated fat: 0.5 g
Carbohydrate: 24.7 g
Total sugars: 10.0 g
Protein: 3.0 g
Sodium: 3 mg
Cholesterol: 0 mg
Dietary fiber: 2.6 g

Baked Apples and Figs

Figs are loaded with fiber—in fact, just one fresh fig has about 2 grams of fiber. Fiber has been shown to be beneficial for your gastrointestinal tract, and may play a role in decreasing colon cancer risk. This recipe is delicious and easy to prepare.

Ingredients:
Nonstick cooking spray
2 tablespoons brown sugar
2 teaspoons cinnamon
1/4 teaspoon nutmeg
2 tablespoons honey
1 teaspoon vanilla extract
4 medium apples, peeled and chopped
10 fresh figs, stems removed and finely chopped
1/2 cup low-fat natural granola

Preparation: Preheat oven to 350°F and lightly coat a 12x12-inch baking dish with nonstick cooking spray. In a large bowl, stir together brown sugar, cinnamon, nutmeg, honey, and vanilla extract until thoroughly mixed. Add apples and figs and stir until well coated in sugar-spice mixture. Pour mixture into baking dish and sprinkle granola on top. Cover with foil and bake about 25 minutes, until apples are tender. Remove foil and bake an additional 5 minutes. Remove from oven and allow to cool 5 to 10 minutes before serving. Makes 6 servings.

This recipe's fiber (figs) and quercetin (apples) may help prevent the following cancers: **colon and lung.**

Nutritional information per serving:
Calories: 191. 7
Fat: 0.9 g
Saturated fat: trace
Carbohydrate: 44.3 g
Total sugars: 34.5 g
Protein: 1.6 g
Sodium: 25 mg
Cholesterol: 0 mg
Dietary fiber: 4.2 g

Black Cherry and Chocolate Frozen Yogurt

Ingredients:
1-1/2 cups (about 8 ounces) fresh or frozen black cherries, pitted, divided
2 cups low-fat cherry-flavored yogurt
1/2 cup honey
1/2 teaspoon almond extract
1 ounce dark chocolate, chopped
2 tablespoons water

Preparation: Frozen yogurt: Coarsely chop 1/2 cup cherries; set aside. In a blender or food processor container, combine remaining cherries, yogurt, honey, and almond extract; process until smooth. Stir in reserved cherries. Transfer mixture to ice cream maker; freeze according to manufacturer's directions. Prepare Chocolate Swirl when yogurt has frozen.
Chocolate Swirl: In a small saucepan, combine chocolate and water. Stir over low heat until chocolate is melted and mixture is smooth. Remove from heat and set aside until ready to use.

When yogurt is frozen, place 1/4 of yogurt in medium container; drizzle with 1/4 of Chocolate Swirl; repeat, in layers, with remaining yogurt and chocolate. Store in freezer until ready to serve. Makes 6 servings.

Nutritional information per serving:
Calories: 212.9
Fat: 2.5 g
Saturated fat: 1.6 g
Carbohydrate: 42.8 g
Total sugars: 26.5 g
Protein: 4.8 g
Sodium: 50 mg
Cholesterol: 4.5 mg
Dietary fiber: 1.7 g

Blueberry Pie

This is a lower-sugar version of traditional blueberry pie. If you want to save yourself a little work, you can use a pre-made 9-inch double pie crust.

Filling Ingredients:
5 cups fresh blueberries
1/4 cup sugar
1/4 cup Splenda®
1/4 cup all-purpose white flour
1 teaspoon lemon juice
1/2 teaspoon grated lemon peel

Pastry Ingredients:
2 cups all-purpose white flour, plus more for preparation
1/2 teaspoon Splenda® or other low-calorie sweetener
2/3 cup trans-fat–free margarine
5-6 tablespoons cold water

Preparation: Preheat oven to 450°F. In a large bowl, gently stir together blueberries and remaining filling ingredients. Set aside. In a large bowl, place 2 cups flour and Splenda® or other low-calorie sweetener. With pastry blender or 2 knives used in scissor fashion, cut in margarine until mixture resembles coarse crumbs. Add cold water, 1 tablespoon at a time, until mixture just holds together. On a lightly floured surface with floured rolling pin, roll out half of pastry and line a nonstick 9-inch pie plate with it. Spoon blueberry mixture into pie shell. Roll remaining half of pastry to fit for top crust; place over blueberry mixture. Fold pastry overhang under, and then bring up over rim and flute edges. Make several 1-inch slits in top crust for steam to escape. Bake 10 minutes. Reduce oven temperature to 350°F and bake another 35 to 40 minutes or until golden brown. Makes 8 servings.

This recipe's pectin (lemon peel) and resveratrol (blueberries) may help prevent the following cancers: **prostate and breast.**

Nutritional information per serving:
Calories: 225.4
Fat: 9.8
Saturated fat: 2.8 g
Carbohydrate: 31.4 g
Total sugars: 10.2 g
Protein: 2.9 g
Sodium: 185 mg
Cholesterol: 0 mg
Dietary fiber: 2.1 g

Nutritional information per serving:
Calories: 129.3
Fat: 0.5 g
Saturated fat: trace
Carbohydrate: 29.8 g
Total sugars: 8.6 g
Protein: 1.4 g
Sodium: 106 mg
Cholesterol: 0.3 mg
Dietary fiber: 1.0 g

Nutritional information per serving:
Calories: 143.8
Fat: trace
Saturated fat: trace
Carbohydrate: 34.9 g
Total sugars: 33.3 g
Protein: 0.7 g
Sodium: 17 mg
Cholesterol: 0 mg
Dietary fiber: 1.1 g

Brownies!

You probably didn't think that you could make a healthy brownie. Well, this is a low-fat and lower-calorie version of one of America's favorite treats. If you want to make peppermint brownies, substitute mint extract for the vanilla extract. For a nutty brownie, substitute almond extract for the vanilla.

Ingredients:
Nonstick cooking spray
1-1/2 cups all-purpose white flour
1/2 cup unsweetened cocoa powder
1-1/2 cups sugar
1/8 teaspoon baking powder
1/2 teaspoon salt
1/3 cup light (reduced calorie and sugar) chocolate syrup
1/3 cup light corn syrup
2/3 cup (about 6 ounces) vanilla nonfat yogurt
2 egg whites
1/4 cup nonfat milk
2 teaspoons vanilla extract

Preparation: Preheat oven to 300°F. Spray a 13x9-inch pan with nonstick cooking spray. In a large bowl, combine flour, cocoa, sugar, baking powder, and salt. Add remaining ingredients to dry mixture and mix well. Evenly pour batter into pan and bake 30 minutes. Cool before cutting into bars. Makes 15 brownies.

Cherry-Cranberry Sorbet

If you can't find fresh cherries to make this sorbet, use 2 cans (16 ounces) of drained, pitted cherries and only 1/2 cup of sugar.

Ingredients:
4 cups fresh ripe sweet dark cherries, pitted
2/3 cup sugar
1/2 cup light corn syrup
2 cups 100% cranberry juice

Preparation: In a blender or food processor fitted with metal blade, purée cherries, sugar, and corn syrup. Add cranberry juice and process about 5 seconds, until just blended. Freeze in resealable plastic container. Makes 1-1/2 quarts of sorbet or 12 servings, 1/2 cup each.

Chocolate-Almond Biscotti

I used to be intimidated by biscotti because I thought it would be difficult to make. Guess what? It's easy. The trick is getting all of the dry ingredients moistened and using a very thin serrated knife to cut the logs into cookies. These delicious biscotti are also full of antioxidants.

Ingredients:
2 tablespoons brewed espresso or very strong coffee
3 egg whites
1/3 cup canola oil
1-1/4 teaspoons vanilla extract
1-2/3 cups all-purpose white flour
2/3 cup sugar
1/2 cup unsweetened cocoa powder
1 teaspoon baking powder
1/4 teaspoon baking soda
1/8 teaspoon salt
1/2 cup almonds, sliced or chopped
1/4 cup dried tart cherries

Preparation: Preheat oven to 350°F. In a small bowl, beat together espresso or coffee, egg whites, oil, and vanilla extract. In a large mixing bowl, combine flour, sugar, cocoa, baking powder, baking soda, salt, almonds, and cherries and stir until well blended. Add coffee-egg mixture to dry ingredients and stir until well mixed and evenly moistened. Shape mixture into two 12x2-inch logs; place both on non-stick baking sheet and flatten slightly, so each log is about 1 inch high. Bake 30 minutes; remove from oven and cool 10 minutes. Transfer one cooked log to cutting board and cut diagonally into 3/4-inch thick biscotti. Arrange biscotti, cut side up, on baking sheet. Repeat with second log; use additional baking sheet if necessary. Bake biscotti 20 minutes; transfer to wire rack to cool. Store in airtight container up to 1 month. Makes about 32 biscotti.

Nutritional information per biscotti:
Calories: 91.7
Fat: 4.1 g
Saturated fat: 0.4 g
Carbohydrate: 11.7 g
Total sugars: 5.2 g
Protein: 2.0 g
Sodium: 34 mg
Cholesterol: 0 mg
Dietary fiber: 0.8 g

Chocolate Chocolate-Chip Zucchini Brownies

The antioxidants in dark chocolate and cocoa have been shown to be more powerful than those found even in red wine. Feel good about eating these brownies!

Ingredients:
Nonstick cooking spray
1/2 cup canola oil
1 cup sugar
1/4 cup plain nonfat yogurt
2 teaspoons vanilla extract
1 cup all-purpose white flour
1 cup whole-wheat pastry flour
1/2 cup unsweetened cocoa powder
1-1/2 teaspoons baking soda
1 teaspoon salt
2 cups zucchini, grated
1/4 cup walnuts, chopped
1/2 cup dark chocolate chips

Preparation: Preheat oven to 350°F. Spray a 9x13-inch pan with nonstick cooking spray. Beat oil, sugar, yogurt, and vanilla together in a large mixing bowl until well combined. In a small mixing bowl, whisk together white and whole-wheat flour, cocoa powder, baking soda, and salt. Fold dry ingredients into wet ingredients. Stir in zucchini, walnuts, and chocolate chips. The batter may seem stiff at first, but if you allow a few minutes for it to soak up the moisture from the zucchini, it will look like typical brownie batter. Spread batter into prepared pan. Bake 25 to 30 minutes or until a knife inserted in center of brownies comes back with just a few crumbs on it. Remove from oven and allow brownies to cool. When completely cooled, cut into squares and serve. Makes 24 brownies.

Nutritional information per brownie:
Calories: 145.3
Fat: 6.5 g
Saturated fat: 1.0 g
Carbohydrate: 19.5 g
Total sugars: 10.1 g
Protein: 2.2 g
Sodium: 101 mg
Cholesterol: < 1 mg
Dietary fiber: 1.6 g

Chocolate "Cream" Pie

I don't remember who gave me this recipe originally, but it is a delicious way to incorporate soy into your diet without even knowing that you are eating tofu. It is delicious with raspberries or chopped nuts (think walnuts or pecans) on top, as well. For a variation, add 3/4 cup cashew or almond butter to tofu in blender to make a turtle pie.

Ingredients:
1 bag (10 ounces) dark chocolate chips (about 2 cups)
1 package (10 ounces) soft silken tofu
1 tablespoon vanilla extract
1 Keebler's Graham Cracker Ready Crust (or other brand)
2/3 cup fresh strawberries, hulled and thinly sliced

Preparation: Boil water in the bottom of a double boiler and remove from heat to cool. Place chocolate chips in top of double boiler over very hot (but not boiling) water until they melt. If you do not have a double boiler, melt chocolate chips in a saucepan over low heat, stirring, or in microwave on 70% heat in 20- to 30-second stages. Place tofu in a blender or food processor and blend until creamy. Add melted chocolate chips and vanilla extract to blender or food processor; blend again until well mixed. Place filling into graham-cracker crust. Refrigerate about 1 hour, add sliced strawberries, and then refrigerate at least 1 more hour before serving. Makes 8 generous servings.

This recipe's catechins (dark chocolate) and isoflavones (tofu) may help prevent the following cancers: **colon and prostate.**

Nutritional information per serving:
Calories: 284.4
Fat: 13.2 g
Saturated fat: 0.7 g
Carbohydrate: 37.5 g
Total sugars: 25.2 g
Protein: 3.9 g
Sodium: 104 mg
Cholesterol: 0 mg
Dietary fiber: 2.7 g

Chocolate Crème Pots

Ingredients:
3 eggs
1/3 cup unsweetened cocoa powder
2/3 cup sugar
2 tablespoons prepared espresso or very strong coffee
1 cup nonfat (skim) milk, heated until very hot
Water as needed to make a hot water bath
Non-fat whipped topping

Preparation: Preheat oven to 325°F. Adjust oven rack to center position. Place 6 demitasse cups, pots de crème cups, or small custard cups (1/3 cup each) into a large baking dish. In a large bowl, beat eggs slightly; add cocoa, sugar, and espresso or coffee; beat until well mixed. Mix in hot milk until blended. Pour egg mixture into custard cups; cover with lids or aluminum foil. Bring water for a water bath to a light simmer on top of stove; carefully pour hot water into baking pan to come at least half-way up the sides of the custard cups. The water should come up to approximately the level of the custard inside the cups in order to protect your custard from the heat. Bake approximately 20 minutes or until custard is set around edges but still loose in center. The cooking time will depend on the size of custard cup you are using. When center of custard is just set, it will jiggle a little when shaken, and it can be taken out of the oven. Remove from oven and immediately remove cups from water bath; remove aluminum foil and let cool to room temperature on wire rack. Cover with plastic wrap, and refrigerate at least 2 hours and up to 2 days. To serve, top with a teaspoon of nonfat whipped topping. Makes 6 servings (depending on size of custard cups).

Nutritional information per serving:
Calories: 153.3
Fat: 2.9 g
Saturated fat: 1.1 g
Carbohydrate: 26.7 g
Total sugars: 11.5 g
Protein: 5.1 g
Sodium: 54 mg
Cholesterol: 93.9 mg
Dietary fiber: 1.6 g

Cocoa Crunch Berry Parfait

This is one of my very favorite desserts. It is light and healthy, with the sweet and crunchy flavor combination of berries and wheat germ. Strawberries or blackberries can be substituted for the raspberries for variation.

Ingredients:
2 cups fresh raspberries, plus 12 fresh raspberries
2 tablespoons sugar, divided
2 cups (16 ounces) plain low-fat yogurt
2 tablespoons unprocessed cocoa powder
1-1/2 tablespoons wheat germ

Preparation: In a medium bowl, place 2 cups raspberries and sprinkle with 1 tablespoon sugar; stir until sugar is evenly distributed. In a separate medium bowl, whisk together yogurt, cocoa powder, and remaining tablespoon of sugar until creamy. In four 8-ounce parfait glasses, spoon alternating layers of yogurt, raspberries, and wheat germ, until 3 layers are formed, ending with yogurt. Top each parfait with 3 fresh raspberries. Makes 4 parfaits.

> This recipe's ellagic acid (raspberries) and vitamin E (wheat germ) may help prevent the following cancers: **pancreas and colon.**

Nutritional information per serving:
Calories: 131.7
Fat: 2.5 g
Saturated fat: 1.5 g
Carbohydrate: 19.4 g
Total sugars: 15.8 g
Protein: 7.9 g
Sodium: 86 mg
Cholesterol: 7.4 mg
Dietary fiber: 2.1 g

Cranberry Poached Pears

Ingredients:
2 cups pure cranberry juice
1/4 cup orange juice
1/3 cup sugar
1 stick cinnamon
4 firm, ripe pears
1/2 cup fresh cranberries

Preparation: Place cranberry juice, orange juice, and sugar in a saucepan large enough to hold the pears. Heat gently, stirring, until sugar dissolves. Add cinnamon and boil 5 minutes. Peel pears and immediately stand them in pan with cranberry syrup. Cover and simmer gently 40 minutes, or until pears are cooked and soft through to center when pierced with a skewer or toothpick. Remove from heat and leave to cool completely. Chill 2 hours or overnight, occasionally turning pears in syrup to achieve an even color. Remove pears from pan and bring cranberry syrup to a boil; cook 10 minutes, or until reduced to a thick syrup. Add fresh cranberries and simmer 5 minutes. Remove from heat and set aside until completely cool. Place pears on separate plates with cranberries and pour sauce over and around them. Makes 4 servings.

> This recipe's resveratrol (cranberries) and vitamin C (orange juice) may help prevent the following cancers: **breast and prostate.**

Nutritional information per serving:
Calories: 252.4
Fat: 0.4 g
Saturated fat: 0 g
Carbohydrate: 60.9 g
Total sugars: 50.0 g
Protein: 1.3 g
Sodium: 5 mg
Cholesterol: 0 mg
Dietary fiber: 5.9 g

Creamy Orange Cupcakes with Dark Chocolate Ganache

Ingredients:

Orange Cream filling:
1/4 cup sugar
1/4 cup calcium-enriched plain soy milk
1/2 cup orange juice
3 tablespoons cornstarch
1 teaspoon vanilla
Zest of 1 orange, finely grated

Cupcakes:
1/3 cup canola oil
3/4 cup granulated white sugar
3/4 cup calcium-enriched soy milk
1/2 cup orange juice
1 teaspoon vanilla extract
1-1/3 cups white whole-wheat pastry flour, divided
1 teaspoon baking powder
1/2 teaspoon baking soda
1/4 teaspoon salt
1 tablespoon orange zest, finely grated

Chocolate Ganache:
1/4 cup soy milk
4 ounces dark chocolate (at least 70% cacao), chopped into small pieces

Preparation: Cream filling: Place sugar, soy milk, orange juice, cornstarch, and vanilla in a saucepan over medium heat. Whisk together until mixture starts to boil. Turn heat down to low and stir continuously until mixture thickens. Once it reaches the consistency of a pudding, remove from heat and add the orange zest. Transfer to a glass bowl and let cool completely. Once cool, refrigerate for an hour. **Cupcakes:** Preheat oven to 350°F. Spray a muffin tin with nonstick spray or line with cupcake liners. Whisk together oil, sugar, milk, orange juice, and vanilla with 1 tablespoon pastry flour. Sift together remaining flour, baking powder, baking soda, and salt. Add flour mixture to wet ingredients, about one third at a time, stirring until batter is smooth after each addition. Fill cupcake liners 2/3 full with batter. Bake 20 to 22 minutes until top springs back when pressed lightly. Remove cupcakes from muffin tins; cool completely. Remove orange filling from refrigerator and put into a gallon-size storage bag or pastry bag. Warm with your hands to make sure pudding is pliable, if necessary. Snip end of storage bag off to make a tip. Make an indentation in center of each cupcake with the handle of a wooden spoon (or your finger). Fill generously with orange pudding. **Ganache:** Heat soy milk in small saucepan over medium heat until bubbles just start to form around the edges. Remove from heat and whisk in chocolate. As soon as mixture is smooth, place a dollop in the center of each cupcake. Makes 12 cupcakes.

Nutritional information per serving:
Calories: 245.8
Fat: 9.4 g
Saturated fat: 2.0 g
Carbohydrate: 37.5 g
Total sugars: 23.4 g
Protein: 2.8 g
Sodium: 11 mg
Cholesterol: 0 mg
Dietary fiber: 2.4 g

Grape-Berry Salad

This sweet and juicy fresh fruit salad is full of antioxidants. The U.S. Department of Agriculture has shown that pterostilbene, found in grapes, may be able to protect people from certain cancers and diabetes.

Ingredients:
2 tablespoons lemon juice
2 tablespoons Cointreau (or other orange liqueur)
2 teaspoons honey
1-1/2 cups fresh strawberries, hulled
1 cup fresh blueberries, stemmed and sorted (throw out mushy ones)
1 cup fresh raspberries, preferably small and firm berries
1/2 cup seedless red or purple grapes, cut in half
1/4 cup seedless green grapes, cut in half
1/4 cup fresh mint leaves, chopped

Preparation: In a small bowl, whisk together lemon juice, orange liqueur, and honey to make the dressing. In a large bowl, combine berries, grapes, and mint. Pour dressing on top of fruit and toss gently. Serve in small glass bowls or martini glasses. Makes 6 servings.

Nutritional information per serving:
Calories: 65.5
Fat: 0.3 g
Saturated fat: trace
Carbohydrate: 14.8 g
Total sugars: 10.0 g
Protein: 0.9 g
Sodium: 2 mg
Cholesterol: 0 mg
Dietary fiber: 2.9 g

Grilled Pineapple Sundaes

Nutritional information per serving:
Calories: 237
Fat: 2.5 g
Saturated fat: 1.2 g
Carbohydrate: 49.9 g
Total sugars: 38.3 g
Protein: 3.9 g
Sodium: 48 mg
Cholesterol: 0 mg
Dietary fiber: 2.3 g

Nutritional information per serving:
Calories: 63.6
Fat: trace
Saturated fat: trace
Carbohydrate: 15.4 g
Total sugars: 12.1 g
Protein: 0.5 g
Sodium: 14 mg
Cholesterol: 0 mg
Dietary fiber: 2.6 g

Pineapple contains an enzyme called bromelain that British researchers have shown to be able to stop the growth of various tumor cells. It also has anti-inflammatory effects and helps to keep platelets from clumping together and forming blood clots.

Ingredients:
1 medium pineapple, peeled and cored
1 teaspoon cinnamon
1/2 cup orange juice
1 tablespoon raw sugar
1 teaspoon cornstarch
1 teaspoon vanilla
1/4 cup maple syrup
1 tablespoon extra-virgin olive oil
1-1/2 pints vanilla (or flavor of your choice) nonfat frozen yogurt
3/4 cup fresh blueberries or strawberries

Preparation: Slice peeled pineapple into six 3/4-inch-thick slices (there will be some remaining). Place slices on a large plate. Sprinkle cinnamon over both sides of each pineapple slice, and rub to distribute. Set aside. To make pineapple sauce, mince reserved pineapple and place it in a medium saucepan. Whisk in juice, sugar, cornstarch, and vanilla. Over medium heat, bring to a simmer and cook until thickened. Chill to cool completely. Preheat grill. Just before grilling, combine maple syrup and olive oil, and brush onto pineapple slices. Place pineapple on grill grate and grill over medium fire until grill marks appear. Turn and cook until soft. Place a grilled pineapple slice on each dessert plate and top with a scoop of frozen yogurt, 2 tablespoons of fresh berries, and pineapple sauce. Makes 6 servings.

Lemon-Mint Strawberries

These strawberries have such a gourmet presentation and sweet flavor that your guests will never realize how easy this dessert is to prepare.

Ingredients:
1/4 cup sugar
1/4 cup lemon zest, cut into thin strips
1 tablespoon lemon juice
1/4 cup water
2 cups strawberries, hulled and halved
1 tablespoon fresh mint, chopped

Preparation: Bring sugar, lemon zest, lemon juice, and water to a boil in a heavy saucepan over medium high heat. Simmer 5 minutes, stirring frequently. Remove from heat and place saucepan in cold water to cool. Pour syrup over strawberries. Sprinkle with mint and toss. Makes 4 servings.

Lemon-Tofu Cheesecake

Courtesy of the United Soybean Board's website, www.unitedsoybean.org, this scrumptious cheesecake is high in protein and isoflavones. How many desserts can say that?

Ingredients:
Nonstick cooking spray
Crust:
1 cup reduced-fat vanilla wafers, crumbled
2 tablespoons pecans, finely chopped
2 tablespoons trans-fat–free butter or soy margarine, melted
Filling:
2 packages (24 ounces total) silken tofu
1 pound (16 ounces) low-fat cream cheese
3/4 cup sugar
1/4 cup all-purpose white flour
1 tablespoon grated lemon peel
1 tablespoon vanilla extract
3 eggs
3 egg whites
Garnish: 1/2 cup sliced strawberries and 1 sectioned orange

Preparation: Preheat oven to 375°F and lightly spray a 9-inch springform pan with nonstick cooking spray. Combine vanilla wafers, pecans, and melted butter in a bowl and mix well. Press mixture into bottom of spring form pan. Bake crust about 8 minutes or until golden brown. Cool on a wire rack. In a medium mixing bowl, beat tofu with a hand or stand mixer until smooth. Add cream cheese, sugar, flour, lemon peel, and vanilla; mix until well blended. Beat in eggs and whites, one at a time; mix well. Pour filling into crust and bake 50 to 60 minutes or until filling is set and edges around top are lightly browned. Cool on a wire rack; refrigerate several hours or overnight until completely chilled. Remove from pan and cut into slices, dipping the knife blade into hot water between each slice. Garnish with strawberries and orange sections. Makes 10 servings.

This recipe's isoflavones (tofu) and calcium (cream cheese) may help prevent the following cancers: **breast and colon.**

Nutritional information per serving:
Calories: 266.6
Fat: 13.4 g
Saturated fat: 5.8 g
Carbohydrate: 25.2 g
Total sugars: 16.4 g
Protein: 11.3
Sodium: 241 mg
Cholesterol: 78.7 mg
Dietary fiber: 2.3 g

Light Lemon Pie

Compared to most cream-filled pies, this pie is low in calories and saturated fat and has a delicious lemony flavor.

Ingredients:
1/2 cup cholesterol-free egg substitute (such as Egg Beaters®)
3/4 cup sugar or granulated Splenda®
1/4 cup cornstarch
1/8 teaspoon salt
1 cup water
1 cup low-fat buttermilk
2-1/4 teaspoons grated lemon rind
1/2 cup lemon juice
1 reduced-calorie ready-made graham-cracker pie crust
Garnish: Lemon curls (thin slices of lemon peel) and mint leaves
Nonfat whipped topping

Preparation: Pour egg substitute into a Pyrex measuring cup. Combine sugar or Splenda®, cornstarch, and salt in saucepan; gradually stir in water and buttermilk. Cook over medium heat, stirring constantly, until mixture begins to boil. Once boiling, cook 1 minute. Gradually stir about 1/4 hot mixture into egg substitute, mixing well. Add egg mixture back to hot mixture, stirring constantly. Cook over medium heat, stirring, approximately 2 minutes, until mixture thickens and large bubbles begin to pop up. Remove from heat; add lemon rind and lemon juice and stir to blend. Allow to cool about 1 to 2 minutes. Pour mixture into prepared pie crust. Chill thoroughly—at least 2 hours, but preferably overnight. Garnish with lemon curls and fresh mint and serve with a dollop of nonfat whipped topping. Makes 8 servings.

Nutritional information per serving made with Splenda®:
Calories: 184.7, Fat: 5.9 g, Saturated fat: 2.1 g, Carbohydrate: 28.0 g Total sugars: 12.1 g, Protein: 4.9 g, Sodium: 209 mg, Cholesterol: 6.6 mg, Dietary fiber: 0.4 g

---

This recipe's calcium (buttermilk) and vitamin C (lemon juice) may help prevent the following cancers: **colon and lung.**

Nutritional information per serving made with sugar:
Calories: 256.7
Fat: 5.9 g
Saturated fat: 2.1 g
Carbohydrate: 46.0 g
Total sugars: 30.2 g
Protein: 4.9 g
Sodium: 209 mg
Cholesterol: 6.6 mg
Dietary fiber: 0.4 g

Low-fat Cheesecake with Fresh Strawberry Sauce

This crustless cheesecake is light and delicious and a perfect way to end a healthy meal. If you want to forgo the strawberry sauce, simply top the cheesecake with fresh berries of your choice.

Ingredients:
Nonstick cooking spray
16 ounces nonfat cream cheese, softened
2/3 cup plus 3 tablespoons sugar
1-1/2 teaspoons pure vanilla extract, divided
3/4 cup cholesterol-free egg substitute
1 cup nonfat sour cream
1 pound fresh or frozen whole strawberries
1/2 cup seedless strawberry all-fruit preserves
1/4 cup sugar
2 teaspoons lemon juice

Preparation: Cheesecake: Preheat oven to 350°F and lightly coat a 9-inch pie plate with nonstick cooking spray. In a large mixing bowl, use a hand or stand mixer to beat together cream cheese, 2/3 cup sugar, and 1/2 teaspoon vanilla until fluffy. Gradually add egg substitute and beat until smooth. Pour mixture into pie plate and bake 30 to 35 minutes or until puffy and light brown around edges. Cool on a wire rack 10 to 15 minutes. Meanwhile, in a small bowl, combine sour cream, remaining sugar, and vanilla. Spread over cooled cheesecake. Bake an additional 15 minutes. Cool completely on a wire rack, and then refrigerate at least 2 hours before serving. **Strawberry Sauce:** Combine strawberries, strawberry preserves, sugar, and salt in a medium saucepan. Cook, stirring frequently, over medium heat, until sauce has thickened, about 8 or 9 minutes. Remove from heat, stir in lemon juice, and transfer to a medium bowl. Cool for 30 minutes, then loosely cover with plastic wrap and refrigerate until chilled, at least 2 hours. Prior to serving, remove cheesecake from refrigerator for at least 15 minutes and pour fresh strawberry sauce on top. Makes 8 servings.

This recipe's calcium (cream cheese) and anthocyanins (strawberries) may help prevent the following cancers: **breast and bladder.**

Nutritional information per serving:
Calories: 249.5
Fat: 1.5 g
Saturated fat: 0.6 g
Carbohydrate: 47.6 g
Total sugars: 36.1 g
Protein: 11.4 g
Sodium: 347 mg
Cholesterol: 4.2 mg
Dietary fiber: 1.4 g

Mango and Green Tea Sorbet

Nutritional information per serving:
Calories: 144.7
Fat: 0.3 g
Saturated fat: trace
Carbohydrate: 34.9 g
Total sugars: 32.0 g
Protein: 0.6 g
Sodium: 2 mg
Cholesterol: 0 mg
Dietary fiber: 1.9 g

Ingredients:
2/3 cup water
1/3 cup loose green-tea leaves
1/2 cup sugar
3 ripe mangoes, peeled, pitted, and cut into large chunks
3 tablespoons fresh lemon juice

Preparation: Combine water and tea leaves in a saucepan. Bring just to a boil. Remove from heat and let steep 5 minutes. Strain, discarding leaves. (Do not press leaves to extract liquid; it will make the liquid bitter.) Return tea to clean saucepan; add sugar and bring to a boil. Boil until sugar dissolves, about 1 minute. Remove from heat and cool about 30 minutes. In a food processor or blender, purée mangoes and lemon juice. Add tea and blend until smooth. Pour into a glass 9-inch baking dish and freeze about 3 hours. Transfer mango mixture to a food processor or blender. Pulse or blend until smooth, 30 to 40 seconds. Serve at once or store in freezer up to 2 months. Soften 10 minutes before serving. Makes 6 servings.

Mixed-Berry Cheesecake Parfait

This low-fat parfait is made with yogurt, keeping it relatively low in fat and calories. It can be made with a single berry type, or a combination of any berry in season.

Nutritional information per parfait:
Calories: 260.6
Fat: 4.2 g
Saturated fat: 2.5 g
Carbohydrate: 41.9 g
Total sugars: 35.9 g
Protein: 13.8 g
Sodium: 173 mg
Cholesterol: 14.7 mg
Dietary fiber: 3.6 g

Ingredients:
4 cups plain low-fat yogurt, divided
3 tablespoons honey
1 teaspoon vanilla extract
1 cup fresh blueberries
1 cup fresh raspberries
1 cup fresh strawberries, hulled and sliced

Preparation: The night before (or a few days ahead of time), place two cone paper coffee filters over two large mugs. Place 2 cups (16 ounces) yogurt into each filter and place mugs in refrigerator overnight. Liquid will drain into mugs; discard liquid and keep the 'yogurt cheese.' Combine 1/2 yogurt cheese with vanilla extract and honey in a medium bowl and whisk until thoroughly mixed. Add remaining yogurt cheese and whisk again until well combined. In 4 large wine glasses or parfait glasses, place 2 tablespoons yogurt cheese and alternate with berries in layers. You can choose to combine all berries in a bowl or layer each type separately. Serve immediately or chill before serving. Makes 4 parfaits.

Orange-Cranberry Oatmeal Cookies

Ingredients:
1/2 cup (1 stick) trans-fat–free margarine, at room temperature
1 egg
1/4 cup ripe banana, mashed with a fork (about 1/2 medium banana)
1 teaspoon vanilla extract
1/2 cup brown sugar
1-1/2 teaspoons orange zest
1 cup whole-wheat pastry flour
1/4 teaspoon salt
1 teaspoon baking powder
1-1/2 cups rolled oats
1/4 cup unsweetened shredded coconut
1/3 cup pecans, chopped
1/2 cup dried cranberries

Preparation: Preheat oven to 350°F. With a stand or hand mixer, cream margarine and egg together until smooth and well blended. Gradually beat in mashed banana, vanilla, and brown sugar. Add orange zest and mix well with a wooden spoon until ingredients are thoroughly blended. In a large bowl, combine flour, salt, baking powder, rolled oats, coconut, pecans, and dried cranberries. Stir with a wooden spoon until ingredients are evenly distributed. Stir dry ingredients into wet ingredients and mix thoroughly until there are no dry areas or clumps. On a nonstick baking sheet (or a regular baking sheet sprayed with nonstick cooking spray), drop heaping tablespoonfuls of batter 2 inches apart, and press down lightly to flatten. Bake 20 minutes or until lightly browned. Cool on a wire rack. Makes 15 large cookies.

This recipe's fiber (oats) and resveratrol (cranberries) may help prevent the following cancers: **colon and pancreas.**

Nutritional information per cookie:
Calories: 180.9
Fat: 9.7 g
Saturated fat: 4.6 g
Carbohydrate: 20.9 g
Total sugars: 8.9 g
Protein: 2.5 g
Sodium: 47 mg
Cholesterol: 28.6 g
Dietary fiber: 2.3 g

Pecan Ice-Cream Roll with Raspberry Sauce

You can easily make this dessert ahead of time if you are planning a party. Wrap it tightly, and it can be stored for up to 2 weeks in the freezer.

Ingredients:

Pecan Roll: Nonstick cooking spray
1/3 cup all-purpose flour
1/4 cup unsweetened cocoa powder
1 teaspoon baking powder
1/4 teaspoon salt
4 egg yolks
1/2 teaspoon vanilla
1/3 cup plus 1/2 cup sugar
4 egg whites
Sifted powdered sugar as needed
1 quart fat-free vanilla ice cream, softened
1/4 cup pecans, chopped or broken in pieces
Raspberry Sauce: 2/3 cup seedless raspberry spreadable fruit
1 tablespoon lemon juice,
1/4 teaspoon almond extract
Garnish: 1/2 cup fresh raspberries

Preparation: Pecan roll: Preheat oven to 375°F. Lightly spray a 15x10x1-inch baking pan (also called a jelly-roll pan) with nonstick cooking spray. Stir together flour, cocoa powder, baking powder, and salt. Set aside. In a small mixing bowl, beat egg yolks and vanilla with an electric mixer on high speed about 5 minutes or until thick and lemon-colored. Gradually add the 1/3 cup granulated sugar, beating on medium speed about 5 minutes until sugar is almost dissolved. Thoroughly wash beaters. In a large mixing bowl, beat egg whites on medium to high speed until soft peaks form (curled tips). Gradually add the 1/2 cup granulated sugar, beating until stiff peaks form (straight tips). Fold egg-yolk mixture into the egg-white mixture. Sprinkle flour mixture over egg mixture; fold in gently, just until combined. Spread batter evenly into prepared pan. Bake 12 to 15 minutes or until top springs back when touched lightly. Immediately loosen cake edges from pan; turn out onto a clean dish towel sprinkled with sifted powdered sugar. Starting with a narrow end, roll up cake and towel together. Cool on a wire rack. When cool, unroll the cake. Spread softened ice cream onto cake to within 1 inch of edges. Sprinkle with pecans. Reroll cake without towel. Wrap and freeze at least 4 hours before serving. **Raspberry Sauce:** In a small saucepan, combine seedless raspberry spreadable fruit, lemon juice, and almond extract. Cook and stir over low heat until just melted. Cool slightly. To serve, drizzle Raspberry Sauce over the serving plates. Slice the cake; place on plates. Garnish with raspberries. Makes 10 servings.

Nutritional information per serving:

Calories: 277.5
Fat: 5.1 g
Saturated fat: 1.2 g
Carbohydrate: 51.5 g
Total sugars: 37.3 g
Protein: 6.4 g
Sodium: 131 mg
Cholesterol: 83.9 mg
Dietary fiber: 1.9 g

Pumpkin Oatmeal Cookies

These cookies are low in fat and sugar, but have a rich, moist texture and a delightfully spicy flavor. They are great around the holidays or just for occasional snacking or dessert.

Ingredients:
Nonstick cooking spray
1 cup 100% pumpkin purée
2 egg whites, lightly beaten
1 cup packed brown sugar
1 cup all-purpose white flour
1/2 cup whole-wheat pastry flour
1 teaspoon baking soda
1 teaspoon cinnamon
1/4 teaspoon nutmeg
3 cups rolled oats
1/2 cup raisins
1/2 cup pecans, chopped

Preparation: Preheat oven to 350°F and spray a baking sheet with nonstick cooking spray (or use a nonstick baking sheet). In a large bowl, combine pumpkin purée and egg whites. In a separate bowl, combine sugar, flour, baking soda, cinnamon, nutmeg, oats, raisins, and pecans. (Batter will be very dry at first.) Mix ingredients together until just moistened. Use a tablespoon to drop batter onto baking sheet, 2 inches apart, and flatten slightly before baking. Bake 15 minutes. Makes 24 cookies.

Nutritional information per cookie:
Calories: 134.4
Fat: 2.4 g
Saturated fat: 0.3 g
Carbohydrate: 25.1 g
Total sugars: 11.2 g
Protein: 3.1 g
Sodium: 62 mg
Cholesterol: 0 mg
Dietary fiber: 2.1 g

Raspberry Crepes

You can either make the crepes ahead of time and freeze or refrigerate, or practice the timing of this recipe so that the sauce and crepes are ready to eat at about the same time. Raspberries are full of antioxidants, and the low-fat dairy products provide protein as well as the valuable nutrients calcium and vitamin D.

Crepes ingredients:
1/4 cup all-purpose white flour
1/2 cup nonfat (skim) milk
1 egg
Nonstick cooking spray

Filling ingredients:
1/2 cup nonfat cottage cheese
1/2 cup nonfat cream cheese
3 tablespoons sugar
3 tablespoons nonfat sour cream
2 teaspoons grated lemon rind
1 teaspoon vanilla extract
1/4 cup low-sugar, seedless raspberry jam
1 tablespoon fresh or bottled lemon juice
2 teaspoons Chambord (or other brand raspberry liqueur)
1 cup fresh or frozen unsweetened raspberries

Preparation: Crepes: Process flour, milk, and egg in a blender for 1 minute. Transfer batter to a small bowl; cover and refrigerate at least 1 hour. Coat a 6-inch crepe pan or skillet with nonstick cooking spray and place over medium heat. Pour 3 tablespoons batter into pan, and quickly tilt pan in all directions so batter covers pan in a thin film. Cook 1 minute. Flip crepe (using a plastic spatula) and cook about 30 seconds. Place crepe on wax paper to cool. Repeat process until batter is used. Stack crepes between layers of wax paper to prevent sticking. Makes 4 crepes.

Filling: Position knife blade in food processor bowl; add first 6 ingredients. Process until smooth. Transfer cheese mixture to a small bowl; cover and chill. Combine raspberry jam, lemon juice, and Chambord in a small saucepan and place over medium heat. Heat until jam melts, stirring constantly. Remove from heat; cool. Stir in raspberries; set aside.

Final preparation: Spoon 3 tablespoons cheese mixture down center of crepes. Fold right and left over filling. To serve, place crepe, seam side down, and spoon raspberry mixture evenly over crepes. Makes 4 servings.

This recipe's calcium (milk) and vitamin C (raspberries) may help prevent the following cancers: **colon and cervical.**

Nutritional information per serving:
Calories: 203.1
Fat: 2.3 g
Saturated fat: 0.9 g
Carbohydrate: 34.5 g
Total sugars: 22.3 g
Protein: 12.1 g
Sodium: 322 mg
Cholesterol: 57.1 mg
Dietary fiber: 2.6 g

Ruby Red Grapefruit Brulee

Grapefruit and other citrus fruits contain fiber as well as vitamin C, which promotes healthy teeth and gums as well as wound healing. But red grapefruit also contains lycopene, and higher lycopene consumption may be associated with a decreased risk of some cancers.

Ingredients:
3 large ruby red grapefruit
4 tablespoons packed dark brown sugar
1 tablespoon trans-fat-free butter, cut into tiny pieces
Approximately 1/2 teaspoon ground cinnamon

Preparation: Place oven rack about 5 inches from broiler and preheat broiler. Slice the stem and opposite end off of each grapefruit. Stand each grapefruit, one cut end down, on a cutting board and slice off the rind and pith with a sharp knife; make certain to remove all the white rind. Cut each grapefruit into 4 round, parallel slices about 1/2 inch thick. Place slices in a single layer in a large baking pan. Top each slice with a teaspoon of brown sugar (more if desired) and dot with butter; sprinkle cinnamon on top. Broil grapefruit slices about 6 to 8 minutes, until bubbling and beginning to brown. Drizzle pan juices over each slice when serving. Makes 6 servings, 2 grapefruit slices each.

> This recipe's lycopene and naringenin (grapefruit) may help prevent the following cancers: **pancreas and lung.**

Nutritional information per serving:
Calories: 110.9
Fat: 2.1 g
Saturated fat: 1.2 g
Carbohydrate: 22.1 g
Total sugars: 17.3 g
Protein: 0.9 g
Sodium: 4 mg
Cholesterol: 5.1 mg
Dietary fiber: 2.1 g

Stuffed Peaches

Ingredients:
4 large ripe peaches, cut in half and pitted
1/4 cup walnuts, finely chopped
1 tablespoon raisins, chopped
1 tablespoon brandy (can substitute fruit liqueur or 2 teaspoons almond extract)
4 teaspoons honey, divided

Preparation: Preheat oven to 375°F. In a small bowl, combine walnuts, raisins, and brandy. Spoon mixture into the center of each peach and drizzle 1/2 teaspoon honey on top of each peach half. Place on a cookie sheet or in a large baking dish and bake 10 minutes until peaches are soft. Let cool slightly before serving. The peaches are delicious alone or with some vanilla frozen yogurt on the side. Makes 4 servings (2 halves per serving).

> This recipe's vitamin C (peaches) and fiber (walnuts) may help prevent the following cancers: **lung and colon.**

Nutritional information per cookie:
Calories: 151.1
Fat: 5.1 g
Saturated fat: 0.5 g
Carbohydrate: 23.7 g
Total sugars: 20.3 g
Protein: 2.6 g
Sodium: < 1 mg
Cholesterol: 0 mg
Dietary fiber: 2.9 g

Tofu Pumpkin Pie

Nutritional information per serving:
Calories: 237.6
Fat: 8.8 g
Saturated fat: 2.1 g
Carbohydrate: 35.5 g
Total sugars: 21.4 g
Protein: 4.1 g
Sodium: 268 mg
Cholesterol: 0 mg
Dietary fiber: 2.8 g

Ingredients:
1 can (16 ounces) 100% pumpkin puree
3/4 cup sugar
1/2 teaspoon salt
1 teaspoon ground cinnamon
1/2 teaspoon ground ginger
1/4 teaspoon ground cloves
1 package (12 or 12-1/2 ounces) soft tofu, processed in blender until smooth
9-inch unbaked, whole-wheat pie shell

Preparation: Preheat oven to 425°F. In a mixing bowl, use a stand or hand mixer to cream together pumpkin and sugar. Add salt, spices, and tofu; mix thoroughly until smooth. Pour mixture into pie shell and bake 15 minutes. Reduce heat to 350°F and bake for an additional 40 minutes. Chill and serve. Makes 8 servings.

Tropical Fruit Salad with Rum

Nutritional information per serving:
Calories: 237.9
Fat: 10.3 g
Saturated fat: 8.2 g
Carbohydrate: 33.7 g
Total sugars: 22.0 g
Protein: 2.6 g
Sodium: 8 mg
Cholesterol: 0 mg
Dietary fiber: 7.5 g

This is a delicious dessert salad from south of the border that is full of vitamins A and C.

Ingredients:
2 mangoes, peeled and cubed
1 papaya, peeled and cut into chunks
2 medium ripe but firm bananas, peeled and sliced about 1/2 inch thick
1/2 fresh pineapple, peeled, cored and cut into chunks
2 oranges, peeled and sectioned
1 star fruit, sliced
1/4 cup light rum
Garnish: 1/2 pint fresh raspberries
1/2 cup unsweetened coconut, shredded and toasted

Preparation: In a large glass bowl, combine mango, papaya, bananas, pineapple, oranges, and star-fruit pieces. Pour the rum over the fruit and stir until well mixed. Allow fruit salad to sit 20 to 30 minutes before serving. Serve in glass martini dishes, with raspberries and toasted coconut sprinkled on top. Makes 8 servings.

Recipes Suitable for Individuals Who are Receiving Cancer Treatment

In parentheses are ingredients that you may want to omit or decrease in quantity, depending on the degree of treatment side effects that you are experiencing. Please check with your treating physician for guidance on establishing your most suitable diet and whether these dishes would be appropriate for you.

Selected References:

1. Calle EE, Rodriguez C, Walker-Thurmond K, Thun MJ. Overweight, obesity, and mortality from cancer in a prospectively studied cohort of U.S. adults. New England Journal of Medicine 2003;348(17):1625-38.

2. Ericson U, Sonestedt E, Gullberg B, Olsson H, Wirfalt E. High folate intake is associated with lower breast cancer incidence in postmenopausal women in the Malmo Diet and Cancer cohort. American Journal of Clinical Nutrition 2007;86(2):434-43.

3. Benavente-Garcia O, Castillo J, Alcaraz M, Vicente V, Del Rio JA, Ortuno A. Beneficial action of Citrus flavonoids on multiple cancer-related biological pathways. Current Cancer Drug Targets 2007;7(8):795-809.

4. Chan JM, Wang F, Holly EA. Whole grains and risk of pancreatic cancer in a large population-based case-control study in the San Francisco Bay Area, California. American Journal of Epidemiology 2007;166(10):1174-85.

5. Adebamowo CA, Cho E, Sampson L, et al. Dietary flavonols and flavonol-rich foods intake and the risk of breast cancer. International Journal of Cancer 2005;114(4):628-33.

6. Pelucchi C, La Vecchia C, Chatenoud L, et al. Dietary fibres and ovarian cancer risk. European Journal of Cancer 2001;37(17):2235-9.

7. Stoner GD, Wang L-S, Zikri N, et al. Cancer prevention with freeze-dried berries and berry components. Seminars in Cancer Biology 2007;17(5):403-10.

8. McCann SE, Moysich KB, Mettlin C. Intakes of selected nutrients and food groups and risk of ovarian cancer. Nutrition & Cancer 2001;39(1):19-28.

9. Sapone A, Affatato A, Canistro D, et al. Cruciferous vegetables and lung cancer. Mutation Research 2007;635(2-3):146-8.

10. Bommareddy A, Arasada BL, Mathees DP, Dwivedi C. Chemopreventive effects of dietary flaxseed on colon tumor development. Nutrition & Cancer 2006;54(2):216-22.

11. Byers T, Nestle M, McTiernan A, et al. American Cancer Society guidelines on nutrition and physical activity for cancer prevention: Reducing the risk of cancer with healthy food choices and physical activity. CA: a Cancer Journal for Clinicians 2002;52(2):92-119.

12. Clinton SK, Giovannucci E. Diet, nutrition, and prostate cancer. Annual Review of Nutrition 1998;18:413-40.

13. Fraser ML, Lee AH, Binns CW. Lycopene and prostate cancer: emerging evidence. Expert Review of Anticancer Therapy 2005;5(5):847-54.

14. Feigelson HS, Jonas CR, Robertson AS, McCullough ML, Thun MJ, Calle EE. Alcohol, folate, methionine, and risk of incident breast cancer in the American Cancer Society Cancer Prevention Study II Nutrition Cohort. Cancer Epidemiology, Biomarkers & Prevention 2003;12(2):161-4.

15. Fernandez E, Gallus S, La Vecchia C. Nutrition and cancer risk: an overview. Journal of the British Menopause Society 2006;12(4):139-42.

16. Giovannucci E, Stampfer MJ, Colditz GA, et al. Multivitamin use, folate, and colon cancer in women in the Nurses' Health Study. Annals of Internal Medicine 1998;129(7):517-24.

17. Martinez ME, Willett WC. Calcium, vitamin D, and colorectal cancer: a review of the epidemiologic evidence. Cancer Epidemiology, Biomarkers & Prevention 1998;7(2):163-8.

Valuable Resources:

1. The American Cancer Society (ACS): www.cancer.org: The American Cancer Society is devoted to understanding all aspects of cancer and provides a user-friendly format for finding valuable information on all cancer types. Causes, treatment (including clinical trials), research and volunteer opportunities are all described on this useful website.

2. The American Institute for Cancer Research (AICR): www.aicr.org: This organization is devoted to studying nutrition, diet, obesity, and cancer. Their website provides specific information on various foods and nutrients and cancer risk, the latest research related to diet and cancer, and a variety of healthy recipes.

3. The National Cancer Institute (NCI): www.cancer.gov: This governmental site provides information on all the major cancers for clinicians and the general public and has links to other useful websites, such as those involving specific clinical trials and therapeutic options.

4. The American Association for Cancer Research (AACR): www.aacr.org: This Philadelphia-based association supports research for clinicians and basic scientists, and also provides a wealth of information for the general public on recent research findings related to cancer. They have a particular interest in the genetic and molecular causes of cancer.

Index

Index

Also Available from Sunrise River Press:

Conquer Back & Neck Pain: Walk It Off!
A Spine Doctor's Proven Solutions for Finding Relief Without Pills or Surgery
by Mark Brown, MD, PhD

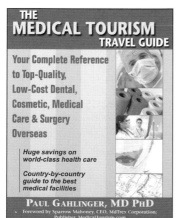

Every human being suffers from back pain at some point in life. In an effort to find relief, people turn to a wide variety of treatments, and to doctors who will prescribe narcotic painkillers. What they don't realize is that many of these treatments — especially narcotic drugs — actually interfere with their body's own ability to heal and overcome pain. When these treatments fail to help, they desperately conclude that surgery is their only option for relief. In his new book Conquer Back and Neck Pain: Walk It Off!, renowned spine surgeon Dr. Mark Brown, MD, PhD, explains exactly what causes back pain and why humans are so predisposed to spinal problems. He provides a detailed questionnaire that allows you to identify which of seven types of back pain you are experiencing, and then he explains each of those types in clear and easy-to-understand language.

Contrary to what you might expect from a spinal surgeon, Dr. Brown actually advocates against turning to surgery in most cases of spinal pain. In his 35 years of experience, he has found that the vast majority of back pain cases will resolve with minimal treatment. In fact, the very best thing you can do is to simply allow your body to heal itself by avoiding the many treatment pitfalls that people with back pain commonly fall into when looking for relief. Avoiding these mistakes, along with incorporating gentle aerobic exercise, will almost always allow you to "walk off" your back or neck pain naturally.

With an interesting collection of anecdotes and a frank discussion of the pitfalls that come with many of the back-pain treatments out there, Conquer Back and Neck Pain: Walk It Off! will give you fresh, new insight into how your back really works and how to finally find healthy relief from your back pain. Softbound, 6 x 9 inches, 168 pages. **Item # SRP601**

The Medical Tourism Travel Guide: Your Complete Reference to Top Quality, Low-Cost Dental, Cosmetic, Medical Care & Surgery Overseas
by Paul Gahlinger, MD, PhD

What if you could get top-notch medical care by highly skilled, U.S.- trained physicians in a world-class medical facility, all at a cost far less than treatment in the United States? It is called medical tourism, and hundreds of thousands of Americans each year are doing it.

They go for dental treatment in Mexico, for hip replacement in Thailand, for heart surgery in India, and for cosmetic and weight loss surgery that costs as little as a tenth what they would pay in the United States.

This is the first really authoritative book that will tell you almost everything you need to know—hundreds of clinics, hospitals, and spas in about 50 countries, how to travel, how to pay for it, how to prepare—what to do and what to avoid.

Dr. Paul Gahlinger brings his experience as physician, anthropologist, hospital director, and professor of public health and medicine to explain how it really works. Dr. Gahlinger has personally visited a great number of these hospitals, clinics, and doctors. You cannot always trust what you see on the Internet—but you can trust this book.

While many medical tourism "referral services" take your money and send you to low-quality providers, this book shows you how to do it directly, with all addresses, phone and fax numbers, and everything you need to know to obtain superb health care at an affordable cost. Softbound, 7 x 9 inches, 328 pages. **Item # SRP600**